# TREATISE ON THE GODS

Titles by H. L. Mencken published by
The Johns Hopkins University Press

*Happy Days: 1880–1892*

*Newspaper Days: 1899–1906*

*Heathen Days: 1890–1936*

*On Politics: A Carnival of Buncombe*

*Prejudices*
Selected by James T. Farrell

*Thirty-five Years of Newspaper Work*
edited by Fred Hobson, Vincent Fitzpatrick, and
Bradford Jacobs

Also available:

*Mencken: A Life*
by Fred Hobson

Maryland Paperback Bookshelf

# Treatise on

# The GODS

*H. L. Mencken*

❧ Second edition: corrected and rewritten

The Johns Hopkins University Press
Baltimore and London

Copyright 1930, 1946 by Alfred A. Knopf, Inc.
All rights reserved
Printed in the United States of America on acid-free paper

First published as a Borzoi Book by Alfred A. Knopf, Inc., New York
First edition 1930
Second edition 1946
Reprinted by arrangement with Alfred A. Knopf, Inc.
Johns Hopkins Paperbacks edition 1997
9 8 7 6 5 4 3

Works published as part of the Maryland Paperback Bookshelf are classics of a kind. While some social attitudes have changed and knowledge of our surroundings has increased, we believe that the value of these books as literature, as history, and as timeless perspectives on our region remains undiminished.

The Johns Hopkins University Press
2715 North Charles Street
Baltimore, Maryland 21218-4363
www.press.jhu.edu

**Library of Congress Cataloging-in-Publication Data**

Mencken, H. L. (Henry Louis), 1880-1956.
    Treatise on the gods / H.L. Mencken. — 2nd ed., corr. & rewritten
       p.    cm. — (Maryland paperback bookshelf)
    Originally published: New York : A.A. Knopf, 1946.
    Includes index.
    ISBN 0–8018–5654–X (pbk. : alk. paper)
    1. Religion—Controversial literature.   2. Christianity—Controversial
literature.   I. Title.   II. Series.
BL2747.M45   1997
200—dc21                            96-51594
                                     CIP

A catalog record for this book is available from the British Library.

# Contents

*Preface to the Revised Edition*                               ix

1  *The Nature and Origin of Religion*              3

2  *Its Evolution*                                                    51

3  *Its Varieties*                                                     109

4  *Its Christian Form*                                         174

5  *Its State Today*                                              246


*Bibliographical Note*                                         294

*Index*                                                               303

# Preface to the Revised Edition

THIS *book was first published early in 1930. The first and second printings were sold out before publication, and during the years following there were eight more, including a cheap edition for victims of the prevailing Depression. The regular edition continued to sell more or less until 1945, when Mr. Knopf notified me that it had gone out of print at last, and suggested that a revision might be in order. That revision, undertaken willingly, is now offered to the nobility and gentry, and I am in hopes that it will stand until long after I am bustled off to bliss eternal. In the first four sections I found no need of more than a few small changes, so they remain substantially as originally written. But Section V had to be reworked rather elaborately, for in its first form it was full of contemporary references that had become stale and irrelevant, and in some cases almost unintelligible. The Bibliographical Note, on the contrary, asked for but little revision, for there have been few contributions of any significance to the enormous literature of the subject since 1930. The efforts of speculative men, during that time, have been concentrated mainly upon the invention and discussion of secular theologies — the Economy of Plenty, Technocracy, the More Abundant Life, Fascism, Naziism, Communism, Democracy, Semantics, Racial Equality, World Union, and so on — and these theologies, and others like them, promise to keep the world agog until World War III bursts upon us. Whether, after they have all been tried and failed, there will be a return to the Old Time Religion I do not offer to predict, but from the pages following it is possible that the reader of prophetic gifts may be able to deduce some notion of his own. My book is mainly factual. Its purpose is simply to get together, in handy and I hope readable form, the material data about the embryology, anatomy and physiology of theology, with an occasional glance at its pathology.*

*Naturally enough, I give more attention to Christianity than to any other faith, for I was myself educated in its doctrines in youth, though not urged to believe them, and most readers, I assume, are in the same case. I try to rid it of the metaphysical flummery that has so long encased it, and to consider it realistically and dispassionately, as one might consider any other human artifact. The notion that it differs from the rest, and is somehow superior to them, is one that seems to me to be very dubious. Religion was invented by man just as agriculture and the wheel were invented by man, and there is absolutely nothing in it to justify the belief that its inventors had the aid of higher powers, whether on this earth or elsewhere. It is, in some of its aspects, extremely ingenious and in others it is movingly beautiful, but in yet others it is so absurd that it comes close to imbecility. What the faithful Christian professes to believe, if put into the form of an affidavit, would be such shocking nonsense that even bishops and archbishops would laugh at it, but as a practical matter he need not bother about any such test, for it is enough, when doubts assail him, if he hold his tongue, leaving the rest to the professional theologians — a class of men for whom I have an unashamed partiality, as I have for politicians. They are the most adept logicians in the modern world, and once their premises are granted the rest is easy sailing. All I venture to hint in the pages following is that their premises are probably unsound, and this, I assume, will also be the position of nine-tenths of those who undertake to read me. There is no purpose here to shake the faithful, for I am completely free of the messianic itch, and do not like converts. Let those who believe, and enjoy it, heave this book into the dustbin, and go on reading the War Cry. The world is very wide, and there is room amidst its dermatitis for all of us.*

*It would be folly to underestimate the power of religion upon the unhappy Simidiiae known as man, even today. That its grip is lessening I show by plain evidence, but this lessening is to be seen only in relatively small minorities, admittedly damned. The great masses of people still follow theologians as they follow politicians, and seem doomed to be bamboozled and squeezed by both for many long ages to come. Having been born without any capacity for moral indignation, I can only record this fact in a scientific spirit, letting others, if they choose, deplore it — or rejoice in it. Religion itself is commonly thought of as a moral engine, but I am convinced that that aspect of it is largely fortuitous. (I have dealt with the subject of ethics at some length in a companion volume called "Treatise on Right and Wrong".) Men do not derive their ethical ideas from the powers and principalities of the air; they simply credit those powers with whatever laws they evolve out of their own wisdom or lack of it. Religion, in its essence, is thus not a scheme of conduct, but a theory of causes. What brought it into the world in the remote days that I try to conjure up by hypothesis in Section I were man's eternal wonder and his eternal hope. It represents one of his boldest efforts to penetrate the unknowable, to put down the intolerable, to refashion the universe nearer to his heart's desire. My belief is that it is a poor device to that end — that when it is examined objectively it testifies to his lack of sense quite as much as to his high striving. But that belief is only a belief. The immense interest and importance of the thing itself remain.*

H. L. M.

Baltimore, January 1, 1946

# TREATISE ON THE GODS

# I   The Nature and Origin of Religion

THE ANCIENT and curious thing called religion, as it shows itself in the modern world, is often so overladen with excrescences and irrelevancies that its fundamental nature tends to be obscured. When we hear of it in everyday life, it is usually in connection with some grandiose pretension by its priests or practitioners or some unseemly row or scandal among them, religious only by courtesy. It is employed by such pretenders as a sanction for moral theories, for political and economic dogmas, for reforms (or for opposition to them) in laws and manners, for social protests and revolutions, and even for purely private enterprises, including the commercial and the amorous. In Christian Europe, as everyone knows, it is the plaything of political charlatans, clerical and lay; in America it is used as a club and a cloak by both politicians and moralists, all of them lusting for power and most of them palpable frauds. Some of the most bitter religious controversies of this age of hatreds — for example, the war over Prohibition in the United States, the long struggle over the Pope's temporal power in Italy, and that between church and state in Germany, Russia and Mexico — have had little to do with religion, properly so called. But it serves so conveniently to give a high dignity and authority to this or that faction, otherwise plainly in want of a respectable case, that it is constantly lugged in by the heels, to its own grave damage and discredit and the complete destruction of common sense and common decency. The fact, no doubt, accounts at least partly for the slowness with which some of the capital problems of mankind approach solution, especially in the fields of morals and government: their discussion is often so contaminated by pseudo-religious considerations that a rational and realistic dealing with them becomes impossible. It accounts unquestionably for the general feeling that religion itself is a highly complicated and enigmatical thing, with functions so diverse and sinister that plain men had better avoid thinking of them, as they avoid thinking of the Queen's legs and the King's death.

Nevertheless, it is quite simple at bottom. There is nothing really secret or complex about it, no matter what its professors may allege to the contrary. Whether it happens to show itself in the artless mumbo-jumbo of a Winnebago Indian or in the elaborately refined and metaphysical rites of a Christian archbishop, its single function is to give man access to the powers which seem to control his destiny, and its single purpose is to induce those powers to be friendly to him. That function and that purpose are common to all religions, ancient or modern, savage or civilized, and they are the only common characters that all of them show. Nothing else is essential. Religion may repudiate every sort of moral aim or idea, and still be authentically religion. It may confine itself to the welfare of the votary in this world, rejecting immortality and even the concept of the soul, and yet hold its character and its name. It may reduce its practices to hollow formulæ, without immediate logical content. It may imagine its gods as beings of unknown and unknowable nature and faculties, or it may

4

imagine them as creatures but slightly different from men. It may identify them with animals, natural forces, or inanimate objects, on the earth or in the vague skies. It may credit them with virtues which, in man, would be inconceivable, or lay to them vices and weaknesses which, in man, would be unendurable. It may think of them as numerous or as solitary, as mortal or as immortal. It may elect them and depose them, choose between them, rotate them in office, arrange them in hierarchies, punish them, kill them. But so long as it believes them to be able at their will to condition the fate of man, whether on this earth or elsewhere, and so long as it professes to be capable of influencing that will to his benefit, that long it is religion, and as truly deserving of the name as the most highly wrought theological system ever heard of.

2

In its pure and simple form religion is not often encountered today. It is almost as rare, indeed, as pure democracy or pure reason. It tends inevitably to gather the accretions that I have mentioned, some of them suitable to it and some not. The first man who sought to propitiate the inimical and impenetrable powers of the air must have done it with certain outcries and certain gestures of abasement, and thereby he laid the foundations of liturgy and ceremonial. His first apparent success, observed by his marvelling and perhaps envious fellows, made a priest of him, and straightway theology was born. There are, in truth, psychological impediments to pure religion, deeply implanted in the common nature of man. He is not, ordinarily, capable of the profound and overmastering feeling that its practice demands. His discontents, in the main, are transient, and his yearnings come and go with easy fluency, changing day by day. Nor has he the intellectual resolution and audacity, the hard drive of character, needed for a direct onslaught upon the gods. The thought of facing them in their rainbow crowns and robes of lightning appalls him; his inferiority complex gets in the way; he has all he can do to face the policeman on the beat and his own wife. Thus the business of wrestling with Omnipotence tends to fall into the hands of specialists, which is to say, into the hands of men who by habit and training are subnormally god-shy and have a natural talent for remonstrance and persuasion. These specialists, by the method of trial and error, develop a professional technique, and presently it is so complicated and so highly formalized that the layman can scarcely comprehend it. He may retain a lively sense of its purpose, and even lend a hand in some of its procedures, but he is quite content to leave the general management of the business to priests.

The Catholic Mass offers a case in point. Every adult Catholic has been instructed in the nature and meaning of that ceremonial, and is supposed to participate in every important step of it. At a certain place he is admitted by a sacerdotal miracle into the actual presence of the Son of God, and there, in theory, performs an act of personal worship, directly and without any further priestly intervention. But it would surely be too much to assume that the average Catholic, at this place, really does anything of the sort. The hortatory literature of the church, in fact, is largely devoted to upbraiding him for failing to do so. The Mass, with its strange language and esoteric ceremonials, is simply too much for him: he comes to regard it less as

6

a means of worship than as a symbol and witness of his willingness to be worshipped for. He resorts to it on Sunday morning as a public notice that he is of a generally religious cast of mind, and of specifically Catholic views. When he thinks of it seriously at all, he thinks of it as principally the priest's affair, not his own. His bare presence, with due regard to certain matters of etiquette, is enough in his mind to establish his piety, and so get him his fair share of grace, *i.e.,* his fair share of the Almighty's special favor, reserved for the faithful.

Within all the great religions there arise, from time to time, cults which seek to rid worship of this formalization and artificiality. One of the most familiar of them is called mysticism. It has appeared not only in all three of the principal branches of Christianity, but also in Moslemism, Buddhism, Brahmanism, and Taoism, and even in the barbaric shamanism of Central Asia and the crude animism of the North American Indians. There were mystics among the ancient Jews, and their ideas give pungency and glamour to the Book of Revelation. St. Augustine inclined toward mystical practices, and the cult was prosperous so early as the Fourth Century, especially in the Eastern church. It came into the Western church with monasticism, which was originally grounded upon it, and found adherents in such magnificoes as Ekkehard of St. Gall, Bernard of Clairvaux, Francis Assisi, Ignatius Loyola, Thomas Aquinas, St. Catharine of Siena and St. Teresa. Luther, in his early days, was a mystic, and later on there were many more among the Protestants. There are survivors in our own day, despite the general decay of religion. The Holy Rollers, when they are possessed by the Holy Ghost and address God directly in the tongues, practise what may be called a form of mysticism, and so do the Trappists when they engage in their silent and interminable grovellings. The Calvinistic process of redemption that dour Presbyterians visualize is essentially private and mystical, and so is the process of spiritual purification imagined by the Christian Scientists.

The essence of mysticism is that it breaks down all barriers between the devotee and his god, and thereby makes the act of worship a direct and personal matter. In theory, no ceremony is required, nor any priest, nor even any teacher. The mystic brings himself into contact with Omnipotence by any device which pleases his fancy, and can be demonstrated to work in his case. He may resort to magical formulæ, to narcotics, to violent physical activity, or to painful ascetic practices, or he may accomplish his purpose very simply by introspection and prayer. The main thing is that, without the aid of any human agent, he comes face to face with his god, and can make his wants known directly. The intervention of a liturgy, as of a priest, would be absurd; not even articulate speech is necessary. Here we have religion in a nearly pure form, with god and suppliant in the easy posture of physician and patient or parent and child.

The priests of all faiths naturally view such practices with suspicion, for they tend to discount the value of dogma and to make the devotee self-reliant and intractable. Open any treatise upon pastoral theology and you will find the author warning his sacerdotal readers against old women who pray too much and are otherwise too intimate with God. If all of the faithful inclined to mysticism, and had a talent for it, there would be empty pews in the churches and the whole ecclesiastical structure would begin to rock. But the taste for it, while very far from common, is still too powerful when it is encountered to be put down altogether, so the gentlemen of the cloth have usually tried to keep it within bounds by countenancing it and regulating it. The rules of the various Catholic orders are ingeniously drawn to that end. Piety is encouraged and protected, but the devotee is kept under the eye of judicious superiors, and thus restrained from any indecorous familiarity with the Most High. Further than this discreet policing it would be unsafe to go, for a downright prohibition of mysticism would be only too plainly a prohibition of religion.

But there is really no need for the gentlemen of the cloth to be alarmed, for not many human beings, as we have seen, are fit for private encounters with the gods. The rest prefer to transact their business at a distance and through intermediaries. Thus mysticism (and every other form of pure religion with it) tends to yield constantly to liturgy, dogma and priestcraft. In the end, the way the thing is done begins to count for more than the aim in doing it, and that aim itself is converted, by the magnificent rationalizations of theology, into something that it is not. The process is familiar in everyday life; it is encountered at every step in the history of religion, and especially of Christianity. Protestantism itself, in its earliest phases, was plainly a movement toward mysticism: its purpose, at least in theory, was to remove the priestly veil separating man from the revealed Word of God. But that veil was restored almost instantly, and by the year 1522, five years after Wittenberg, Luther was damning the Anabaptists with all the ferocious certainty of a medieval Pope, and his followers were docilely accepting his teaching. The Lutherans have been horribly priest-ridden ever since. They are even more subservient to sacerdotal authority, indeed, than the Catholics, for most of them take theology more seriously.

Their fellow abhorrers of the Roman Harlot have gone down the common road almost as far. I point to the Baptists. The theology of the Baptists, theoretically, is simple to the point of austerity. Their sole repository of the truth is the King James Bible, and once he has assented to a few simple principles of faith, every Baptist is free to interpret the revelations therein as he pleases. The church has no hierarchy, nor indeed any ecclesiastical organization. Every congregation hires its own pastor, and may ordain anyone to the office. The highest denominational body is a mere steering committee and has no authority in canon law over even the meanest cross-roads church. Nevertheless, it must be plain that the Baptists, at least in the United States, submit to an ecclesiastical tyranny of extraordinary pretensions. Their pastors not only expound Holy Writ to them with great assurance and indignation, but also presume to lay down regulations governing their private conduct in many far-flung fields, including the moral, the political, the connubial and the convivial. These regulations, speaking generally, are respected and obeyed; there are Baptists, to be sure, who protest against them as *ultra vires,* but there are not many who openly flout them. The reason is not far to seek. The majority of Baptists, like the majority of non-Baptists, have very little private talent for religion. They have neither the intrepidity necessary for gaining access to God and making their wants known to Him, nor the erudition needed to interpret His dark wishes and commands. Thus they are forced to resort to professionals. In other words, they are thrown into the arms of priests, as the pious have been thrown since the memory of man runneth not to the contrary, at all times and everywhere.

## 3

It is highly probable, indeed, that the first priest appeared in the world simultaneously with the first religion; nay, that he actually invented it. We know nothing positive, of course, about what happened in that remote and creepy time, but we do know something — though maybe not as much as we ought to know — about the nature of man, and that knowledge teaches us that great inventions are always made, not by men in the mass or even by small groups, but by extraordinary individuals. The Greek mythographers sensed the fact, and so transferred the invention of books from the vague Phoenicians to the concrete Cadmus. In all other mythologies there is the same astute recognition of leaders and innovators. The invention of fire-making apparatus is never ascribed to a whole tribe, nor even to a group within it, but always to a single Fire-Bringer, and usually he is felt to be so unusual that he is credited with a divine character. In later ages the acquired imbecility of the learned made war upon this primeval good sense, and there was much weighty gabble about folk-art, and, what is worse, about folk *works* of art. But now even pedants are aware that nothing of the sort has ever been seen in the world. The very myths themselves are the compositions, not of the folk, but of professional artists — humble, perhaps, but gifted more than most. So with folk-songs. So with theological dogmas. So with theories of government. So, indeed, with college yells.

Certainly religion must be granted to be one of the greatest inventions ever made on earth. It not only probably antedated all the rest, including even fire-making; it was also more valuable to the Dawn Man than any or all of them. For it had the peculiar virtue of making his existence endurable. For many generations, perhaps for many thousands of years, he had been finding life increasingly unpleasant, for the cells of his cortex had been gradually proliferating, and the more they proliferated the more he was afflicted by a new curse: the power to think. Having escaped his enemies and eaten his fill, he could no longer take his brutal ease under a kindly tree. The dog-like beasts who were his playmates and the apes who were his sardonic cousins were far happier. Their minds were empty; they could not generalize experience; they were innocent. But man suffered under the stealthy, insidious assaults of his awakening brain, now bulging and busy like a bulb in Spring. It not only caused him to remember the tree that came near falling upon him last week; it also enabled him to picture the tree that might actually fetch him tomorrow. He began to live in a world of multiplied hazards and accidents, some of them objectively real and some residing in the spooky shades of his burgeoning consciousness. Once he had been content, like his faunal inferiors, to rejoice over the danger escaped; now he was harried by a concept of danger in general, and tortured by speculations about its how and why.

Three devices for dealing with this accumulating unpleasantness lay before him. There was, first, the device of seeking out the causes of things, and endeavoring either to modify them or to anticipate their consequences, so that the tree would not fall, or, if it fell, its fall could be foreseen and evaded. This was the device of knowledge, and with it came in the beginnings of the scientific spirit, the dawn of invention and discovery. There was, second, the device of getting rid of unpleasantness by denying that it was unpleasant — the adoption of the theory that the tree, falling on a man, really did not break his head, or that a broken head, for some reason imagined and stated, was better than a sound one. This was the device of poetry. There was, third and finally, the device of trying to halt the falling of trees by appealing or protesting to the unseen but palpable powers which resided in their branches, or somewhere else aloft, and caused them to fall. This was the device of magic or religion.

I incline to believe that the third device was adopted before either of the other two. It made very little demand upon the imagination and almost none upon the nascent faculty of reason. The sequence of cause and effect that it presented was completely natural and self-evident. Who has not seen a baby, bumped by toddling into a chair, strike at it angrily and jabber anathemas upon it? Who has not seen a puppy, pricked by a thorn, snap at it and get pricked again? All mammals, in truth, seem to have an inborn tendency to identify causation with volition. They are naturally pugnacious, and life to them consists largely of a search for something or someone to blame it on. Every dog, as a sage once observed, has found its god, and worships him with its tail; it might be added that the same god, if young, male and of high spirits, has a dreadful facility for changing suddenly into a demon. The creatures of other classes and phyla attack the unfriendliness of the world with different weapons. The birds and the insects, to name but two, are highly scientific. There is no evidence that they practise any form of religion, but in inventiveness they are far superior to all mammals save man. The common sparrow builds a nest which surpasses anything ever shaped by an elephant or a lion, and the ant and the bee engage in engineering operations which make the ingenuities of even the higher apes seem puerile. If ants and bees have any conception of religion at all, they are probably atheists. They never cry over spilt milk; they proceed diligently to lick it up. But in the veins of primitive man ran none of their cold, acrid, persevering blood; he was a mammal, and as a mammal he naturally made his first attempt to better his lot, not by adding labor to his other pains, but by seeking to placate or destroy his enemies and by courting his friends. Of these enemies and friends the most potent were those who lay beyond his mortal eye.

## 4

The earliest religion, I daresay, arose out of some extraordinary series of calamities, unprecedented and intolerable. As the cells of his cortex multiplied, primitive man found even the ordinary discomforts of life increasingly disagreeable, but it is probable that he was still too close to his infra-human forebears to do anything about them. When it rained, and there was no cave or thicket handy, he simply got wet, as the other mammals got wet. When food was scarce he chewed on twigs. When it was cold he shivered. When a rival stole his wife he went without the domestic consolations until the rival tired of her, or he could make and wive a widow. All such misfortunes were unpleasant, and the new trick of thinking made them more so, but they tended to be transient, and they were not often fatal, nor even disabling. Beyond them lurked others of a greater fearsomeness: drowning, dropping sunstruck, getting killed by lightning, by wild beasts or by falling rocks and trees, dying in general. An inimical volition seemed to lurk in all of them. It was not hard to imagine some evil will throwing down the avalanche, or sending the lightning, or drawing the drowning man down to death. In fact, it was easier to imagine it than not to imagine it.

But I find myself doubting that any of these disasters was sufficiently poignant and shocking to arouse the Dawn Man to anything resembling general measures against them. They came, as a normal thing, too infrequently for that, and they had the peculiarity that those who suffered them commonly died in the process, and were thus unable to think of remedies and preventives. If the survivors gave earnest thought to them at all, it was probably to the effect that they themselves had escaped once and would likely escape the next time. That attitude is common to this day. When it is encountered in soldiers it is called bravery and when it is encountered in philosophers it is called optimism. Under it there lies a certain rationalization, conscious or unconscious, of the probabilities, but its main constituent is simply a lethargic habit of mind, a disinclination to think. To primitive man thinking was even more unpalatable than it is to modern Christians. He did it badly, as they do, and his brief experience of it had taught him that it brought him only woe.

What was needed, to arouse him to the immense feat of ratiocination which gave birth to religion, was a calamity so vast that he could not put it out of mind, and yet so merciful that it left him alive and thinking. No one, of course, will ever know what it was, nor when or where it came, nor whether it took the form of a single shocking blow or of a long series of smaller but accumulating disasters. In the folk-lore of most races there are what seem to be echoes of it — greatly distorted, perhaps, but still seeming to point to some actual experience. The Flood story is a common example. It is encountered, not only in the Old Testament, but also in the mythologies of peoples as far apart as the Persians, the ancient Greeks, the Hindus, the primitive Peruvians and Mexicans, and the Polynesians. Only the tribes of Africa seem to lack it, and no doubt it will be found there as ethnological research advances. As we have it from the Jews, who got it from the Babylonians, who got it from the Sumerians, it is placed in a relatively advanced stage of human progress, and so the effect of the deluge is represented as being, not the invention of religion, but the mere reform of a religion already existing. But that detail is unimportant, for it is always the habit of man to reincarnate his heroes and divinities, so that Barbarossa and Odin tend to become indistinguishable, and Moses is forever reappearing — in our own time as Joseph Smith, Mary Baker G. Eddy and a long series of lesser prophets. No doubt Noah, as a small boy, heard in his *Chedar* school of an *Ur*-Noah, and played with a toy ark. And the *Ur*-Noah that he heard of probably had predecessors of his own.

The persistence of this Flood myth suggests a hypothetical reconstruction of the invention of religion. It remains, to be sure, only hypothetical, and if any facts are in it then the chances are that they only repeat parallel facts at other times and places, but it will serve the present purpose well enough. I pitch on a stretch of grassland for the scene — a stretch of grassland in a wide valley, with a small river bisecting it. On one bank of the river there was a bit of higher land, broken by rock masses and covered with trees. The people of the valley found this higher land very attractive. There were caves on it for shelter, there were nuts and berries to eat, and there were birds and small game. They came to regard it as their refuge and citadel, as the center of their common life, as what we would call their home. When dangerous beasts roved in the grassland, or there were heavy rains, or it was cold and windy, or the lightnings flashed, or the sun was intolerably hot, they took shelter in its caves. Therein they devoured their food, housed their sick, had their babies, rested from their labors, and dreamed their murky dreams.

One Spring there came great rains in the valley, and on their heels a flood of melting snow. The little river turned into a big one, and was presently over its banks. Foot by foot it spread across the grassland, until there was water everywhere, as far as the eye could see. But still the rains kept falling. Soon the flood lapped at the base of the higher ground, and by and by it began creeping near the top. One night it rolled into the lowermost cave, cut off the occupants, and drowned a mother and her child. The next morning it was making for other caves, higher up the slope, and before dark the people deserted all of them, and gathered on the summit, huddled, wet and half dead with terror. One can scarcely think of them as silent. They took counsel, they gave voice to their distress, they cried out. The rising water seemed to them like a living thing. It moved upon them like one, it menaced them like one, it would devour them like one. Already a mother and her child had gone into its maw, wiped out as if gobbled by a tiger. Who would go next? Would all go, one by one?

17

In terror they wailed and protested, seeking to dissuade the water, to placate it, to scare it off. But always it came nearer, and soon famine was added to the greater horror, for all their food was gone.

It is not hard to imagine the hideous scene — the paralyzing fright, the despair, the false hopes, the bitter desperation. Nor is it hard to imagine one man more desperate than the rest — more desperate, and hence braver. Maybe he was the mate of the woman devoured, the father of the lost child. One pictures him resolved upon a last, violent, fantastic attempt to dissuade the monster. The rest, pressed together on the summit, are silent and hopeless by now, but he steps boldly forth. He stands out and hurls his objurgations across the flood. He goes close to the edge and bombards the enemy with stones. Growing bolder, he stalks into the water and belabors it with his club. His fellows, appalled, shrink back: at every instant they expect to see him drawn in, following the mother and her child. But he comes back safely. He comes back proudly, shaking himself. He has at least done something. The terror of the others begins to be tempered with the sneaking envy called admiration. Rough men, facing all their lives a world of hazards and enemies, they know courage when they see it. . . . And next morning the flood begins to recede.

## 5

I like to think of religion as beginning thus, not with propitiation but with remonstrance, not with grovelling but with defiance. The hypothesis is certainly as good as another. It accounts for all the necessary facts, and leaves out of account all irrelevant refinements and sophistications, by theology out of poetry. It does not reason backward from the complicated wants and aspirations of civilized man, like so many of the theories advanced by the learned; it assumes that the Dawn Man actually stood at the dawn, and was but one remove from his indelicate uncle, the ape. It depicts him as keeping within the bounds of his probable observation and experience, as making no dizzy and unlikely leap into a world of transcendental shapes. The concept of the supernatural, indeed, must have come much later. To primitive man all things were natural. He did not think of waters and lightnings, winds and avalanches as differing in essence from tigers and wolves; he thought of them as substantially identical to tigers and wolves. Not until ages later, in all probability, did his children formulate the concept of a category of beings quite unlike ordinary beings, and qualitatively superior to them. Thus the earliest imaginable religion, in the strict sense, had no gods; it simply had powers of an extraordinary potency, to be dealt with as ordinary powers were dealt with, but with a certain exaggeration of effort. If, as I have assumed, remonstrance and intimidation were the first weapons used against them, then it is also reasonable to assume that something akin to propitiation, or at all events of thanksgiving, soon followed. For it is hard to think of early man upbraiding the waters which made his world a desolation and then neglecting to laud the sun which warmed him back to life.

But if these waters did not constitute a god, the brave fellow who bawled and flogged them down was still unquestionably a priest. He had discovered what seemed to be a way to inflict his will upon powers that were otherwise immovable, and had thus rendered a vast service to the whole tribe. You may be sure that this service got its reward in adulation, and that he did not shrink therefrom. The power to think was still a novelty in the world, but vanity was already ancient, and so was the yearning for power. This first priest was the owner of a valuable arcanum. He could accomplish something that other men were incapable of. One may fancy him slowly developing his technique, no doubt by the method of trial and error. One may fancy him, too, slowly widening the field of its efficacy. If he could stop floods, then it was easy to believe that he could also ward off the lightnings. Here there was a chance for his public repute to increase more quickly, for of every thousand, or two, or ten thousand persons menaced and alarmed by lightning flashes only one was hit. Thus he made devotees, and was presently in receipt of gratifying revenues. People came to him with all sorts of troubles, as they go to priests today. He took on the aloof, philosophical air of a dermatologist contemplating an eczema: he learned how to avoid making promises and yet hold the confidence of his customers. He gave some thought to the form and content of his incantations, and thereby invented the first ritual. He devised, perhaps, a distinctive costume for himself, to mark him off from the common run of men. He made friends with the women especially, for women are always the chief custodians of woe. He did no work.

But it was not all easy sailing. The gift of blarney went with the sacerdotal office, in the earliest days as now, but there must have been failures occasionally which even the richest blarney could not explain away. One can imagine the rage of a hunter who, on going on *safari,* paid a stiff fee for the protection of his wife and children, and then returned from the hills to find them all drowned, or struck by lightning, or devoured by a saber-toothed tiger, or crushed by a falling tree, or done to death by snakes or ants. It was a delicate situation for the primeval priest, and he was lucky if he got out of it with nothing worse than a cracked head. To this day, in the remoter parts of Italy and Polynesia, the simple folk, when one of their gods fails them, take it out by smashing his image. Even on higher levels there is the same unpleasant resort to the axiom that it is unfair to exact something for nothing, and one hears that soldiers wounded in the wars are commonly very suspicious of their regimental chaplains. No doubt the first priest made some narrow escapes. If he survived to die naturally, as natural death was understood in that gory era, it was probably only by the aid of casuistry, which is thus as old as theology, and remains its chief staff in our own enlightened day.

But there was something that gave the pioneer pastor even more concern than the murmuring of dissatisfied clients, and that was the appearance of rivals. They must have come upon the scene at a very early stage, for the new trade of priestcraft had attractions that were plainly visible to any bright and ambitious young man. It carried an air of pleasing novelty; there was daring in it, and thrills therewith; it made for popularity and a spacious and lazy life; dignity belonged to it; above all, it seemed easy. To be sure, we may assume that the first practitioner hastened to spread the word that there was vastly more to it than appeared on the surface — that under his facile whoops and gyrations glowed a peculiar inward illumination, highly refined in its nature and hard to achieve. Hints of the same sort still come from the holy men: it is not, they let it be understood, their overt acts which count, nor even the arcanum to which they are privy, but their own singular state of interior grace, partly engendered by the apostolic laying on of hands, and partly the fruit of an inborn gift for holiness.

But the first priest probably found it much harder to support such pretensions than it is today, for the science of theology was still in its infancy. One can easily imagine rivals essaying to talk him down, and even laughing at him. Was the tribe as a whole with him or against him? The chances are that it was more or less divided, for in the domain of religion the human mind is naturally somewhat flighty, and what one man believes another is sure to doubt. If the first priest was prudent, as he probably was, he soon grasped the fact that his monopoly could not last, and sought to save what he could of it by compromise. That is to say, he sought to dispose of his most formidable rival by admitting him as an apprentice and so gaining his help. Thus two priests bloomed where only one had bloomed before, and presently there was a whole guild of them, and they began to act in coöperation, pooling their professional secrets and equipment, accumulating a tradition, and acquiring a definite place in society.

This organization of their business no doubt saved their necks on more than one occasion, for it enabled them to defend themselves to some effect when their ghostly technique failed and they faced an indignant clientèle. They could not only make a better physical resistance; they could also make a better forensic resistance, for the ideas that occurred to them in the course of their professional deliberations *in camera,* and were therein labored to a high state of finish, would operate against the plain people with extraordinary force. Thus theology got on its legs, both as a science and as an art, and with it its faithful hand-maiden, homiletics. The sacerdotal office began to be associated with eloquence, with learning, with a smooth and ready plausibility, with the trick of getting out of tight corners neatly.

But though the first priests, by resorting to coöperation, thus escaped disaster, they made it impossible, by the same stroke, for any of their number to become king. The eldest among them, at the start, had been plainly headed for that office, and without rivals at his heels he would have got it. Anyone could see that he was superior, in more ways than one, to the Old Man who then held it, or what passed for it. Was the Old Man a mighty hunter? Then so was the priest, and a far mightier than any who hunted wolves, tigers or other men, for his quarry was the dreadful shape that rode the lightnings and the baleful presence that caused the waters to rise, and caves to be flooded, and people to be drowned. He had a kind of wisdom that was palpably rarer and more delicate than any Old Man's. He had, too, the charm of strangeness; his feats were new in the world; he was, in a sense, like a being from another planet; he shared some of the dark, exquisite mystery of the powers he professed to rule. Moreover, he probably had youth, or, at all events, less hoariness of age than the Old Man, and that fact would not pass unnoticed among the women.

## 6

But the moment one priest turned into two all these qualifications for kingship went for naught, for one was destroyed that was greater than all of them, and that was the character of a single and indivisible man. The simple savages of those days had not yet formulated the concept of government by committee; they wanted to be led, when there was leading to be done, by a leader who could come to decisions instantly, and whose familiar frame, heaving into battle, was his sufficient ensign and guidon. They were yet close cousins to the brutes who hunted in packs, always with one leader, not two, or three, or a dozen. They had no communal policy save that of forthright attack upon whatever seemed to menace them; they had not yet invented congresses, plebiscites or even councils of war: their minds were still too primitive to be equal to the colossal intellectual feat — perhaps the most revolutionary, when it was achieved at last, in the whole history of man — of lifting reflection from its natural place after action, or, at best, alongside, and putting it in front.

So the priests, powwowing and quarrelling among themselves, failed to wrest kingship from the Old Man. The theology which saved them also ruined them. The Old Man knew less than even the least of them, but what he knew had a higher practical value, and was instantly applicable, and needed no argument to support it. As human society developed he was challenged by other and less purely biological leaders, but always they came one by one, bringing the same homely goods that he had to offer and speaking his own simple language. The earliest history that we know of tells us of single kings; never of boards and commissions. Not infrequently they succumbed to rivals, but always the rivals who beat them reigned alone. But the first priests to leave definite records were already organized in droves, with complicated gradations of rank.

Among the early Egyptians and the peoples of Mesopotamia they had elaborate hierarchies, and constituted a separate caste, clearly superior to the rest of the population but still subject to the king. In India they constitute such a separate caste to this day — the Brahmans. The ancient Jews had a whole tribe of them — the Levites, who were later shouldered out by the Aaronites. These Aaronites became so powerful that even kings could not take away their high privileges and prerogatives; but though they were immensely lordly they never became actually royal. Now and then, in history, we hear of kings who were also priests, or even gods, but almost always it turns out on investigation that they were kings first and became priests only afterward. The case of David is familiar, and that of the Egyptian pharaohs will be recalled. The former Czar of Russia was a sort of high priest, but only *ex officio*. The King of England is another.

The common people have always rejoiced over a show of piety in their rulers: it flatters them to have a sign that the inferiority they must suffer on this earth has its compensation in equality before God. There are many examples in history of rulers who were ardent devotees. The late Queen Victoria was of that company, and so was Kaiser Wilhelm II when he was on the throne: in the rôle of head of the state church of Prussia he not infrequently delivered sermons, and some of them revealed a pretty gift for theology. It seems to be generally felt that the President of the United States ought to be a member of some church or other — safely Protestant, of course — and that he should attend its public ceremonials more or less regularly. Roosevelt II began praying fervently as soon as he got to the White House though before that his devotions had been inconspicuous. Hoover, after years of back-sliding, became a passionate Quaker the moment he was nominated. And so on back to George Washington, a vestryman. Thomas Jefferson and Abraham Lincoln seem to have been the only Presidents of a definitely irreligious cut, and they were discreetly silent upon the subject while in office. When a ruler thus submits gracefully to the religious ideas prevailing among his people he greatly augments his prestige and popularity. Believers are consoled and even skeptics are reassured, for skepticism commonly distrusts iconoclasm quite as much as it distrusts orthodoxy. It is felt to be dangerous, in modern states, to make religious speculation a public matter.

The clergy repay this friendly recognition of their place in society by an almost unfailing devotion to the constituted authorities. When they take part in rebellions, it is almost always against subversive usurpers, not legitimate rulers. At all times and everywhere they have been the bulwark of orthodoxy in politics — in England during the long constitutional struggle that culminated in the Reform Bill of 1832, in Russia during the three-cornered war between autocracy, democracy and Communism, in Italy during the Risorgimento, in Germany in 1848, and in Spain yesterday. Their prayers always go up for kings, not for rebels and reformers. During the American Revolution the priests of the established church were almost unanimously loyal to King George, and during the Civil War the clergy of the South remained faithful to the Southern economic system, and to slavery as a part of it. The great religious reformers have never preached the liberation of the masses. Luther, Calvin and John Wesley were all on the side of authority. The Catholic church is for it everywhere today, and the more intransigent it is the better the church likes it. Thus the patriotism of a priest is hard to distinguish from the patriotism of a stock-broker. When he is found questioning the established order it usually develops, upon inquiry, that he is also questioning the tenets of his church, and is on his way to heresy.

## 7

Among the learned there is a frenzy to differentiate between religion and magic, and whole shelves of books have been written upon the theme. The magician, it is explained, is one who professes to control the powers he deals with; the priest attempts only to propitiate them. The magician pretends to be able to work evil as well as good; the priest works only good. The magician deals with all sorts of shapes, some supernatural and others not; the priest deals only with gods and their attendant angels. The magician claims a control over material substances; the priest confines himself to spiritual matters.

Such distinctions have been set up in great number, but, as it seems to me, to no useful purpose. It may be that there are magicians who are not also priests, but it would be hard to find a priest who is not, in some sense, a magician. Let us turn, for illustration, to the rev. clergy of Holy Church. When the celebrant of Mass comes to the Consecration, and, in the words of the Fourth Lateran Council, "the whole substance of the bread is changed into the body of Christ, and the whole substance of the wine into His blood, the species alone remaining" — when this daily miracle is performed, it must be plain that there is an indubitably magical quality in it. The simple carbohydrate of the bread, a purely material substance, is changed into a complicated congeries of other material substances, and so with the alcohol of the wine. Only the "species," or "accidents," *i.e.,* the outward appearances, of the bread and wine remain; otherwise they are completely transformed into flesh and blood. Here we have all the characteristics of a magical act, as experts set them forth: the suspension of natural laws, the transmutation of a material substance, the use of a puissant verbal formula, and the presence of an adept. If it be argued that the essential miracle is performed, not by the priest but by God, then it may be answered that, as a matter of historical fact, God has never performed it since the Last Supper save at a priest's behest and with his aid, and that if the priest should neglect any important part of the prescribed formula the whole transaction would fail.

But the point needs no laboring, for it doesn't make much difference what a thing is called, so long as its intrinsic character is clearly apprehended. Magic or religion: it is all one. Theologians themselves dispose of the matter by calling everything they do an act of religion, including even such operations as bedizening themselves with high-sounding titles and dignities, superior to any ever claimed by Christ, and laying taxes upon the faithful for their own aggrandizement; if that is how they feel about it, let them have their way. Their earliest forerunners, we may be sure, wasted no time upon any such bandying with words. They were aware of no difference between magic and religion, but practised both with easy consciences. The first priest,. indeed, by any modern definition, was far more the magician than the priest. If he saw the flood that he put down as a living thing, then he saw it as a living thing differing in no essential from himself. It plainly had free will, as he had, and, having free will, it must have had consciousness, but that will and that consciousness were not transcendental; they responded to ordinary terrestrial stimuli, and could be controlled by human means. I suppose the first priest, if he thought about it at all, thought that he had overcome the flood by scaring it. Its subsidence followed his volley of objurgations: the logic in that fact was strong enough to convince any theologian ever heard of. There was no intervention by a higher power, summoned to the business by the priest's words, for no higher power had yet been imagined. Purpose and malignancy could be detected in floods and tempests, as they could be detected in tigers and hyenas, but there was no evidence that they differed in any manner from the purpose and malignancy of man.

This naïve view of the matter, however, could not last. As the new art of thinking developed and primitive man began to feel somewhat at ease in its exercise, it must have occurred to more than one speculative mind that the power exercised by the priest was really of an extraordinary character. He could do things that no other man could hope to do; he could force his will upon other wills that were notably sturdy and recalcitrant. The best hunter thought he had performed a not inconsiderable feat when he had brought a tiger down, but here was a man who could bring down the dreadful forces residing in the waters and the lightnings. Was he, in fact, an ordinary man? If the vast powers he professed to possess were real, then how did he come to possess them? And why were they not found in other men?

I suspect that the early priests, facing this dawn of the critical spirit, soon found themselves in the situation in front of Pope Pius IX in 1870. Confronted by a revival and epidemic of Gallicanism which menaced not only his temporal power but also his spiritual authority, he was forced to seek a ground for his pretensions that would be beyond the reach of challenge and denial. He found it in the doctrine of papal infallibility. In other words, he found it in the doctrine that he was not, in fact, an ordinary man. No doubt the early priests went much the same route. It had become increasingly difficult for them to convince skeptics that the gifts they exercised were like the gifts of other men, but only greater and grander; it was necessary for them to pretend to gifts which differentiated them from other men in kind as well as in degree. That step, it is probable, took them further than they had any intention of going, and maybe to their embarrassment. Its effect was to make them, for all practical purposes, gods.

If I suggest that they were embarrassed thereby, it is for a plain reason. So long as they were ordinary men their occasional — or even frequent — failures were not fatal to their pretensions, for other men also failed at times. Everyone knew of a hunter who had gone out to kill a tiger, and got killed himself. Everyone knew of failures in other enterprises, some of them easy. It was thus not unnatural that priests, facing the potent shapes that they habitually dealt with, should also come to grief now and then. But the minute they began to pretend that there was something in them that was superior to anything in those shapes, and differed in kind from anything in ordinary men, that minute it became unreasonable for them to fail. Failure now took on the appearance, not of an ordinary human calamity, but of proof of false pretenses. They found themselves in the unpleasant situation of the popes after 1870, with the riddle of organic evolution confronting their newly won infallibility, and no doubt they tried, for a time, to get out of the difficulty as the popes have sought to dispose of the riddle: by delicate evasion. But the subtleties suitable to modern theologians did not fit their realistic time: the reasoning that went on among their clients, in so far as any went on at all, was of the harsh, literal variety observed among children. Either they were superior beings or they were not superior beings. Either they had within them wills which could best the wills of flood and storm, and hence stood clearly above the wills of ordinary men, or they were frauds. I daresay that while this question was being debated, perhaps over a stretch of thousands of years, there was a high mortality among priests, and every great public catastrophe was followed by a massacre. And if not by a massacre, then at least by an unpleasant disgorging of spoils and a painful running of the gauntlet.

## 8

The way out was plain enough. What the priest couldn't prove himself, he could prove very easily of the powers he dealt with. Their extraordinary puissance was admitted by the very skeptics who were his enemies; it was, indeed, the foundation of the case of the skeptics. What was easier than to grant it — and then add something to it? That addition produced the first gods, in the true sense. The priest himself had been transiently a god, and some trace of his early divinity has clung to his heirs and assigns ever since, but it is only too obvious that he was also a mere man, and, as men ran in the world, of none too savory a kind.

The concept of a being both god and man was still beyond the nascent imagination of *Homo sapiens:* millenniums would have to come and go before even specialists in theology would pretend to be able to grasp it. But it was easy for the simplest of men to imagine a category of beings who were superior to any beings in human form, even including priests, and it was a logical step to acknowledge that dealing with them was a complex and difficult matter, and that an occasional failure was thus no disgrace. They could be intimidated at times, given the proper technique, and they could be wooed and bamboozled at other times, but there were yet times when they refused to yield for any reason that pleased them or for no reason at all.

This view of them, as it gained acceptance, vastly increased the security and influence of the priests. On the one hand, it saved them from accountability when they failed, and on the other hand it gave a new dignity and authority to their technique when they succeeded. One may be sure that they did not neglect to refine that technique in the light of experience. What worked once — whether genuflection, or outcry, or *passacaglia* — was cherished to be tried again, and when it failed on that second trial steps were taken to remedy the deficiencies that it revealed. Priestcraft thus became a more and more complicated discipline, with characters suggesting both an art and a science. A native talent was no longer sufficient for its practice; the practitioner also had to be trained. To this day, whether upon the low level of savage superstition or upon the shining heights of Christian culture, his training remains a tedious and laborious process. Even a Baptist pastor, though he may preach without knowing anything else, cannot preach until he knows the Bible.

The primitive priest, as we have followed him, had now come to the point where, when luck ran his way, he could fight and conquer beings of a supernatural potency — in fact, nascent gods. But as yet he had to fight them alone, or, at all events, with no aid save that of his fellows, and so the business, though it was safer than it used to be, continued to be full of unpleasant hazards. If there were times when he prevailed brilliantly, there were still times when he failed dismally. What he needed, obviously, was reinforcement from the high realm of his awful antagonists, that the chances of battle might be more equitable. In other words, what he needed was the aid of other gods. I suspect that he got it, when it came at last, quite fortuitously, and perhaps to his considerable surprise. There was, let us say, a great forest fire or a grass fire, and he went into action against it as in duty bound. The people, trembling, were helpless; if he could not stay the monster disaster was upon them. He stood out bravely, trying his most trusted gesticulations one by one, and hurling his blackest imprecations at the flames. But his magic simply would not work. The fire came on and he retreated before it, along with the Old Man, the hunters and the rest. Then, to the joy and amazement of all, something happened. Clouds rolled up; the skies darkened; there was a splutter of rain. Anon there was a downpour — and the fire god was routed.

What more natural than to give thanks? What more logical than to hail and praise the good god who had overcome the bad one? True religion, in the most modern and delicate sense, was born at that moment. If the worker of marvels, in the past, had been no more than a magician, he was now genuinely a priest, with gods working for him. That is the hallmark of a priest to this day; he has a god working for him. He is a public expert in all that pertains to that god. He knows what is pleasing to it and what offends it. He interprets and expounds its occult desires, and executes its dark and arbitrary mandates. He has avenues of approach to it that are closed to ordinary men. He can, by appropriate representations, induce it to change inconvenient decrees, and he can summon its aid when his own decrees are flouted.

One may be sure that the first priest to manacle a god was not slow to see the advantages in his new situation. He became, at one stroke, infinitely more powerful than he had ever been before. Hitherto, despite the steady advances in his art, there had remained something equivocal and uncomfortable about his position: he had been, when he succeeded, almost a god himself, and when he failed, no more than a poor charlatan, laughed at by the very children. But now, with a god in his service, and then another, and then a whole hierarchy, he was securely somebody and what he had to say was attended to. When he let it be known that there were certain things, done by the people, that would gratify the gods and insure their aid, these things began to be regarded as virtuous, upright, moral. When he announced that other things were frowned upon, they straightway became sins. The two categories were carefully marked off by the priest. The acts in the first he commanded, and those in the second he forbade. Religion ceased to be a mere trembling before unsearchable enmities, and became a way of life. The priest found himself a law-giver.

True enough, there were still failures, but they were no longer dangerous to him. His day of taking the blame had passed; he could now throw it upon the people. Did fires rage and the sky remain dry? Then it was because the faithful had forgotten their plain duties. They had done something that they ought not to have done, or left undone something that they ought to have done. They had neglected some act of obligation, bungled some formula of devotion, yielded to some sin. Above all, they had failed in their obedience to the priest. At great pains he had taught them what would please the gods, but in their days of ease they had gone gadding after false lures. Now, with calamity upon them, they were paying for it. It was not the priest's fault. He was not only innocent; he was actually injured, for they had rewarded all his trouble with ingratitude. This ingratitude itself soon became a sin. It was just as bad, it appeared, to flout the priest as it was to flout the gods. It remains so to this day, and in the fact lies the chief dignity of the sacerdotal office. The priest, as such, cannot err, for his mandates are the mandates of the gods, and, being unable to err, he cannot really fail. When the gods blast the faithful it is not a sign that the priest's ministrations have gone for naught; it is a sign that the people have not been worthy of them. The ire of the gods is the penalty of human weakness. If there were no sin there would be no sorrow.

There is every reason for believing that this emergence of the priest as infallible law-giver goes back to the earliest days of religion. At the very dawn of recorded history he was already secure in the rôle. There were other law-givers, to be sure, but within the field of his peculiar interests and capacities he was not often challenged. His rivals, however powerful, could not hope to unhorse him, for behind him stood the omnipotent gods. If, put to the test of defiance, he could not induce those gods to send down their punitive lightnings instanter, he could always rely upon them doing it soon or late. The first ensuing calamity justified him, and got him back whatever authority he had lost — and calamities were plentiful in those remote days, as they are now. They remain the most potent weapons in the armamentarium of the priest. He may rest assured that, soon or late, they will come, and he may rest assured that when they do come their victims will turn to him for aid and consolation. Whenever there is blood upon the moon, and multitudes of human beings are heavy laden and sore beset, religion revives and flourishes. It was so when the Roman Empire began to disintegrate and the whole Western world was plunged into chaos; it was so when the wars of nationalism began, at the close of the Middle Ages; it was so when the Industrial Revolution made slaves of half the people of England. Always, in time of bloodshed, pestilence and poverty, of misery and despair, there is what theologians call a spiritual awakening. But when peace and plenty caress the land the priest has a hard time keeping his flock at prayer, and great numbers desert him altogether, as they desert his colleagues in cheer and comfort, the poet and the political reformer.

## 9

So far I have said nothing whatever about the soul, nor about the theological theory, so familiar to modern man, that it never dies, but goes on serenely after the death of its owner, maybe in Heaven, maybe in Hell, and maybe lingering somewhere between. The omission has not been accidental but deliberate, for I can find no reason to believe that early man had any conception of such an entity, though he plainly had a more or less clear notion of the psyche, or, perhaps more accurately, of the will. The will he could easily sense and savor, as even dogs sense and savor it. He felt within him the stirrings of his own, and he observed the operation of wills of the same kind in other men, in the lower animals, and even in inanimate things. When a stone on a hillside, hitherto motionless, began suddenly to roll downhill, it was natural and inevitable for him to conclude that it had will to do so. In the same way he saw the workings of will in thunder and lightning, in rain and fire, in snow and hail, in the rising and setting of the sun, and in the seasonal leafing and decline of trees. To this day children reason in the same way, as Jean Piaget sets forth instructively in " The Child's Conception of the World." They begin their conscious lives by assuming that all things are likewise conscious, and then revise that assumption to include only things that move, and then, coming to the border of critical thinking, cut it down to things that move of themselves.

Primitive man was surely not critical. His mental habits, in so far as we can determine them across the void of millenniums, were those of a child just barely able to think at all. It was thus easier for him to imagine will in things than not to imagine it, and so a concept of conscious purpose probably went into the first law of causation that he formulated. But this will that he imagined (or psyche, or consciousness, or spirit, or personality, or Ka, or whatever you choose to call it) was certainly not the thing that modern theologians think of as the soul. It moved the body in which it lived, but it was still bound by that body. When the body was destroyed, it also was destroyed. There is no reason to believe that primitive man, in the first days of his muddled grappling with the unknown, ever thought of it as existing independently. All the evidence before him ran in the other direction. A dead man could no longer fight; a fire put out could burn no more; when the sun went down for the night its will to warm and comfort went with it. Was the will of the first god in a different category? It is not likely. That will, too, had its corporeal embodiment: its operations could be apprehended only physically. To have imagined it as existing outside and apart from that corporeal embodiment would have strained the nascent imagination of early man beyond its reasonable and probable capacity. And what he could not imagine of the gods he could scarcely imagine of himself. The soul was to be invented in due course, but not yet.

Virtuosi of theology, who, as we shall often see in this work, are sometimes far from critical in their ways of thought, ground their theory that a belief in the soul goes back to the first days of religion upon two very dubious pieces of evidence. The first is the fact that something somehow resembling it is believed in almost universally by the savages of today, even the lowest. The second is the fact that in some of the caves once inhabited by early man there are indications that he carefully buried his dead brothers, or otherwise put them away, and as carefully surrounded them with objects which suggest that he expected them to rise again. But there is nothing in either of these facts of a genuinely persuasive nature. To begin with the first, what savages believe today is by no means a safe indicator of what primitive man believed, for their ancestry is just as long as our own, and they have been exposed to the same processes of change that we have been exposed to, though perhaps in lesser degree. Some of them, perhaps, have been living, ever since the dawn of human history, on a plane but little above that of the apes, but others show abundant evidence that they have been up in the world and then come down again. The superstitions of the latter represent, not only ideas that they have evolved themselves, but also ideas inherited from forebears of a superior and now half-forgotten culture. Even the former always show signs of outside influence, for there is no tribe in the world that is completely isolated. Thus what savages believe about the soul tells us next to nothing about what our earliest progenitors believed. The lowest African tribesman of today is far above the first priest, for he is the heir and assign of long generations of highly subtle and ingenious theologians. It is, indeed, reported by missionaries that he sometimes criticizes the salient Christian dogmas with such skill that it is difficult to argue him down. Not infrequently, percipitating his criticism into overt acts, he has to be dealt with by the secular arm.

The evidence from the cave burials is even more shaky. In the first place, they do not appear until a relatively late date — perhaps tens of thousands of years after primitive man had begun to support priests. In the second place, it is plainly not necessary to assume, from what they reveal about his disposition of the dead, that he had any conception of an immortal soul. All they show is that he did not abandon his fallen comrades to the hyenas. But do atheists today? Do even animals? Surely not always. All of us have seen a dog watching by the carcass of its dead mate, and the books of big game hunters are full of stories to the same effect. Köhler (or is it Yerkes?) tells of a mother baboon who, when her baby died, clutched it to her breast for days and weeks — until, in fact, its poor body was reduced to leather and bones. Primitive man, I suspect, did little more. He had still to be convinced of the irrevocability, in all cases, of somatic death. He saw an occasional fellow, struck by clubs or stones, fall unconscious, and yet revive and survive. He knew that he himself went to sleep at night, and yet awoke again in the morning. It must have been hard for him to decide, in any given case, that a dead man was actually dead forever. So he prudently cherished the body in his cave, and when the process of decay convinced him at last that there would be no awakening he got rid of it by sinking it into the floor. Perhaps he continued to hope even when decay was far gone, for his graves were shallow, and a sleeper come to life in one of them might have got out very easily.

The things that he deposited with the dead offer no evidence that he believed in an immortal soul, separate from and independent of the body. Their significance has been exaggerated by thinking of them in terms of the funerary objects in vogue among far later and more sophisticated peoples. What more natural than to put a fallen hunter's weapons by his side? Suppose he should awake when no one was by — wouldn't he need them? So with food. So with clothing. There remains the red ochre that certain peoples of the Stone Age smeared over corpses: in some graves large amounts of it have been found. Long treatises have been written to prove that it had some profound and transcendental significance, but it seems to me to be far easier to believe that primitive man saw it as no more than a surrogate for lost blood.

The dead man, more often than not, had met his death by violence, and to the accompaniment of hemorrhage. The causal connection between that hemorrhage and his loss of consciousness must have been plain to even the most unreflective, as it would be plain today to a child. What more reasonable, then, than to try to replace it with something that, to primitive eyes, closely resembled it, even to the extent of substantial identity? Blood and ochre were both red, and redness was a character that was considerably more salient and arresting than any other that primitive eyes could detect in either substance. It took mankind tens of thousands of years to get past such superficialities to the more important realities beneath; the process is not yet complete. The whole history of religion, indeed, and of magic with it, is a history of objects looked upon as essentially alike because they shared, to use the theological terminology, the same " species " or " accidents." To this day the wine used at the Eucharist is almost invariably red, not white. I have heard of Mississippi Baptists who, in fear that even unfermented grape-juice might deliver them to the Rum Demon, used coca-cola, but I have never heard of them using soda-pop.

## 10

The learned, in their speculations regarding the genesis of religious ideas in primitive man, would get farther and fare better if they disregarded the dubious analogies presented by the thinking of relatively advanced savages, prehistoric or of today, and addressed themselves to an examination of the thinking of very young children. Much remains to be ascertained and charted in that field but not a little is already known. The behaviorists, for example, have made great progress in the study of infantile emotions. They find that the only recognizable one in the newborn child is fear. The world it inhabits, like the world of the lowest savages, is filled with inscrutable and forbidding shapes. It can see things only dimly, and what it sees is seldom reassuring. Further than that it is simply an automaton, with a few primitive instincts to get it through the day.

Its first muddled attempts at observation, as we have seen by Piaget's studies, lead it into a naïve animism. Everything that it is cognizant of seems to be animated by a conscious purpose, usually inimical but sometimes friendly — its rattle as well as its nurse, the bottle that satisfies its hunger as well as the fly that disturbs its sleep. As it becomes aware of more and more objects, the number of wills is simply increased. Its toys begin to take on definite personalities; it divides them into good and evil as it divides its elders or other children. So with natural phenomena. The clouds, hiding the moon, have killed it. The thunder is a voice. The sun is alive "because it keeps coming back." Even when, with the dawn of the critical spirit, some of these concepts are abandoned, it is usually only to make way for others that are but one degree removed from the animistic. The sun, ceasing to be alive, now moves "because someone pushes it."

The principal someone in this world of unfathomable presences is the mother, and after her comes the father. To the child gradually tightening its grasp upon reality they inevitably take on the character of gods. They are, as Pierre Bovet says in "Le Sentiment Religieux," both omniscient and omnipotent. Nothing seems to be beyond

42

their powers. They are not only gods; they are also priests, which, as a practical matter, is often something higher. They can control all the evil purposes that lurk in things; they are masters of the unknown and unknowable. Children have no other gods. When, later on, domestic pedagogy introduces them to an unseen Presence who lurks in the skies there ensues a simple transference of faith and credit. This Presence, at first, is comprehended only dimly, and sometimes He is confused transiently with the sun or the moon, but in His final shape He is always a grandiose Father, watching over little boys and girls. He accumulates reality and authority in two stages. The first is marked by the discovery that the actual mother and father are not really omniscient and omnipotent — that they may be deceived and their will resisted: this discovery had its parallel in primitive man's dawning doubts about the might of the priest as a prime mover. The second stage is marked by the observation that God demands a *quid pro quo* for His favors — that, like mother and father, He functions only according to certain patterns, often uncomfortable to the votary; the parallel is to be found in the primitive priest's invention of moral duty and pious obligation.

The likeness might be pushed further: I point to it only to suggest that in it may be found a clue to the origin of the soul. Piaget supplies some significant facts. The child, at one stage, is unable to take in the concept of death as final. It is simply a departure into that murky realm whence babies issue, and in the face of it certain questions inevitably suggest themselves: " Do people turn back into babies when they get quite old? . . . When you die, do you grow up again? " There may be an echo here of the speculations of primitive man, once he had begun to think at all: it seems, indeed, more likely than not. To him, as to the child, the mysteries of birth and death must have seemed almost identical. A child that, in its mother's body, had had no visible will issued into the world and developed one, and a man who plainly had one lost it by dying. It was probably a philosophical impossibility, as we have seen, for the earliest man to imagine it existing independently — that is, without some bodily investiture. Naturally, then, he thought of it as transferring itself from one body to another. It left an old man as he was dying and entered into a baby as it was born.

This belief, in one form or another, survives into our own day. Among the Papupo-Melanesian savages described by Bronislaw Malinowski in " The Father in Primitive Psychology " (as among many savages in other parts of the world) there is no understanding of the physiological rôle of the father. He is the mother's husband, her lover and provider, but is not thought to share with her in bringing forth the child. She becomes pregnant by the act of ancestral spirits, who insert a spirit into her womb: it is not a new creation, but simply the spirit of one who, being dead, tires of life on Tuma, the island of the departed, and craves another whirl on earth. Nor are such beliefs confined to savages. They have been entertained by civilized man for many centuries, and lie at the bottom of some of the most subtle and elegant of modern religions — for example, Brahmanism. Christianity, for reasons that we shall see in a moment, has never toyed with them, but there are traces of them in the more occult and extravagant parts of the Jewish Cabbala and in the doctrines of the Shiite sect of Moslems. The theosophists, as everyone knows, ground their whole system upon such a concept of transferable psyches. But a transferable psyche, though it has begun to show some of the characters of a soul, is not yet a true one. The essential qualities of a soul, as the most authoritative Christian theology views the matter, are, first, that it is personal to one individual, and, second, that when he dies it goes on existing indefinitely. If it were imagined as common to two or more individuals, then the Last Judgment would present judicial difficulties beyond the ingenuity even of God. And if it could die, then it might escape Him altogether, and so make His jurisprudence ridiculous. So Christianity has no traffic with metempsychosis.

The soul, I believe, has been a thing of slow growth. It has probably had a phylogenetic history almost as long as that of man himself. Our remote ancestors, when they began to speculate about the great mysteries of birth and death, and gradually formulated the notion that the will which went out of a man dying entered into a child new born, must have presently asked themselves just how the transfer was effected, and where the will lingered while awaiting it. Children, obviously, were not born every day. There might be a death, and no woman near her term. No doubt it was long held, as I have said, that the psyche of a dead man lingered in his carcass, or at all events in the vicinity. In case he should revive he would need it again; in case he was doomed to revive no more it would be in waiting for the next birth. Maybe the care of the dead, in the course of time, was inspired by the second notion quite as much as by the first. The stock of psyches had to be kept sweet, and treated with respect. In all this, dreams would reinforce speculation. Everyone, sleeping, had conversed with the dead. They could be seen plainly, always in a shape substantially identical with their earthly form; they talked freely and showed all of the desires and habits of mind of the living; they could be consoling, chatty, instructive, bellicose, threatening, vengeful, lustful, heroic; moveover, they could move about. Thus the ghost was born, a sort of anthropoid ancestor of the soul. It began almost at once to be dreaded, for though it was in many respects like a living man, it yet had ways of its own, and some of them were unpleasantly mysterious and menacing. People took to blaming ghosts, and especially the ghosts of unpopular men, for a variety of minor calamities, too trivial to be laid to the gods. Quite naturally, the business of dealing with them was handed over to the priests, who were already experts in whatever was disagreeable.

But the ghost was still far from the thing that modern theologians call a soul, for it was bound to an earthly investiture and could be restored to that investiture or to another, and it was anything but immortal. The ghosts that men saw in dreams — and pretty soon, by an easy step of the fancy, when awake, especially at night — were all relatively recent, for the memory of man was yet somewhat infantile and hazy, and there was no history to reinforce it. A mother might dream of a baby dead a dozen years, and a man traversing a dark wood might encounter his slain father, but that was as far as it went. He seldom encountered his father's father, and never the grandfather of his grandfather. The ghost thus had a limited span of life, and it continues to show that defective durability to this day. Among savages there is a practically universal belief that, by appropriate devices, it may be killed, or, at all events, reduced to inertia and impotence. Even on

46

higher levels ghost lore is largely a lore of exorcism and extermination. So long as a given ghost behaves with reasonable decency it is viewed with more or less equanimity, for experience teaches that it can't last indefinitely, but if it shows any active unpleasantness steps are taken to put it down. Its life is thus precarious, as man's is. And when it dies, either by natural senility or as a result of operations by the priest, it is dead in bitter reality, for so far as I know there is no concept anywhere of a ghost of the second degree, or ghost's ghost.

## II

There must have been active speculation at a very early day about the precise duration of a ghost's life, for it was a matter of practical concern to primitive man. How long could spirits be preserved in or near the bodies of the dead, that there might be a ready supply when children were born? How long was it necessary to put up with a ghost who made a nuisance of himself, and resisted the efforts of the priests to make away with him? The priests, appealed to for authoritative information on these points, probably showed the usual theological division of opinion. There was a party which held that all ghosts die very soon; there was an opposition party which gave them longer life. As the memory of man improved this second party naturally tended to prevail, for he could now remember men long dead, and so dream about them and see their ghosts. History, getting on its legs, helped too; there began to be traditions of heroes in the remote past, and uneasy sleepers occasionally saw them and had talk with them. Thus the life-span of the ghost was gradually stretched out, and there arose a new speculation as to how it was spent, and where.

Did ghosts continue to hang about their earthly clay, sometimes making themselves visible to man and sometimes withdrawing into invisibility, or did they have quarters of their own, remote from those of man, from which they issued intermittently, as the impulse moved them? It was a pretty question, and it fevered theologians for thousands of years. Even in the great days of Egypt, when the cult of the dead reached its apogee, they were far from agreeing. So far apart, indeed, did the Right and Left parties stand that for practical purposes they were forced into a sort of compromise, whereby the soul was divided into two halves, one of which remained by the body and the other of which departed to some vague bourne in the Nile Delta, of indefinite situation and extent. This habit of thinking of the soul as multiple is common among savages today, so common that the professors of comparative religion have invented a special name for it: polypsychism. Some of the American Indian tribes, in the days before they became realtors and Rotarians, recognized two souls, and some of the African tribes three. The Malays, to this day, think they can distinguish no less than seven. There is the psyche proper, which dies when a man dies; there is the ghost which issues from its corpse; there is a shadow-soul corresponding to the shadow that followed him while he was alive; there is the reflection-soul which he saw in woodland pools, and so on.

But primitive man, it is probable, was far less inventive. The thing he thought of, when he speculated about the dead, was simply the psyche turned ghost. Wherever that ghost lurked, whether by the corpse or far away, it was plainly more or less uncomfortable, else it would not be so often on the prowl. It certainly must have known, having been a man itself, that its grisly appearances in the night were far from pleasant to those it accosted; thus it must have been impelled to make them by discontents sufficiently sharp to overcome its natural decency. It is likely that we have here the beginnings of Heaven and Hell. The two, at the start, were probably indistinguishable, as they still were in the time of the Egyptians. Certain ghosts, inhabiting the vague region of the dead, were unhappy and walked the night, to the terror of the living; others, more comfortable, were never seen or heard from. This vague place of their abiding, under the name of Sheol, survived into the day of the Jewish prophets. It survives into our own day, somewhat embellished by the advances of theological science, as the Catholic Purgatory.

The Swiss-American, James H. Leuba, after a lifetime spent in investigating the psychology of religion, held that the belief of primitive man in the more or less limited survival of ghosts, still almost universal among savages, had very little relation to the belief of the so-called civilized races in the immortality of the soul. The former was based upon what, to our remotest ancestors, must have seemed sound objective evidence — the evidence of shadows, of reflections, of shapes seen at night. The latter, in the jargon of psychology, is only a sort of wish neurose: it is grounded, not upon objective evidence, but upon a despairing, colicky feeling that this world we live in is hopeless, and that there must be another beyond to correct its intolerable injustices. It is, said Leuba, " a child of the craving for rationality." Thus it could not have come into acceptance until a relatively late period in the history

49

of man, after he had begun to speculate elaborately and painfully about the nature and aims of his existence. I incline to think that its authors were not theologians at all, but metaphysicians, which is to say, men professionally devoted to concocting recondite and gratuitous theories about man and the universe.

Theologians, as a class, avoid such puerile exercises; they are practical men, dealing daily with harsh and pressing realities. Immortality, as they preach it in the modern world, is but little more than a handy device for giving force and effect to their system of transcendental jurisprudence: what it amounts to is simply a threat that the contumacious will not be able to escape them by dying. Not many of them, I am sure, can actually imagine the life eternal, and most of them, in all probability, waste no effort trying to do so. They leave that feat to the aforesaid metaphysicians, to the class of scientists who try to reconcile science and revelation, and to spiritualists, all of whom have greatly damaged the dignity and authority of theology by trying to enrich its ideology. I am myself a theologian of considerable gifts, and yet I can no more imagine immortality than I can imagine the Void which existed before matter took form. Neither, I suspect, can the Pope.

## II    Its Evolution

### I

Religion, in its first form, was naturally a very simple thing, and had no need of the complicated theologies which now adorn it and make it dark and bewildering. Primitive man, we may assume, did not concern himself greatly with the origin and nature of his gods; it sufficed him to observe that they were very powerful, and could at their will work good or evil. All he asked of them, taking one day with another, was common politeness, and, to borrow a phrase from an American folk-tale, damned little of that. So long as things were going well with him he gave them little thought, and when thought of them was forced upon him by their own acts, he no doubt regarded them with uneasiness and aversion, as a rat regards cats. When he approached them, either directly or through his priests, it was not to assure them of his admiration or to inquire their wishes, but to get immediate favors, mainly of a homely and highly material character. He wanted more blackberries or fewer mosquitoes. He wanted his dead wife to come back, or his living wife to die. It is so among savages to this day. "The Central Australian," says C. H. Toy in his "Introduction to the History of Religions," "conducts his ceremonies . . . without the slightest emotion of any sort except the desire for gain." The Pueblo Indians, says W. J. Perry in " The Origin of Magic and Religion," quoting an unnamed authority, "look to their gods for nourishment and for all things pertaining to their welfare in this world, and while the woof of their religion is colored with poetic conceptions, when the fabric is separated thread by thread we find the web composed of a few simple, practical concepts. Their highest conception of happiness is physical nourishment and enjoyment, and the worship of their pantheon of gods is designed to this end."

The Pueblo Indians, compared to early man, stand on a high level of culture. They are the degenerate descendants of a race which, in its time, must have been almost civilized, and even as they stand today they know and practise many intricate arts, including weaving, architecture, and a kind of agriculture involving irrigation. Their wants are thus relatively complicated and various. But early man, as he emerged from the simian shadows, knew no arts save such as had to do with food-gathering, so his wants were austerely simple, and mainly of a defensive character. He craved protection against falling trees and rocks, against storms and floods, against snakes and venomous insects, against the beasts he hunted, against other men, and, perhaps after a while, against ghosts. Thus his religion was no more than a scheme of propitiation, and the first priests who served him were simply champions who professed to know better than he did how to stay the malignancy of evil forces. These forces, as we have seen, were the first gods. In character they were mainly satanic; they could be good, but it took some argument to make them so. That primeval satanism continues to show itself in gods to this day. Even the kindly Virgin Mary, in places where there is a genuine faith in her, retains a lively capacity for evil, and the innocent peasants of Italy, when she fails them, do not hesitate to smash her image.

Primitive man probably had no special names for his gods. The one that lurked in the lightning was simply Lightning, and so on. The god Flood was not a definite personality, but simply the baleful will residing in the rising waters. But the thing became more complicated as the priests, advancing to the second step in the art sacerdotal, began to pit one god against another. When Rain was summoned to put down Fire, differences in personality between the two necessarily began to be noticed. The one, at least on occasion, was obviously hostile and hence evil; the other, on the same occasion, was friendly and good. Thus the gods, acquiring personalities, began to resemble persons, and it was only natural for primitive man to credit them with the diverse and complicated peculiarities which he noticed in men and women, in the dogs who hung about his cave-fire, and even in wild beasts. This one was generally testy, and had to be handled cautiously. That one inclined to be benign, and could be relied upon. When the god A, in a combat visible to everyone, beat the god B, it was logical to suppose that B was discomfited and unhappy, and might be expected to show it at the first chance by taking a fling at the beneficiaries of A's victory. In a generally dry country the god Rain would be esteemed above all others, and so gradually acquire all of the qualities that were admired in salient and well-regarded men. Elsewhere Rain would be put below the god Sun, and the talk about him would be mainly unfavorable, and even contemptuous.

The priests, it goes without saying, took a leading part

in the formulation of such judgments. They were, in the first place, acknowledged specialists in the ways of gods, and in the second place they had plenty of leisure for speculation. It was not every day that they were called upon to perform their prodigies, for it was not every day that primitive man was menaced by forces beyond his own powers of resistance. On most days he went about his business without any conscious load of care, gathering herbs and berries, pursuing game and fish, chipping flints, policing his wife and children, criticising the Old Man, and laughing at the apes. Thus the priests, between professional calls, had plenty of time to loll in the sun, as their successors have today, and no doubt they employed their well-fed and comfortable idleness, like their successors again, in considering the two principal problems of their trade: the nature and character of the gods, and the quality of the service they demanded from men. Out of the latter half of the discussion arose the great science of moral theology, with its vast armamentarium of revealed duties, inescapable responsibilities, nicely graduated sins, impenetrable graces and atonements, and implacable punishments. Out of the former came that equally vast store of speculation and dogma about the genesis, genealogy, daily life, philosophy, politics, love affairs, ethical predilections and æsthetic tastes of the gods which remains today, after millenniums of steady enrichment, the most gaudy intellectual treasure of the human race.

As time passed the gods multiplied and took on sharper outlines. The god Rain divided into two gods, one bringing the fearful downpours that flooded the caves and swelled the streams, and the other bringing the gentler showers that cooled the air in Summer. The god Fire, at the start, must have been more terrible than any other, save maybe his brother Lightning, but when his flames began to be harnessed to man's uses he begat a benevolent son. The priests doubtless took the lead in this confection of new gods from the ribs of old ones, for it was to their interest to have as many as possible, and to differentiate them as clearly as possible. The more they had at their command, the better they could meet the demands of any given professional call; and the more they had to say about the idiosyncrasies of this one or that one, the more entertaining their discourse was, and the higher their repute.

Gods began to be credited with all sorts of prejudices, weaknesses, tastes, appetites and humors. They were given the qualities and attributes of men — generosity, pride, wrath, resolution, enterprise, perhaps even a kind of tenderness. And of the beasts that men hunted — the wiliness of the fox, the ferocity of the saber-toothed tiger, the huge strength of the mammoth, the courage of the lion, the foulness of the hyena. This way of thinking of them survives into our own time. The Yahweh of the Old Testament, still worshipped by millions, is called a lion therein, and the Devil, still feared, is a serpent and a dragon. In the New Testament Jesus is both a lion and a lamb. The God of the Episcopalians is an elderly British peer, courtly in manner, somewhat beefy, and, in New York, vaguely Jewish. The God of the Mormons shaves his upper lip, and believes in large families and a protective tariff. The God of the Methodists is an *agent provocateur,* forever fingering His pad of blank warrants. The God of the Baptists is amphibious, and, in some of His aspects, almost identical with the Neptune of the Greeks.

Early man, like the savages of today, whether in Africa

or on Long Island, admired all the more showy of the lower animals. He spent most of his time trying to kill them, but he nevertheless admired them, and so aspired to be like them. His first works of art, still preserved in the caves he inhabited, are portraits of them: he drew and carved them, if the chronology of the archeologists is to be trusted, even before he drew and carved women. From this it has been argued that he worshipped them — that they were, in fact, his gods. But that is not likely, for he would not have drawn a god as a multitude of identical individuals, as he drew deer and mammoths, nor would he have shown gods brought ignominiously to their knees, with spears in their hearts. The concept of gods suffering death and humiliation had to wait for many centuries. When primitive man covered the murky walls of his cave with drawings of the animals he hunted, it was simply because he respected their prowess, and was proud when, by the favor of his gods, he was able to overcome them. But that this admiration induced him to transfer some of their qualities to the gods themselves is not improbable, for in the earliest known images of undoubted gods they are shown wearing animal masks, and even have hooves and tails.

Early man went further. He sought to identify himself with the animals that he specially admired, and when he ate their flesh it was not alone to nourish his body but also to enrich his psyche with their virtues. He yearned to be as cunning as a fox and as bold as a tiger. That aspiration, in the centuries to come, was to lead his descendants, by diverse paths, to the physical horrors of cannibalism on the one hand and to the intellectual horrors of transubstantiation on the other. At a much earlier period it was to set up the curious institution of the totem, which yet remains widespread among savages. A totem may be anything, but is commonly an animal. That animal becomes sacred to the tribe or clan that has adopted it, though it is not precisely a god. They may eat it ceremoniously or they may hold it to be untouchable. In either case they believe that they get from it whatever qualities they are proud of, and that it is the chief repository of that *mana* (= luck, destiny, life-force, place in the sun) which enables them to survive in the world. The falcon-god Horus, of the Egyptians, probably began as such a totem, and so did the cow Hathor and the serpent Neith.

2

As man increased in numbers he became a traveller, and came into contact with strangers of his kind. There was trade of a sort in the earliest days of which we have any record. Shells from the Red Sea are found in some of the pre-historic graves of Western Europe, and tin from England seems to have made its way to the Eastern Mediterranean at a very remote time. Missionaries, I suppose, followed the traders, then as now, for it is a peculiarity of *Homo sapiens* that he is a teaching animal, and longs always to instruct and improve his fellows. And if there were no actual missionaries, it may be safely assumed that the traders themselves were not lacking in the common zeal. If nothing else urged them to preach their gods, then they must have been inspired by mere boastfulness. Their very presence in far places was proof enough that the gods at home had the power to aid and protect them, and the will to do it. One may imagine violent debates around distant campfires, with the visitors whooping up their own gods and running down the gods of the home-folks, and the home-folks, their vanity touched, arguing it the other way.

This naïve pride in the home gods, more than any revealed command from them, is responsible for missionary effort in our own day. When a Georgia Baptist drops ten cents into the plate of a touring rhetorician for the Foreign Missions Board, it is not primarily because he yearns to save the Chinese from Hell, but because he likes to dwell upon the fact that his own god is much more potent and respectable than the Chinese gods, and that he himself, *per corollary,* is a high-toned and enviable man, hookworm or no hookworm. Thus the art of the missions collector is mainly an art of subtle flattery. It is his function to warm his victims into charity toward their inferiors. If he is a genuine virtuoso, he is quite capable of hinting that proofs exist that a Georgia cracker is superior to a Chinese philosopher.

But despite this self-esteem which makes every man put his own gods above all others, the early matching of gods must have led now and then to conversions, for some of them, when the plain facts were examined, surely came out better than others. Here was a god, Wind I, who kept an upland valley pleasantly cool, and here was another, Wind II, who battered the flint-miners down at the seashore with hurricanes. Here was a new and highly puissant god, perhaps thought of as a sort of gaseous tiger, who drove deer in great herds into the clutches of the hunters of Cave A, and here was another of the same sort who sent the hunters to Cave B nothing but a few miserable rabbits. I daresay that many converts, not content with acknowledging that the god over the hills was better than the one at home, went to the length of moving into his territory, that they might be sure of partaking of his favors. But this, in most cases, was probably inconvenient, and maybe prohibited, and so the custom arose of importing outlander gods, or, at all events, a sort of share in them. The number of gods in practice in a given community thus threatened to become enormous, for every returning traveller had news of a new one. We find, indeed, by the earliest records, that most tribes had endless hierarchies, some borrowed and some bred on the spot. There are savages, even today, who have hundreds, some belonging exclusively to small groups, or even to individuals. The semi-civilized Hindus have thousands.

But in the presence of such multitudes, the less potent tend to be deposed for incompetence, or to be forgotten as trivial and unnecessary, or to be reduced to the rank of mere domestic divinities. Whenever a really potent new god is introduced, he clears off shoals of lesser rivals. The whole history of religion in early Egypt is a history of the absorption and destruction of rivals by Rê, the sun-god; in the end, running the cycle that gods follow as well as men, he was himself challenged and badly damaged by the great goddess Isis. Similarly, the air-god of the Aztecs, Tezcatlipoca by name, did powerful execution upon their other gods, and at the time of the Spanish conquests he was threatening to drive many of them out. Even in Christendom we see the process going on. The Catholic saints, who, from the standpoint of the comparative theologian, are substantially gods, have their heyday and their decline. Some of those who were most esteemed in the Middle Ages are now seldom heard of. Even in our time the cult of the Little Flower has done palpable damage to other celestial personages, if only because the faithful can't give over all their time to their devotons, and must thus neglect one saint in order to honor another. Among the Protestants there is a like combat between the ferocious Yahweh of the Old Testament and the gentle Jesus of the New, with Yahweh, of late, usually victorious.

When primitive man began to practise agriculture his need of gods was greatly increased, for his means of subsistence were now exposed to new and very serious hazards. He was never sure, when he planted his barley and millet seeds, that they would yield him a crop. The birds might pluck them out of his shallow furrows; insects might destroy them; they might be washed out by the rain or parched and ruined by the hot sun. Once they sprouted, there was a whole series of new dangers, running from droughts to wind-storms. It was natural for the first farmers, facing all these disheartening and inexplicable difficulties, to turn to the gods for relief: their successors tend to be more religious than other men to this day, if only because they are closer to the elemental forces. Out of the fertility cults that were thus set up there gradually arose the concept of a god specially devoted to the care of the fields, and in the course of time this god began to be thought of as a woman, for it was women who brought forth children, and there was an obvious suggestion of that dreadful and mysterious function in the way the earth brought forth food. Moreover, it was women who did most of the field labor, as among savages today, for the men still had to devote a large part of their time and energy to the chase, and perhaps a bit later on, to war. Thus a goddess called the Earth Mother, the Corn Mother, or something of the sort began to be heard of in the world, and in the course of time she became a divinity of the highest rank, and had her following throughout the vast region stretching from the Indian Ocean to the Baltic. In Greece she was Gaia, in Babylon she was Ninlil, and in the wilds of the North she was Freya.

The earliest records of all the historical peoples, from the Sumerians to the Celts, are full of references to this Earth Mother, and she survives among savages today, and even in Christendom. The Virgin Mary, in all probability, descends from her, for in very remote times she was already looked upon as the mother of the other gods. She gradually assimilated the special powers and prerogatives of various rivals, and even came to be identified with them. Thus, in some places, notably in the Eastern Mediterranean region, she swallowed the moon-goddess, and among the Celts she became confused with the gods residing in trees, and among the ancient Mexicans, whose gods were both good and evil, she became the serpent-goddess, and the source of both disease and healing. The first man-made images which seem, with any plausibility, to have been representations of gods were apparently images of her. They show her protuberant in front, as if pregnant, and with wide hips and enormous breasts.

In the course of time she came to have a host of satellites. When cattle were domesticated and man began to milk cows, he gave her a sacred cow as an attendant, and in some places this cow became her invariable symbol, and was identified with her. Later on trees came under her jurisdiction as well as field crops, for their sap was mistaken for milk. She became the protector of the dogs which policed the camp, and, when irrigation was in-

61

vented, of the waters which prospered the crops. In times of war she turned warlike and was borrowed by the fighting men; in times of peace she reverted to the *Frauenzimmer,* and concerned herself chiefly with women's arts. "As civilization developed," says Perry, "and the people acquired fresh ideas about givers of life, the Great Mother, as the great life-giver, came to be associated with each new development. In herself and her attributes she reflects the increasing complexity of early thought." Thus in Babylonia she became the Carpenter, the Coppersmith, and the Lady Potter, and finally the Mother of Men, and even the Mother of Gods.

But this Earth Mother, though she thus came to have enormous prestige everywhere, was never without the challenge of competitors. The old gods, Rain, Wind, Fire, Lightning, and their kind, survived beside her, and multitudes of new divinities were being invented all the time. The pantheons of all the early peoples whose records have come down to us were densely populated; they fairly swarmed with gods, some trivial and unimportant, but others of immense potency. These gods were so numerous that even the priests could scarcely call the names of all of them, just as a Catholic archbishop of today would be stumped if he were asked to recite a roster of the saints. The Celts alone seem to have had thousands. They ranged from craft divinities, such as Gofannon, the patron of the metal-workers, to Vintius, the god of the wind, and from Mogounus and Sulis, the lowly protectors of certain remote military outposts, to Albiorix, who had the sonorous title of King of the World. Among the Celts, as among many other early peoples, the lesser gods were often put into groups for convenience, and their individuality tended to disappear. Thus there were the *dervonnæ,* who were oak-spirits; the *niskai,* who were water-spirits; and the *quadriviæ,* who were goddesses of the cross-roads. The early Greeks, as everyone knows, had multitudes of subordinate gods and goddesses who were similarly classified: nereids, naiads, dryads, hamadryads, oreads, oceanids, fauns, and so on. These mediatized and regimented divinities survive today as fairies, gnomes, jinns, sylphs, trolls, fays, nixies, and kobolds. Every civilized race has its battalions of them, and usually they are thought of as being of no definite number.

It was not, however, the competition of such hordes of standardized godkins that menaced and finally dethroned the Earth Mother, nor that of the thousands of divine lions, wolves, goats, cats, serpents, dragons, and basilisks who raged everywhere, nor even that of her great predecessors, Rain, Fire, and Wind, but that of an old-timer suddenly clothed with a new dignity and power. He was the sun-god. Sun-worship goes back to a very remote time, and is one of the primeval cults that have flourished uninterruptedly through all the vicissitudes of theological evolution. The predynastic Egyptians worshipped the sun under the name of Horus, and later on he reappeared under the name of Rê, and became the supreme lord of the Egyptian pantheon. Rê came from the north and was soon so powerful that he absorbed the chief god of the south, the mighty Amon. Eventually he absorbed so many other gods that he became corrupted, and the great pharaoh, Amen-Hotep IV, tried to supplant him with a new and purer sun-god, Aton. That was in the Fourteenth Century B.C. Amen-Hotep failed, and Amon-Rê continued to reign in Egypt for many centuries, though eventually he was disposed of. He was, in his great days, gorgeously regal. He was the special god of kings, and the pharaohs pretended to be his children, as their colleagues of Babylonia pretended to be descended from Merodach, another sun-god. "Thou hast the form of thy Father Rê," says a hymn to a king of the Thirteenth Century, "when he rises in the heavens; thy rays penetrate all the lands of the earth; without thy beauties may no place exist. . . . If any man shall perform a secret art, thine eye shall perceive it, O king, gracious lord, who giveth to all the breath of life." "Thou art like Rê," says a stele of Rameses II, "in all that thou dost. . . . If thou wishest for a thing in the night, in the dawn it is by thee."

## 3

Rê and Merodach, like the Earth Mother, had their counterparts among all the ancient peoples, including the Mayas, Aztecs, and Incans of the New World. The Mayan sun-god was Kinichahau, who came out of the East and was the father of the whole human race. The Incan sun-god, Inti, had a long struggle with the pre-Incan jaguar-god, but in the reign of the eleventh Inca, Huayna-Kapac, finally conquered him and ruled Heaven and earth. Above this Inti, to be sure, stood a still greater god, Pacha-Kamac, but he was remote and impalpable: Inti was his son, and accessible, and it was to Inti that the Incans addressed their prayers. He was their intercessor, their Christ. Among the Aztecs the sun-god was Tonatiah, a divinity so powerful that he was commonly referred to simply as Teotl, or God. "He was," says A. Hyatt Verrill in "Old Civilizations of the New World," "the ever-present background of the worship of all the Aztec deities." It was to him that the appalling human sacrifices described by the early Spanish explorers were made: his altars ran blood for weeks on end. Nor was he satisfied with the wholesale butchery of human beings: on great days he also demanded that the other gods be sacrificed to him, and devotees dressed up to represent them were gloriously done to death.

This prosperity of the sun-god spread in all directions, until it almost covered the earth. The early Jews knew him as Shamash, a name borrowed from the Babylonians. He penetrated to Persia and India, and thence to Central Asia. He appeared in Australia and in the islands of Polynesia. The primitive peoples of North America heard of him, and when white men first visited them they were worshipping him. He is still worshipped by some of the Indian tribes, as he is by many tribes in Africa, and in the uncivilized parts of Mexico. In Persia and in India sun-worship flourished for many centuries, and in both countries traces of its influence still survive. Both the Avesta and the Vedas speak of a sun-god, Mithra or Mitra by name. In the Bad Lands beyond Persia and Mesopotamia he coalesced with the Babylonian sun-god, Merodach, and became the national god of the Armenians. Their kings, pretending to be his sons, adopted Mithradates as their royal name. When Alexander of Macedon plunged into that wild country, in the Fourth Century B.C., many of his soldiers were converted to the worship of Mithra, and thereafter, for six centuries, he had his devotees throughout the Mediterranean world. His cult, taking on Phrygian and Chaldean embellishments, became secret and obscene, and military men, in particular, seem to have been addicted to it. The Roman troops, following the Greeks in Asia Minor, brought it to Rome, and it became so popular that it threatened, in the first centuries of our era, to crowd out both the old Roman religion and Christianity. So late as the Third Century the Emperor Valerian was a Mithraist, and had *Sol, Dominus Imperii Romani* stamped on his coins. His mother, indeed, is said to have been a priestess of Mithra.

The old Persian devotion to the sun developed, in the course of time, into a highly intellectualized monotheism, and its prophets predicted the coming of a messiah. It was Persian priests, or magi, who came to Bethlehem to worship the infant Jesus, as Matthew records. The Parsees of India carry on the old faith to this day. They have still further intellectualized it, but they yet maintain ceremonial fires and they yet pray on the seashore to the rising and setting sun. These Parsees are the descendants of Old Believers who refused to yield when the Calif Omar conquered Persia in the year 641 and ordered the whole populace to turn Moslem. They fled to islands in the Persian Gulf, and later on to Bombay, where they have prospered vastly. The old religion is by no means extinct in Persia itself. On the contrary, it has infected Mohammedanism, there as elsewhere, and so late as the Seventeenth Century, after a thousand years of Islam, a Persian reformer, Akbar by name, proposed formally that it be revived. He was put to death for his pains — but every Moslem, facing Mecca when he prays, recalls the days when his ancestors faced the East and the risen sun, just as every Christian goes to church on Sun-day, celebrates Christmas on the *dies natalis solis invictus* or birthday of Mithra, and employs symbols and ceremonials borrowed from the ancient sun-worship at Easter, the time of the vernal equinox.

The fires that are lighted by the peasants of Europe on Midsummer Eve go back to the time when their barbaric forebears, seeing the sun-god beginning to lose power, sought to offer him reinforcement.

In the Old Testament the sun plays an important rôle. Yahweh Himself is often compared to it, and His command of it, both directly and through agents, is counted as one of the greatest of His glories. Certain of the Israelites, indeed, continued to worship the sun-god long after the True Faith was revealed to them. In Deuteronomy one finds Moses denouncing the practice with great eloquence; it was not until the time of Josiah that the priests and trappings of the cult were thrown out of Solomon's temple. As I have just said, the magi who came from the East to worship the infant Jesus were not the kings that pious art has made them, nor even the metaphysicians that Matthew speaks of, but simply Persian priests of Mithra. For many years it had been believed that the sun-god would one day send his son down to earth, or come himself, and they were looking for him. When the alarmed Herod sent them to Bethlehem to "search diligently for the young child," it was a magical star from their own East that guided them — that East which was sacred to all sun-worshippers, as the quarter whence the sun came of a morning.

A form of sun-worship but little different from that of ancient Egypt survives in Japan as Shinto, the state religion. The queen of its pantheon is Ama-terasu no Oho-kami, a sun-goddess, and the mikado is her chief priest and prophet. More, he is of her blood, for his remote ancestor, the first mikado, was her son. The Chinese name for Japan is Jih-pun-Kwoh, the sun-origin kingdom, and to the Japs themselves, as everyone knows, it is the Land of the Rising

Sun. The sun-disk is the official emblem of the country, as the lion is of England and the eagle of the United States. Shintoism has room for many other gods or *kami,* including sea-gods, mountain-gods, animal-gods, tree-gods, house-gods, a moon-god, a fire-god, and several heirs of the Earth Mother — some of the last named, curiously enough, being male. There are also gods who are deified human beings — emperors, war heroes, statesmen, philosophers, and so on; one of them, Temmangu, who shed this flesh in 845 A.D., is the special god of schoolboys. But the sun-goddess is above all the rest. Her worship goes back to a very early day, and at the beginning she was undoubtedly male. In the Sixth Century of our era the infiltration of Buddhism into Japan corrupted her cult, but twelve centuries later there was a Shinto revival, and at the time of the revolution of 1865–68 an appeal to the ancient faith of the people helped to depose the shoguns and restore the mikados. Since then Shintoism has been the established religion of the country, and all of the ceremonials of state are carried on according to its rituals. It is, of course, too idiotic to be taken seriously by a people pretending to be civilized; hence most Japanese reserve their devotion to it for state occasions, and at other times toy with more plausible faiths, including especially Buddhism and Confucianism. They are not, indeed, a religious folk. Patriotism serves them in place of supernaturalism.

The transformation of the sun-god into a goddess, just noted in Japan, is not unique there. Something of the same sort happened in ancient Egypt, where, by the beginning of the Christian era, Isis had completely displaced Amon-Rê. Nearly all religions, in fact, show a pull toward goddesses as they decline: the case of Christianity and its mariolatry is familiar. But the sun-god, at the start, seems to have been male everywhere; as we shall see, he was probably the very incarnation of maleness, as the Earth Mother was of femaleness. The beginnings of his high eminence came with the development of agriculture. He had existed, to be sure, long before the first peasant turned the first sod, but it was only as one among many: the rain-god and the wind-god, to name no more, were his equals and rivals. But with the beginning of orderly sowing and reaping it must have been evident to early man that the kiss of the sun was more important to their success than anything else that the powers and principalities of the air had to offer, not even excepting the kiss of the rain. The sun warmed all growing things as it warmed man himself; it made them leap up joyously. Moreover, it was spectacular, lordly in mien, dramatic, brilliant, overwhelming. Only the lightning could match it there, and the lightning came only at long intervals, whereas the sun came every day. It arose in the morning with the air of a king condescending to expose himself to his lieges, and it went down in the evening to the accompaniment of incomparable fireworks. Its genial caress could be felt by all; even the dumb brutes shared in it and appreciated it. When that caress was vouchsafed, life was cozy and comfortable; when it was withdrawn, life was bleak and unpleasant. At night, when it was gone, men shivered, for the air grew damp and cold, and all sorts of evil shapes were abroad.

Thus it is no wonder that the early kings called the sun their father, and tried to emulate its blinding splendors. It was the very model and pattern of all gorgeousness, as of all beneficence. The days on which it lurked behind the clouds were days of gloom and foreboding, and the thought that it might one day vanish altogether was enough to terrify the stoutest heart. Among all primitive peoples an eclipse of the sun is still a calamity of the first water, and when it occurs the priests bring up their heaviest artillery to rout the demons responsible for it. It was one of the chief duties of the early pharaohs of Egypt, as it was of the Incas of Peru, to rescue the sun from those demons. The pharaohs went further: they undertook, as the sons of the sun, to bring it up every morning, and their people believed that if they neglected that august duty it would not appear. Thus a pharaoh had to arise every day before dawn, and long before his subjects got to breakfast he and his priests were worn out by their complicated and fatiguing incantations.

## 4

But in all this we have forgotten the Earth Mother. How did the sun manage to beat her for first place among the gods? The question looks easier than it is, and so the learned have often fallen into the imprudence of answering it facilely and foolishly. Not a few of them, for example, reason backward from the sun-god's situation in the days of his prime. He was then the patron of kings, and they argue that he became the primate of Valhalla by royal fiat. A conqueror, coming in with banners flying, simply imposed him upon the people, as the Protestant Reformation was imposed upon the people of England by act of Parliament in 1571, and upon half the people of Germany by the Peace of Augsburg in 1555. *Cujus regio, ejus religio:* the lord of the land determines its faith. But that answer only begs the question, for it leaves us still asking how the sun-god became the patron and pattern of kings.

I suspect that when they adopted him he was already high in honor and potency — that they got far more out of the alliance, in fact, than he did. In the remote days of his first triumphs over the Earth Mother there were few kings who could pretend to anything plausibly describable as splendor, and even rough conquerors were rare in the world and went about somewhat cautiously. We find no memorials of them in the earliest relics of man. The Earth Mother was limned, and her symbols were cherished, but it was apparently a long while afterward before man began to cherish the baton that was the symbol of kings. Is there no significance in the fact that this baton was a baton, and not something else? If the early kings were under the protection of the sun-god, why didn't they use his image as their trade-mark, as their successors did in later ages? Why the banal and clumsy baton, of wood or bone or stone, instead of the gorgeous sun-disk, with its jutting rays? And why did the baton bring with it the phallus, so nearly identical to it that the learned now dispute endlessly whether a given object is a phallus or a baton? I think the answer is that baton and phallus were one and the same, and that both came into the world with the greatest single discovery ever made by man, to wit, the discovery that babies have human fathers, and are not put into their mother's bodies by the gods.

It would be impossible to imagine anything more revolutionary. At one stroke, it changed the whole structure of human society, and started history off upon a new tack. Primitive society, like many savage societies of our own time, was probably strictly matriarchal. The mother was the head of the family. Her relationship to her children was known to all, but the relationship of their father, for long ages, was not so much as suspected; as we have seen, it is not suspected by many savage tribes to this day. He was free of her favors, and he had a duty to her and to her children, but with that duty went very few substantial rights. What masculine authority there was resided in the mother's brother. He was the man of the family, and to him the children yielded respect and obedience. Their father, at best, was simply a pleasant friend who fed them and played with them; at worst, he was an indecent loafer who sponged on their mother. They belonged, not to his family, but to their mother's. As they grew up they joined their uncle's group of hunters, not their father's. This matriarchal organization of the primitive tribe, though it finds obvious evidential support in the habits of the higher animals, has been questioned by many anthropologists, but of late one of them, Briffault, demonstrated its high probability in three immense volumes. It is hard to escape the cogency of his arguments, for they are based upon an almost overwhelming accumulation of facts. They not only show that, in what we may plausibly assume about the institutions of early man and in what we know positively about the institutions of savages today, the concepts inseparable from a matriarchate color every custom and every idea: they show also that those primeval concepts still condition our own ways of thinking and doing things, so that "the social characters of the human mind" all seem to go back "to the functions of the female and not to those of the male."

Thus it appears that man, in his remote infancy, was by

no means the lord of creation that he has since become. Abroad, he could barely hold his own against the dreadful beasts that roamed the fields, and at home he was no more than a compound of butler and *gigolo*. His wife, if his hunting failed or she espied another who struck her fancy, could turn him out at her will. His children were not his, but hers alone. He had no property save his spear, and no rights save the bare right to exist. We may savor his lowly situation by turning to his current successors among the obscurer islands of Polynesia, where the male share in generation is still unknown. These successors lead laborious and gloomy lives. They do all the rougher, more hazardous work, in peace as in war, for the women are bound to the hearth and the garden-patch by their children, but they are homeless until the women take them in. They may set up as priests and magicians, but the authority of a priest is determined by woman suffrage. They may consecrate themselves to politics and aspire to be chiefs, but no chief can function if the women laugh at him. If they travel, they are not sure that their wives will take them in when they come back. If they stay at home, they run a constant risk of being turned out. The men's club is their one refuge, as it is the refuge of men without women in Christendom, but, like its Christian counterpart, it is dull and clammy. Dying, they issue into space as homeless ghosts, and wander about disconsolately until the prayers of women enable them to be born again, and the whole sorry round is resumed.

Primitive man must have been much like that. We picture him as a glorious hunter engaged daily in heroic combats with saber-toothed tigers, but it is highly probable that he clubbed a thousand rabbits to death for every

73

tiger that he so much as trailed, and that when he came home he was not infrequently given a caustic dressing down. The invention of agriculture, far from improving his status, must have damaged it gravely, for women could plant and reap as well as men, and they thus became independent economically, as they had always been independent politically and socially. It is very likely, indeed, that agriculture was a feminine discovery, for women monopolized it for countless centuries. We think of their work in the fields as slavery; in reality, it gave them the upper hand of men, especially in regions where the hunting was going off. No wonder the Earth Mother was the earliest really first-rate divinity! She represented dramattically the high position of women in the world. Her broad bosom was like the body of a woman. She gave forth her fruits as woman did, without the intervention of man. She was at once the mother with child and the power that put the child in the womb. The whole round of nature, as primitive man conceived it, was embodied in her. True enough, she had some helpers: the sun that warmed the crops and the rain that watered them. These helpers were useful and deserved some gratitude, but after all they were only helpers. Even the brilliant sun was not a prime mover in the wonders of seed-time and harvest. He had his place, as man had his place in the domestic scheme of things, but that place, for all his florid magnificence, was yet only a subordinate one. Crops did not come out of the sun; they came out of the earth. Children did not issue from men; they issued from women. Man was a bystander, useful on occasions, but not a sharer in the miracle, not a contributor of his flesh. Neither, in the miracle of the fields, was the sun.

74

All this depressing inferiority, this lingering half welcome at the second table of life, disappeared at one stroke when some primeval and forgotten Harvey discovered the physiological rôle of the father. It was, as I have said, the most profound and revolutionary discovery ever made in the world: its consequences were endless and colossal. It not only altered completely the fundamental structure of the family, and hence of tribal government, and hence of human society in general; it also introduced a wholly new concept into religion, and one that was destined to take first place among them all. The gods had started out as mere malign presences, with no visible purpose save to do evil; they had developed, step by step, into powers who could be both evil and good, and might be persuaded, by remonstrance and propitiation, to choose good; they had come to be personified, finally, in a beneficent mother-spirit, nourishing the needs and heeding the aspirations of man. Now they were ready to take the grandiose form of a gracious and all-powerful father — maker and guardian of Heaven and earth.

It was, in fact, more than a revolution; it was a new beginning. Man's view of the entire cosmic process changed as his view of the process of life changed. He needed a new god to mirror his new sense of importance, his new dignity, his new glory. He must have a symbol of his own share in the great miracle of birth and growth — a divine inseminator and fructifier to stand beside the germinal Earth Mother, as he himself stood by his woman. If there was any competition for that great place it must have been short. Was the rain-god a contender? Then his claims got no more than a hearing. The obvious candidate was the sun-god. It was he who caressed the fields and warmed and prospered the crops. He was kind, watchful, generous, diligent, reliable. He was the Father foreordained. Moreover, he was splendid beyond compare: no other god could match him there. Thus man saw in him, not only a symbol of the fatherhood that was so charmingly new in the world, but also a symbol of all the new dignities and prerogatives that went with it. The sun-god in his robes of light represented dramatically and inescapably the deliverance of the male from ancient burdens and ignominies, and his rise to the high place of head of the house. It is no wonder that, with the collapse of the matriarchate, he leaped ahead of the Earth Mother, and that the Old Man, now turned king, adopted him as patron and pattern.

## 5

His dominance, of course, was never complete. There remained a welter of other gods, and they survive among savages to this day, and even among peoples higher up the scale. The concept of a single omnipotent god, reigning in the heavens in solitary grandeur, had to wait for long ages, and when it came in at last it was probably devised, not by theologians, but by metaphysicians. They proved that there could be but one god, not by bringing up any overt evidence to that effect, but simply by appealing to what they conceived to be the logical necessities. The human race, on its more refined and exalted levels, has accepted their proofs with the head, but never with the heart. All the great religions surround their chief deity with lesser presences, some of them potent enough to defy him. Christianity, as everyone knows, goes to the length of separating him into three gods, all theoretically parts of a single whole, but each, nevertheless, more or less autonomous. But though the early sun-god, like these later divinities, did not and could not sweep the firmament of all rivals, he yet managed to seize the first place among them. He was the special god of the now dominant and prancing male; he was the god of captains, kings, and other such lofty men; he became inevitably the god of conquerors. These conquerors imposed him upon their new lieges; they claimed to be his agents on earth; in widely separated regions, East, West, North, and South, they began to speak of themselves as Children of the Sun.

Children of the Sun appear with such regularity in the early chronicles of man, lording it over subjugated peoples and shedding a solar effulgence upon history, that certain anthropologists, especially of the English school, have come to the conclusion that they must have all come from one place, and brought their politico-theological baggage with them. But it is not necessary to assume anything so improbable. If it was natural for man to have gods at all, it was surely natural for him to put the sun among them, and once he had got that far, the rest was but two steps away. What went on thus in one tribe went on also in others, near and far. At the dawn of history we find, not one sun-god, but a multitude. The early Egyptians had two that we are sure of, and maybe many more. In Mesopotamia they swarmed like locusts, and every town of any size had one. The Egyptians finally boiled theirs down to a sort of twin, and proceeded to force that twin upon such lesser peoples as came under their hegemony, but along with it went many other gods, great and small. The Children of the Sun, indeed, were nowhere dependent upon the sun-god alone. They gave him a high place and liked to think of themselves as his offspring, but for everyday purposes they used whole squads of lesser gods.

Thus he was never quite omnipotent. Prudent men, in this or that emergency, turned to other helpers. If there were enemies to blast they appealed, perhaps, to the serpent-goddess, who could kill swiftly and horribly. If there was drought, they made supplication to the rain-god, the sun-god's old rival. If hunting was afoot, they had recourse to some god of the chase. Even in his own special domain, where he reigned as fructifier supreme, the sun-god began to meet with competition. The discovery of the physiological rôle of the father exalted more than man alone; it also exalted, especially after animals began to be domesticated, the ram and the bull. They appeared, therefore, as gods, often with rays or wings, no doubt to show their kinship to the sun. Man admired all such virile and gaudy animals, and liked to sweeten his reflections with the thought that he was like them. Once, as we have seen, his rôle at the domestic hearth was but little more heroic than that of the sad and laborious ox; now he could compare himself proudly to the haughty and robust, the rakish and splendiferous bull. There were bulls among the gods of all the early peoples, from the North Sea to the Indian Ocean.

One of the chief functions of the gods, at the dawn of trustworthy history, was to give their votaries success in war. The Old Testament is full of accounts of their high feats in that direction, and so are all the other ancient records. At a still earlier period, it seems likely, they were seldom called upon for such bloody work, for the world was wide and men were few, and so there was very little fighting. The first cave pictures depict the chase, but not war. But as hunting weapons and the technique of the pursuit were gradually improved there came an increase in population, and when agriculture was invented there came an even greater one. Thus men began to crowd one another, and there were rival claimants to this or that stretch of land. Presently they were at one another hammer and tongs, and the gods above fought a battle matching the one on earth. It was not always necessary, I take it, for the conquerors to impose their gods upon the conquered by command, though no doubt it was sometimes done. The conquered knew quite well what had happened; their gods, in a fair fight, had turned out to be weaker than the gods of the other fellows. So it was probably common for them to come over to their notion, as many of the Negro slaves in the Old South came over to Christianity, and maybe there were times when that coming over was unpalatable to the conquerors, as it undoubtedly was to some of the Southern slave-owners, and they wished that the converts had stayed at home.

But the transfer of allegiance was not always so facile, for the old gods had a way of hanging on, if only under cover. Even when new ones were imposed by the sword, the old-timers lurked in dark and secret places, like Barbarossa in his cave on Kyffhäuser, ready to burst forth at a convenient time. That happened all over Mesopotamia in the days of the great invasions, and the result was a hierarchy of gods that became enormously complicated, and even more or less antagonistic. Similarly in early America, when the Spaniards imposed Christianity upon the Aztecs and Mayans, the old gods of those peoples were not abandoned, but simply went into retirement and were soon peeping out again. The Indians of Guatemala remember some of them to this day. Theoretically, every Indian is a good Catholic, but the little *santo* that he brings to church to be blessed by the priest is really an image of one of the ancient Mayan gods. At Esquipultas, in Guatemala, there is an image of the Black Christ to which, as Verrill says, "thousands of Indians journey annually from all parts of Central America, and even from Mexico and South America." Many of them call this image the Cristo Eckchuah or the Cristo Hunabku. Eckchuah was the Mayan god of travelers, and Hunabku was "the invisible and supreme god who was recognized by all the Mayan tribes." So in South America and in Mexico. There are remote tribes in the latter country who still look for the return of the old gods, and during the great combat with the Catholic church it was seriously proposed by some of the Mexican intellectuals that they be revived, as the Nazis later proposed to revive Wotan.

The one and only proof of a god, among primitive peoples, is what he can do for his customers. They have short memories, and lack the metaphysical gift which swathes the divinities of more refined folks in a shining armor, resistant to ordinary evidences. The realistic Burgundians of the Fourth Century, menaced by the ferocious Huns under Oktar, made a bargain with Bishop Severus of Trèves. On his assurance that the Christian god could save them, they agreed to be baptized *en masse,* with the understanding that they would be free to go back to their old gods in case the tide of battle ran against them. It ran their way, and so they became faithful Christians, and their descendants remain Christians to this day, though with some falling off of the ancestral confidence. Many of the defeated Huns submitted to baptism also; they were eclectics in religion, and always extremely polite to any god who showed himself powerful enough to resist them. They carried this eclecticism to great lengths, for they were a cynical people and had no settled religion of their own. Sometimes, on conquering a tribe whose ways they fancied, they adopted the local gods, along with the local customs, despite the apparent unwisdom of it. It was by a proceeding of that order that the celebrated Attila got his name. Attila was the name of the river Volga in the dialect of a subject tribe living on the bank, and to that tribe the river was a kind of god. Attila's father, Mundzuk, liked the surroundings so well that he settled down there, and when a son and heir was born to him, named the youngster after the river god. In the same way the famous Sargon I of Akkad, invading and conquering Sumer, adopted the local gods and made his daughter a priestess of one of them.

The chances are that many of the early conquerors, in their hearts, were quite as easy in faith as Mundzuk and Sargon. It added to their glory to have it generally believed that some powerful god or other was working for them, and it made them appear the more invincible. But in their private reflections they no doubt thought of their victories as their own achievements, and were perhaps somewhat discontented *in petto* that the gods got so much of the credit. Thus the elaborate devotions of the Egyptian pharaohs are not to be taken too seriously, nor the pious inscriptions that the Babylonian and Assyrian kings carved upon their monuments. There were skeptics in those days as in these, and they tended to be the more numerous, as now, the higher up one went in society. To the peasant it was plain enough that the national god or the neighborhood god or the nearest city god was omnipotent, but there must have been doubts about it in the G. H. Q. of the army and at court. Whenever a king accomplished a conquest of genuine difficulty and importance, he usually followed it with hints that he himself was a sort of god. Such hints did not fall ungratefully upon his lieges, for man has always been thirsty for heroes, and ever willing to see divine attributes in them. The German and Scandinavian barbarians seem to have got almost their whole gallery of gods in that way. At a time before written record, to be sure, they worshipped the Earth Mother, the sun-god, and all the rest of the primitive deities, but these deities were gradually assimilated to salient chiefs and other worthies, male and female, and when the Teutonic pantheon first became known to the Romans it was full of gods who were hard to distinguish from men and women. They married and begot children; they got drunk and fought one another; they went on travels and met with accidents; they practised trades; they sang and made speeches; they engaged in political intrigues; they were served by multitudes of retainers in the form of valkyries, swan maidens, dwarfs and giants. The lives they led were really more operatic than divine, and when the time for it came they slipped into the music-dramas of Richard Wagner as easily as the Yahweh of John Calvin slips into the incantations at a hanging.

## 6

The Romans were not shocked to encounter gods who were thus more than half men, for they had plenty of their own, as well as hundreds of other kinds. At Rome, the cross-roads of the world, all the gods of East and West were mingled. There were so many of them that no one believed in them any more, not even the priests. Some had been borrowed from the primitive Italian tribes; some had come from Greece or Asia; others were no more than men raised to divinity by a decree of the Senate. When an emperor died, his body was burned on a great pyre, and an eagle was released, to carry his soul to the sky; thereafter he was a god. Some of the later emperors were deified while they still lived, like Alexander of Macedon, the pharaohs of Egypt, and the mikados of Japan. The truth is that any respectable Roman, by the simple act of dying, might become a god; all that he needed was children to worship his *manes*. Thus the Roman pantheon swarmed like the German Valhalla, and was rocked by the same tumults and scandals. In it were traces of every variety of religion ever practised by man, from the bald animism of savages to the most highly sophisticated of the cults of Asia Minor. The primitive Earth Mother, or Terra Mater, under the name of Ceres ($=$ the Greek Demeter), and the sun-god and rain-god, joined in Jupiter, survived side by side with local vine-gods from the Italian hill-towns, strange and fearsome deities brought in by the army from the frontiers of the empire, and man-gods who had been emperors only a few years before, and roaring drunk in the streets of Rome.

It goes without saying that no enlightened Roman believed in any of them. Rome had become the sewer of theology, as the United States threatens to become today. All the streams of superstition ran into it, and all the streams of sacerdotal fraud. To be a priest, in the high days of the empire, was to be set down confidently as a swindler. "Cato mirari se aiebat," said Cicero, "quod non

rideret haruspex, haruspicem cum vidisset" — Cato used
to wonder how one priest can avoid laughing when he
meets another. All the more popular cults were cloaks for
vileness of one sort or another, and it was hard to say of a
given one whether it was actually a religion or only a
scheme to cadge money. Loose women were thrust into
pious sisterhoods to get rid of them, as bad boys were once
thrust into the Navy. All the higher dignitaries of state
had ecclesiastical offices, and with each went a large reve-
nue and a series of valuable immunities from the ordinary
laws. Officially, the cult of the emperor was the state religion, and now and then, when it was desired to harass
them, the people of the provinces and foreigners in Rome
were required to make some show of accepting it, but if
they gave lip service that was enough, as it is in the case
of the parallel flag cult in the United States today. Sacerdotal organizations, at all times and everywhere, tend to
be corrupt, for they naturally attract a scheming and unconscionable type of man, but at Rome they were more
corrupt than anywhere else, before or since. When, issuing
out of the back alleys, the homely decencies of primitive
Christianity impinged upon the capital of the world, they
seemed as fantastic and as fabulous as the Rule of St. Benedict would seem today at Palm Beach.

The Greeks, imitated in all things by the Romans, had
little save rubbish to offer them in the theological department. Greece, for hundreds of years, had been absorbing
gods as readily as it absorbed arts, sciences and philosophical ideas. Taking the sun-god from the Northern barbarians, it called him Zeus and set him to reign over the whole
ghostly realm; taking the Earth Mother from the same
source, it gave her the head of a horse and a wig made of

snakes, and called her Demeter. Many of the other gods of the Athenian Greeks were borrowed in like manner. They got Dionysos from Thrace, Pan from Arcadia, and Asklepios from Thessaly. They made gods of human heroes, of animals, and of natural forces and objects, and gave them grotesque genealogies and even more grotesque powers and duties. Achelous, the river-god had 3000 brothers and was the father of innumerable nymphs. Myiagros was the fly-catcher and had the office of shooing away the flies that gathered when sacrifices were made to Zeus.

All the high gods of the Greek pantheon, like the high gods of the primitive Teutons, had human appetites and human weaknesses, and were lavishly given to murder, robbery, fraud, bribery and adultery. There was scarcely a male among them who hadn't hordes of illegitimate children, and very few of the goddesses were *virgines intactæ*. The worship of some of these divinities, especially Dionysos, involved gaudy and swinish orgies, unmatched in modern times save among savages: it was as if the Christians of today should adore Yahweh by putting on uproarious Follies shows, each with a strip-poker tournament following, and a *Kommers* to top it off. The great masses of the Greeks were immensely ignorant and credulous, and even on higher levels there was a great deal of pious flummery. Every crazy cult that came out of the East was made welcome in Athens, and the town was constantly in the throes of revivals and mission campaigns. So numerous were the importations that the state religion could scarcely maintain itself against them; it was by this very hospitality to theological imbecility, indeed, that the Athenians escaped the burden of an established priesthood.

The first reformer to heave himself against all this non-sense was Xenophanes of Colophon. Colophon was in Asia Minor, the ancient home of seers and fanatics, but Xenophanes was an intelligent man, and when he got to Greece he began denouncing Homer and the other Greek poets for attributing to the gods acts "that were a disgrace and a reproach to men." He argued boldly that the funda-mental theological concepts of the time were palpably ab-surd, and that it was an intellectual impossibility to im-agine more than one god. Other reformers followed him, and in the course of time they were joined by such drama-tists as Euripides and such satirists as Lucian. There were also metaphysicians, notably Democritus and Anaxagoras, who sought to dispose of the prevailing theology by put-ting something more rational in its place. But the great majority of intellectuals, then as now, were very polite to so-called holy things, and spoke against them only with great caution. This was true even of Socrates, though he was condemned to death for what amounted to a sort of agnosticism. "By the testimony of Xenophon and Plato," says Dr. Paul Shorey, "he worshipped the gods according to the law of the city, and approved the consultation of the oracles in matters beyond the scope of human foresight."

His great disciple, Plato, went much further. It is im-possible to believe that he gave sober credit to the pre-vailing theology, for it was inescapably revolting to any educated man, but he nevertheless held, according to the immemorial canons of the uplift, that it was good for other men, and that religion was "an essential bulwark of law and morality." He was willing to make any compromise with what was generally believed in that direction in order to get a receptive audience for his notions about

politics, ethics, metaphysics and æsthetics. This willingness had a curiously modern smack; no doubt it helps to
explain his popularity among such devout sages as Paul
Elmer More. Aristotle leaned in the same direction, and
so did the great tragic dramatists, Æschylus and Sophocles.
Aristotle tried to rationalize the current belief in the gods
by tracing it to dreams, *i.e.*, by smothering it in psychology, but he accepted the spiritism which goes with what
is called natural religion, and he even composed a treatise,
now lost, upon the immortality of the soul. Like Plato, he
was above all a highly respectable man, and as such he
regarded religion as "a useful aid to the laws."

These were the whales. When they vanished there was
intellectual chaos. On the one hand skepticism began to
make some progress, with Arcesilaus, Carneades, and the
Pyrrhonists as its chief leaders, and gradually it came
about that the majority of really enlightened men believed
in neither religion nor philosophy. But they constituted,
of course, only a small faction; lower down the scale, even
among those who were more or less instructed, there was
widespread belief in all sorts of pious absurdities, and in
the long run this belief conquered the lost ground. As
Mary Mills Patrick says in "The Greek Skeptics," Pyrrhonism lasted but six centuries, and academic skepticism
but two. Moreover, the Pyrrhonists, even in their heyday,
were as cautious as Socrates and Plato, and "did not op-
pose custom in religious observances." In the end, metaphysics, instead of going on with the war upon theology,
began reinforcing it with new and fantastic concepts, all
of them of powerful appeal to the believing kind of mind.
The old sun-god, having been reduced by scientific materi-
alism to a red-hot and insensate rock, whirling idiotically

through space, now became a hundred different absolutes and essences, all vague and more or less heady. The other gods, explained away, came sneaking back as emanations and appearances. The Logos was hatched: a sort of transcendental internal-combustion motor, half libido and half inhibition. Zeus, castrated and put under bond to keep the peace, stalked through the twilight in the character of the Demiurge, the Presence, the Whole, the All. Meanwhile, the ever-fertile East kept pouring in its shiploads of prophets and missionaries, mullahs and magi, each with something new and shiny to sell, and the plain people wallowed in endless revivals. The Orphic cult was perhaps typical. It began in a quite orthodox fashion, with Dionysos as its special god, but in the course of time it took on all sorts of excrescences, some of them from places as far away as India, and in the end it became a sort of primeval theosophy, with overtones of spiritualism. Its priests, more than once, indulged themselves in such pretensions that they menaced the security of the disintegrating state.

There were other cults that were still worse. Some of them borrowed respectable names and claimed eminent metaphysicians as their prophets, but they were actually no more related to a rational thinking than Christian Science. Even Stoicism began to admit miracle-mongering and even Epicureanism began to traffic with the decaying gods. As in our own time, there was a furious and fatuous effort to reconcile such exact knowledge as existed with the prevailing theology; there were, indeed, quite as many Robert A. Millikans, A. S. Eddingtons, Henry Fairfield Osborns, and Oliver Lodges in Athens as there have been in Anglo-Saxondom in our own time. Philo of Alexandria, in the last century of the old era, attempted the heroic feat of reconciling the classical Greek philosophy with Judaism. A bit later Paul of Tarsus was to succeed far better with Greek pseudo-philosophy and Christianity.

## 7

As I have said, the inordinate appetite of the Greeks for imported and mutually antagonistic religions had at least one beneficent effect: it kept the official faith on the defensive, and thereby saved them from the curse of a state clergy. That immunity, though they did not know it, they shared with the far-away Chinese, and in a later age it was to be enjoyed by the Moslems and by sundry lesser peoples. It was not, however, to become general in the world. Both in ancient and in modern times the priests have always reached out for power, secular as well as spiritual, and the history of civilization is largely a history of the long and often vain effort to shake them off. Even when, as was the case in most of the great empires of antiquity, they are theoretically subordinate to the head of the state and can function only in his name, they almost invariably manage to invest their operations with so much importance that he is more or less in their hands. That was true in Egypt and it was preëminently true in Babylonia. In the latter country, though the king himself was the official high-priest or pope, and any citizen was competent to act as priest in his own home, and even to take part in the ceremonials in the state temples, the clergy nevertheless attained to a position of immense influence, and their ranks swelled almost beyond belief, so that their support became a crushing burden upon the community.

The Babylonian priests were divided into many classes,

each with its special function. Those of one class devoted
themselves to determining lucky and unlucky days; those
of another delivered people from evil spells; those of a
third were anointers; those of a fourth made music at
weddings and lamented at funerals; those of a fifth interpreted dreams; those of a sixth took care of the sacred
fires; those of a seventh made the sacrifices. It appears that
a given priest, on occasion, might turn from one function
to another, but nevertheless they were primarily specialists,
and each class seems to have had its own name. When a
king came home from foreign parts and the whole order
paraded, there was probably little room left for the army
and the populace. Every time a priest invoked the gods,
of course, he had to be paid. How much went to his temple
and how much into his privy purse we do not know, but
we do know that the temples all became tremendously
wealthy, and that the priests lived on the fat of the land.
In hard times as well as good times their posts were secure,
and when there was actual famine they were the last to
starve.

The priests of Egypt were similarly opulent and perhaps even more numerous. There were so many of them
in the great days of the empire that it was impossible for
all of them to serve at once, so at each temple they were
divided into four squads, and while one was in service
the other three rested. But every temple also had a perma-
nent managing committee, made up of priests of high
degree, usually with a prophet, or arch-priest, as chairman.
To each extensive glebe-lands were attached, and the revenues of some of them must have been very large. The accounts of several such temples have come down to us. Those
of the shrine of Amon at Teuzoi show that the presiding

prophet received 20% of the net income, and that the remaining 80% was divided in equal shares among his eighty assistants. Apparently, twenty of these assistants were on duty at a time, while the others rested from their labors. At another temple the arch-priest received but 10% of the revenues, probably because he had a larger staff. In addition there were many perquisites. Every time a bull was slaughtered the officiating priest received a roast. When beer was offered to the gods, he and his assistants drank it. When there was wine they had it at dinner. If a goose was brought in they first sacrificed it professionally and then consumed it personally. For officiating at funerals, praying to or for the dead, casting out demons, determining lucky days, and other such offices there were special fees, over and above the revenues from their lands. Moreover, there were also salaries for their wives, who were known officially as concubines of the gods, and even for their daughters.

It was an easy and lordly life. Priests escaped both military service and the forced labor that was usual along the Nile. They paid no poll tax and could not be arrested for crime. In ordinary times even the heavy revenues of their temples were not taxed, but when a pharaoh was hard up he sometimes made a levy on them. The priests could afford to pay it, for what the pharaoh took one day they got back from the people the next. Naturally enough, many ambitious young men aspired to holy orders, and the pressure, after a while, got so great that a rule was set up restricting ordinations to candidates of priestly families. In the end, a candidate had to prove that both his father and his father's father had been priests before he could so much as come up for examination.

The ancient Jews, in theory, stood in little need of priests, for every head of a household was a sort of priest on his own account. But a powerful and numerous clergy nevertheless developed among them, and by and by the clerical office became hereditary, as in Egypt. First the Levites exercised it, and then they were displaced by the Aaronites and reduced to the estate of temple attendants. In the days of the Maccabees, when the Jewish state was on its last legs, the whole body of clergy, superior and inferior, was so large that the temple revenues could not support it, and many men born to the cloth were forced to turn to other trades. Even at the time of the return from the Babylonian captivity, four centuries before, no less than one-seventh of all the adult male Jews had been priests of one sort or another.

In many other barbaric nations the proportion was probably quite as high. Among the Aztecs of Mexico the clergy ran to immense numbers, and their support half starved the people. So in Persia. So in Asia Minor. Even among the early Greeks, who gave them only the most dubious official status, they became numerous enough, at more than one time, to constitute a public nuisance. When Henry VII came to the throne in England they numbered between 30,000 and 40,000 in a population of 3,000,000 and had two-thirds of all the votes in the House of Lords, owned one-third of all the land in the realm, and had an income two-and-a-half times that of the King himself. So in Spain. So in Italy. So in most parts of Germany. In Tibet today we observe a nation so priest-ridden that the church has actually swallowed the state, and the sacerdotal career is almost the only one open to an ambitious young man. In India the priestly caste of Brahmans has arrogated to itself the first place in society, putting itself above even the warrior caste that supplies soldiers and rulers. Its members refuse to intermarry with members of the lower castes, or to eat with them, or even to take so much as a drink of water from their hands.

Thus, at all times and everywhere, the clergy have reached out for high and singular privileges, and always they have tended to increase up to the limit of communal endurance, both in numbers and in wealth. The Reformation, at bottom, was quite as much economic in motive as theological; it represented a desperate effort to throw off an intolerable burden. The confiscation of the monasteries in England was an instinctive and inevitable measure of self-preservation, for the common people as well as for nobles and king. True enough, rents still had to be paid, but there were more hands to earn them: the vast hordes of dispossessed monks and nuns were driven into productive industry. The same motive undoubtedly had something to do with the cataclysm in Russia, where a weak and superstitious monarch was the puppet of the clergy of a grasping and unconscionable state church. The battle over such high rights and prerogatives engaged Western Europe for more than a thousand years, at the cost of millions of lives. Ever since the great duel between Henry IV and Gregory VII it has rumbled at the bottom of all continental politics, and the story of the miseries that it has heaped upon mankind is one of the most appalling in the history of the race. Count the priests since Peter and you will come to an approximation, perhaps, of the number of the dead.

This apparently universal tendency of the clergy to seize every sort of power and privilege within the range of their always florid imagination goes back to the earliest times. When we first hear of them they were already men of high puissance and consequence, and on terms of easy confidence with the captains and kings of the beginning states. The very nature of the art they practised made it inevitable that they should move in that direction. Government was usually eager to trade with them, for it needed them doubly. On the one hand, they could give it aid and countenance in its usually hazardous external enterprises, for the gods were at their call and command. On the other hand, they were the best of all agents of domestic tranquillity, for they were experts in the kind of conduct that the gods desired and demanded. The ruler who had them on his side had no need to look to his rear, for they were able, speaking *ex cathedra,* to make every sort of subversion immoral. For its cruel putting down in this world they were ready with divine mandates; more, they could project punishment beyond the grave, and make it endless.

So they naturally got on with kings, and were not overlooked when the budget was drawn up. Nor did they forget the side on which their bread was buttered. One reads in history, now and then, of priests backing a usurper against some sitting monarch who forgot to be polite to them, but one seldom reads of them supporting genuine revolution. In all countries, ancient and modern, the overwhelming majority of them have cast their weight, both as seers and as citizens, against all reforms in government. Their votes have gone to the king, or, by second choice, to the nobles; seldom if ever to the people. In England, for century after century, they constituted the shock troops of the old order, and when, despite their opposition, the new order forced its way in, they banged their pulpits against it to the last, learning nothing and forgetting nothing. When a bishop is not a Bourbon it becomes a sort of marvel, as if he were heavyweight champion of the world. Even Jesus, though He came with a sword, was careful not to draw it against Cæsar.

## 8

It is Hell, of course, that makes priests powerful, not Heaven, for after thousands of years of so-called civilization fear remains the one common denominator of mankind. At the bottom of every approach to the gods, even in the most enlightened societies of today, lies the ancient motive of propitiation; the worshipper seeks avoidance, escape, immunity, pardon, mercy; as the Methodists say in their Book of Discipline, his first desire is to "flee the wrath to come." What remains, however brave, lofty, and metaphysical its terms, is no more than *lagniappe*, and of no serious import. When men cease to fear the gods they cease to be religious in any rational sense. They may continue to mouth pious formulæ, but they are no longer true believers. As some wit once said of Unitarianism, a movement typical of the modern effort to get rid of Hell, it is not a kind of Christianity at all, but simply a mattress for skeptical ex-Christians to fall on. The essence of all priestly morality is retribution, and without a Hell of one sort or another retribution becomes mere rhetoric, signifying nothing. All the great faiths of today, including even Buddhism, teach that an intolerable unpleasantness is possible *post mortem,* and that it may be avoided only by correct conduct in this world.

Priests are professional experts in both that conduct and

that unpleasantness. How, letting their fancy run free, they have limned the latter you may find by examining such works as James Mew's "Traditional Aspects of Hell." The Christian Hell, I incline to believe, is the deepest and hottest of them all. It has gathered in all the hells of antiquity, and bent them to its constabulary purposes. Avernus has become its bottomless pit and Phlegethon its lake of brimstone. It is peopled by demons out of the mythologies of Egypt and Babylonia, Greece and Rome. It has borrowed tortures from the Celts and the Teutons, the Jews and the Persians. Those tortures are the bulwarks of all sacerdotal authority today, whether Catholic or Protestant. They constitute the overwhelming answer to every doubt, whether of theological dogma or parish government. "On the banks of the river of death," says E. B. Tylor in his "Primitive Culture," "priests have stood for ages to bar the passage against all poor souls who cannot repeat their formulæ or pay their fee." "I know a certain holy man," said the good St. Chrysostom more than fifteen centuries ago, "who gave thanks for Hell in his prayers." No wonder!

The priestly concept of correct conduct deserves a great deal more study than it has got. There are in it many rich opportunities for the more ghoulish variety of psychologists. In all countries, save where the clergy are transiently at odds with the state, it naturally ratifies the secular penal system. Thus, whatever is punishable by the ordinary courts is also punishable, additionally and with infinite exaggeration, beyond the grave. But there are, beside, many offenses, unknown to the state, that carry the same inordinate and eternal penalties. They divide themselves, in the main, into two well-marked classes. The first in-

cludes acts which tend to break down the priestly authority and security; the second is made up of acts which priests
themselves, by their very character, are specially forbidden
to commit, and hence feel to be peculiarly corrupting and
obnoxious. Examples of both classes are to be found conveniently in the jurisprudence of Holy Church. Of the
first, there is the mandate that every Catholic, on penalty
of mortal sin, must make his Easter duty, *i.e.,* must go to
confession and take communion at least once a year, pref-
erably between Palm Sunday and Easter. The punishment for wilful and continued failure to do so is genuinely
appalling: it is no less than eternal damnation. In other
words, it is precisely the same punishment, to the last jot
and tittle, that is provided for entering an orphan asylum,
putting all the inmates to tortures worthy of Mississippi
Baptists, locking the doors upon them, and setting fire to
the building.

To the second class belong the various ecclesiastical in-
terdicts of procedures which tend to facilitate acts of sex,
or to make them more charming, *e.g.,* contraception and
divorce. The psychological springs of the savage excess of
virtue here visible are no doubt to be found in the uncomfortable necessities of a celibate priesthood. To a clergyman lying under a vow of chastity any act of sex is
immoral, but his abhorrence of it naturally increases in proportion as it looks safe and is correspondingly tempting.
As a prudent man, he is not much disturbed by invitations
which carry their obvious and certain penalties; what
shakes him is the enticement bare of any probable secular
retribution. *Ergo,* the worst and damndest indulgence is
that which goes unwhipped. So he teaches that it is no
sin for a woman to bear a child to a drunken and worth-

97

less husband, even though she may believe with sound reason that it will be diseased and miserable all its life, but if she resorts to any mechanical or chemical device, however harmless, to prevent its birth, she is doomed by his penology to roast in Hell forever, along with the assassin of orphans and the scoundrel who forgets his Easter duty. To this instructive subject we shall return later on.

The human race is stupid, but it is not so stupid that it can't see the irrationality in such grossly excessive and barbaric punishments for what, at bottom, are quite natural acts. Thus it has always been more or less restive under priestly jurisprudence, and the history of religion is largely a history of its efforts, usually somewhat cautious but sometimes violent and bloody, at rebellion. The uprising against indulgences, at the time of the Protestant Reformation, was not aimed alone at the corrupt traffic in them; it was also aimed at the grotesque scheme of punishments behind them. People had begun to have doubts about the Hell preached by medieval theologians, and they therefore objected to paying heavy fines to escape it. The clergy, confronted by this ever recurring questioning of their penal code, have always sought to keep it within bounds by taking control of the education of the young. They sometimes find it impolitic or even impossible to proceed against the concrete skeptic when he is full grown, but if they can get hold of his children they can at least prepare for battle against skepticism in the next generation. The Catholic church, according to an accepted legend, asks for the tutorial custody of the child only up to its twelfth year; after that, it is regarded as either safe for life or hopelessly lost. All other organized churches make the same effort to impress the faith indelibly upon the innocent and tender.

Among Catholics the parochial school is the chief agency; among Protestants there is the Sunday-school. The Jews have similar devices, and so have the Mohammedans, the Brahmans, and the Buddhists. All seek, by drastic training in youth, to prepare for the doubts that are apt to come with years of reflection.

The priests were psychologists long before Freud. In the most remote ages one finds them alive to the fact that what is forcibly presented in the most impressionable years is bound to endure — if not on the plane of conscious reasoning, then at least in the depths of the unconscious. The clergy of Holy Church see proofs of it every day. When the backslider, after years of contumacious abstention from the sacraments, comes at last to his death-bed, the faith of his nonage oozes out of his marrow to overcome him, and he dies with the holy oils upon him and the crucifix at his lips. Faith, indeed, have been well compared by theologians to the artless confidence of a little child. It enters the human mind most effectively before reason has begun to function, and once it is implanted it is likely to stay. The only safe skeptic is one who was never exposed to faith in his infancy. Converts of more mature years are always more or less unreliable.

Thus, going back through history, we find that priests have always been ardent pedagogues. In many, and perhaps most of the great nations of antiquity they held pedagogy as a monopoly. The young Egyptian, at the age of four or five, was sent of a morning to the nearest temple, and there a priest taught him reading and writing, and instructed him in his duties to the gods. The class-room exercises of many such boys, painfully inscribed upon papyrus, have come down to us: nine-tenths of them are copies of religious texts. So the pupil continued until he was thirteen or fourteen, when his basic education was completed and he was ready to undertake a trade or profession. Whatever he knew the priests had taught him. If he had any doubts thereafter about the nature and desires of the gods and his duties to them, they had to meet and overcome the full weight of his early training. In Babylonia the priest and the teacher were similarly identical. Not a great many Babylonians, it is probable, ever learned to read and write at all, for their system of writing was cumbersome and difficult, but those who became privy to the art were initiated by the clergy. In the empire of the Aztecs, says Lewis Spence in "The Mythologies of Ancient Mexico and Peru," "all the science and wisdom of the country was embodied in the priestly caste. The priests understood [probably a misprint for undertook] the education of the people, and so forcibly impressed their students with their knowledge of the occult arts that for the rest of their lives they quietly submitted to priestly influence." This influence ran to almost incredible lengths. So powerful was it that the priests found it easy every year to induce thousands of devotees to offer their lives to the gods. The Spanish conquerors were astounded to discover these heathen *shamans* baptizing infants, administering communion, hearing confession and giving absolution. But all those rites had been old in the days of the Sumerians.

The earliest recorded codes of laws have a sacerdotal smack, and were probably drawn up by priests. The celebrated Code of Hammurabi, King of Babylonia, which goes back to the Twentieth Century B.C., is often cited as as exception, but it is so only superficially. The authority behind it is that of Shamash the sun-god, and it deals at length with the rights and prerogatives of priests and puts them in the *amelu,* or patrician order. True enough, the greater part of it is devoted to civil law — but priests have never hesitated to concern themselves with civil law. In England, as everyone knows, they still participate, through their bishops, in the framing of it, and it was only yesterday, as time goes in human history, that they ceased to administer it. In the United States they are still able to force their ideas upon the secular lawmakers, despite the constitutional theory that they have no voice, in their professional character, in the conduct of the government. Such legalistic extravagances as national Prohibition, the Comstock section of the Postal Act, and the oppresive Sunday laws and blasphemy laws which survive in most of the States are monuments both to their enterprise and to their power. It is only, indeed, among a few tribes of savages, *e.g.,* the Crow Indians, and on the most enlightened levels of civilization that one encounters a true divorce between ethics and religion. Everywhere else the clergy are the final arbiters of all moral disputes, and everywhere they give authority to their fiats by crediting them to the gods.

This supernatural support relieves them very conveniently of the obligation of consistency, and their jurisprudence is full of instructive paradoxes. The same priest who is himself a celibate insists that his parishioners shall be fecund up to the limit of physiological endurance; the same Bible which teaches that marriage is only a desperate alternative to burning is also cited to prove that it is made in Heaven. Once, in the mountains of Tennessee, I heard an eloquent sermon by a pastor of the Holiness sect of Methodists. He devoted the first half of it to denouncing bootlegging, gun-toting, and fornication, the three favorite sins of his followers, and the second half to expounding the difficult doctrine of the Trinity. My thoughts strayed irresistibly to the miracle at Cana, the ferocious blood vengeances of Yahweh, and the exercise of the *jus primæ noctis* by the Holy Ghost, as described in Matthew 1, 18. But it was a rough, Christian country and I was far from home, so I kept my reflections to myself.

## 9

At all times and everywhere priests have reduced their moralizing to absurdity by their own acts, or by the acts they have ascribed to the gods. So long ago as the Fifth Century B.C. Anaxagoras of Clazomenæ was protesting that they were defaming Zeus by praising him for transactions that would have cost an Athenian his citizenship; as a reward for this quite reasonable caveat he was condemned to death, and it took all the eloquence of Pericles to get him a commutation to banishment for life. The wisdom of the common people, though they may believe, leads them in all lands to regard the moral authority of their spiritual advisers with more or less suspicion: there are countless homely proverbs to that effect. The general distrust of the Jesuits, who show to an exaggerated degree all the special characters of priests, good and bad, is testimony to the same purport. Though they deny it with vehemence, it is almost universally assumed that, in their dealings with an increasingly recalcitrant world, they hold that the end justifies the means, and more than once they have been expelled from this or that country on some such ground.

In all the more enlightened nations of modern times efforts have been made to break the clerical control of education, and with it of moral training; the movement, indeed, is one of the first signs of cultural advancement. But it has never succeeded completely, save maybe in Japan. Everywhere in Christendom the priests retain a voice in the education of the young, and seek diligently to protect their dogmas, both theological and ethical, against the inroads of skepticism. Even where they no longer determine what shall be taught, they are still permitted to make black-lists of things that shall not be taught. Thus in the Catholic areas of the United States the Roman hierarchy effectively prevents all rational instruction in the physiology of sex, for by its ethical system sex is intrinsically a wicked matter and hence ought to be kept as mysterious and painful as possible; and in the Protestant areas of the South the evangelical clergy prohibit the teaching of biological evolution as a fact, for their whole theology is grounded upon the cosmogony of Genesis. Both factions, North, East, South and West, teach the ignorant that the Hell of the medieval theologians really exists, though no enlightened man today believes in it, and both found their power upon fear of it.

Such absurdities put the intellectual dignity of priests in a bad light, but it would be going too far to say that they also lack intellectual integrity. The great majority of them, I am convinced, have always believed in their own magic. If laymen, exposed to their influence in youth, tend to acquire a certain irreducible and ineradicable modicum of faith, they themselves, exposed to heavy professional and public pressure their whole lives long, are surely likely to have more. Like all other men, they inevitably rationalize their practical necessities. Pledged formally to the propagation of definite ideas, they naturally avoid scrutinizing those ideas too narrowly. If doubts arise, they instinctively try to put them away. Here they are helped by the arduous training that they commonly receive, and by the sacrifices that their trade forces upon them. For priests, though in all ages they have sought power, glory, and even fortune, have also in all ages resigned and renounced many pleasant things, including even liberty and life. If, at times, the renunciation demanded of them may seem trivial, as in the case of the Methodist parson who takes oath at his ordination to quit tobacco-chewing, then let us not forget that it may be no mean deprivation to the man himself, simple clodhopper that he is. On higher levels the sacrifices called for may be extraordinarily onerous. It is obviously no fun to be a Trappist, nor even a Jesuit. Nor is it exactly charming to be a Baptist dominie when the jug goes round, and the damned make merry: the very bitterness of his denunciation is proof enough that the renunciation behind it is bitter too. As for the burdens of sacerdotal celibacy, they have been sufficiently set forth by Dr. E. Boyd Barrett, a a Jesuit *a.D.*, in various instructive volumes.

Everywhere, indeed, both in ancient and in modern times, and among both civilized peoples and savages, the priest has been a man apart, with certain harsh duties and disabilities to match his privileges and immunities. A relatively high degree of chastity is commonly demanded of him, even by tribes who avoid it sedulously themselves. Almost universally, save among the meaner varieties of Protestant Christians, he must school himself to fasting and to long and wearying vigils. Like the soldier, he must wear a distinctive and often uncomfortable dress, and adapt the cut of his beard to the fiats of his superiors. He must be free from bodily defect, but often he is tonsured or otherwise mutilated. Among the Egyptians, so early as the time of the Old Kingdom, he had to submit to circumcision, then a novelty in the world and confined to priests: it became obligatory upon all males only when all males began to take over some share in the priestly office, as among the Jews. Among some of the American Indian tribes he must prepare to arrest the attention of a somnolent god by chopping off a phalanx of one of his fingers. In parts of Africa he must sacrifice his ears or his teeth; in Polynesia he must must submit to tattooing of a special elaborateness, often very painful. If the gods of his people are approached by going into a desert, or climbing a high mountain, or entering a sweat-bath, or a sacred pool (maybe with alligators or something of the sort in it), or a haunted wood, or the crater of a volcano, or a den of snakes, he must go oftener than anyone else, and stay longer. He must be ready to face mysterious and loathsome diseases as bravely as a medical man, and the public enemy as bravely as a soldier, and the revolting horrors of death and decay as bravely as a mortician.

"The life of an Aztec priest," says Spence, "was rigorous in the extreme. Fasting and penance bulked largely among his duties, and the idea of the implacability of the gods . . . appears to have driven many priests to great extremes of self-torture." It was the same at the other side of the world. "In Summer," say the Laws of Manu, "let him [the twice-born *snataka, i.e.,* the theologue who has completed his vows] expose himself to the heat of five fires, during the rainy season live under the open sky, and in Winter be dressed in wet clothes. . . . Let him wear a skin or a tattered garment, and let him wear his hair in braids — the hair on his body, his beard and his nails being unclipped. . . . Let him live without a fire, without a house, wholly silent, subsisting on roots and fruits, . . . chaste, sleeping on the bare ground, dwelling at the roots of trees. . . . Let him not desire to live; let him not desire to die; let him wait for his time. . . . Let him patiently bear harsh words; let him not insult anybody; let him abstain entirely from sensual enjoyments."

The laws of Manu were formulated many centuries ago, but the Hindu *sadhus* of today, perhaps three millions in number, follow the ancient rule. They rub ashes on their gaunt bodies, submit patiently to the assault of pediculæ, and sleep on the bare ground. They live on alms for which they must not ask, even by indirection: they may not approach a house at mealtime. Some of them, more austere than the general, lie upon boards set with spikes, or hold their arms above their heads for weeks and months on end, or double their fists until their fingernails pierce their palms, or chew live coals, or thrust skewers through their legs, or sit in water up to their necks, or consort with venomous snakes. They may not kill anything, not even a bee that stings them. They must renounce wines and liquors. They may eat no meal of more than eight mouthfuls.

The Christian chronicles are full of fair matches for these *sadhus*. Observing a Methodist bishop engaged in tracking down sin, a man of eminence and puissance, followed by newspaper photographers, and as proud and prancing as a stallion at a county fair, one forgets his brethren in the back country, serving God laboriously for $250 a year. Observing a Roman cardinal dashing down Fifth avenue in his Rolls-Royce, with bands braying, drums rolling, and cops clearing his regal way, one forgets the Rule of St. Benedict, and the sisters in the hospitals. One forgets, too, the Stylites on their pillars, the Dendrites roosting in trees, the Boskoi who ate only grass, the Euchites who prayed incessantly, the Trappists who never speak. St. Peter Celestine kept four Lents every year, and during each of them ate only black bread, and that only once every three days. St. Joseph of Copertius went five years without a meal and fifteen years without a drink: what he got at communion was enough for him. Father Nicholas de Flue went on a fast lasting twenty years, with no break save at the holy table. St. Aïbert said 150 Ave Marias and 150 Psalms a day. St. John-Joseph de la Croix (who is not to be confused with the mystic, John of the Cross) wore one hair-shirt day and night for forty-six years, and for sixty years never looked into the face of a woman. Father Laurent, a Benedictine of Naples, burned his forehead every Friday in memory of the crown of thorns. Cardinal Damiani of Ostia, the forerunner of the great reformer, Gregory VII, slept on a board, scourged himself daily, and wore an iron collar.

The chronicles of Islam are equally rich in examples. They begin with that Bahlul ben Dhu'aih who retired to the mountains behind Medina, clad himself in haircloth, had his hands tied behind him with a chain, and repeated over and over again: "O my God, see Bahlul, bound and shackled, confessing his sins!" and they end with the swarms of Qadris, Rifa'is, Mauliwis, Shadhilis, Badawis, and other holy sectaries who entertain the Moslem world today, some of them dancing frantically, others brandishing scimitars, and yet others immersed in cells with veils over their heads, howling the name of Allah ten thousand times a day. Nor are such austerities unknown among savages. There are Stylites among the American Indians, and Mauliwis in the jungles of Africa.

# III    Its Varieties

Most persons, looking into the anatomy and physiology of religion for the first time, are struck at once by the vast diversity of sects. They seem to sweep in all directions, taking in ideas of the most remote and fantastic sorts, and their rites and ceremonials are observed to run the whole scale from imperial splendor to the most severe simplicity. There are religions that are gorgeously operatic, and there are others that are inordinately secret and sneaking. Some lay great stress upon magic, and others make an appeal that is almost purely æsthetic. Some are as noisy as a brass band, and others are as *pianissimo* as a seduction. This reaching out for every imaginable device and agent of wonder has led Dr. Lowie, in his "Primitive Religion," to put within the scope of religious interest everything that is extraordinary, *i.e.,* everything that is not instantly explicable as natural and familiar. But it seems to me that it is possible to make a much narrower definition of religion without losing anything of actual significance. It is, in fact, by no means a mere recognition of the extraordinary, nor even of the transcendental, for that may be accompanied by complete indifference; it is essentially a scheme to bend the extraordinary to man's uses — a plan of attack upon the powers which seem to control and condition it.

All religions, whatever their superficial differences, have that purpose at bottom, and so all of them are fundamentally alike. What the Bakua medicine-man seeks to accomplish by rattling stones in a cocoanut-shell, or the Tibetan *lama* by whirling his prayer-wheel, or the Yakut *shaman* by going into a sweat-bath, or the Crow Indian devotee by chopping off a finger is precisely what the Pope seeks to accomplish by saying Mass in St. Peter's. All desire, first, to attract the notice of the gods, and, second, to induce them to be amiable. The differences in method of approach, however radical they may appear superficially, are of little consequence in essence. Every religion, if it survives long enough, changes its ceremonials, and every one of them borrows constantly from the others. It would be hard to discover any act of a Christian priest, of whatever rite, that is not matched in the rituals of a hundred other religions, and there is scarcely a non-Christian usage or solemnity, however barbarous it may appear at first glance, that has no parallel in the operations of Christianity. Everything that Holy Church cherishes as peculiarly its own, from pedo-baptism to auricular confession and from holy communion to the monastic vows of poverty, chastity, and obedience, was hoary with age before Peter ever saw Rome.

Four ideas lie at the bottom of all organized religions, whether ancient or modern, cultured or savage, to wit:

*1. That the universe is controlled by powers of a potency superior to that of man, and that the fortunes of man are subject to their will.*

*2. That these powers take an interest in man, and may be influenced to favor him.*

*3. That certain men have a greater capacity for influencing them than the generality of men.*

*4. That certain words and acts are more pleasing to them, and hence more likely to make them friendly, than other words and acts.*

The first idea, theoretically, may stand alone, but when it stands so it does not make a religion; what it makes is simply a fatalism that, as a practical matter, is almost the negation of religion. No really religious man ever submits himself so abjectly to the divine will; even the most ardent believer in predestination is always an active suitor in the omnipotent court. The most essential article is thus the second: that the gods, whoever and whatever they may be, are susceptible to propitiation. But the third and fourth follow it inevitably, for even cults that have no formal priesthood at least recognize a difference between those men who are in the favor of the gods and those who are not, and the former, it is manifest, thereby become indistinguishable from priests; and even cults that reject all ritual recognize certain obligations of conduct and of thought. If the gods demand nothing else, at least they demand an elaborate deference and politeness. "Always and in everything," says the Chinese Li Chi, the Book of Rites of Confucianism, "let there be reverence." Nor is it believed anywhere, as far as I can make out, that they fail to distinguish between worshipper and worshipper, separating those who are, so to speak, attorneys from those who are mere petitioners. Even the sects that minimize the function of the clergy, *e.g.,* Moslemism, recognize the intercessory power of men of extraordinary holiness, and even those that reject priestcraft altogether, *e.g.,* Christian Science and Quakerism, yet have their prophets and saints.

Some sort of fixed ritual, carried on by such experts, is

thus of the very essence of religion. It is to be found in the rites of the lowest savages, none of whom approach the gods in the way they approach mere men. There is always a special time for the business, and usually a special place, and there must be careful preparations. The priest, not infrequently, makes his addresses in an archaic, foreign or artificial tongue, and to the accompaniment of acroamatic songs, postures and gesticulations. The ancient Assyrians and the Babylonian priests petitioned the gods in Sumerian, which was as unintelligible to their clients as the Hebrew of the holy scrolls is to the modern Jews, or the Latin of the Mass to the Catholic, or the Old Church Slavic of the Greek rite to the peasant of Eastern Europe, or the Sanskrit of the sacred books to the Hindu, or the Arabic of the daily *suras* to the Turk. Even among savages there appears this preference for a secret language of religion; it plainly adds to the impressiveness of ritual, and is moreover a subtle proof of the high and occult learning of the priest. Solemn High Mass would be vastly less solemn if the ancient text were intoned in English, maybe with an Irish or Italian accent; the mysterious Latin, even though it, too, rolls out over Irish tonsils, is far more grave and imposing.

As everyone knows, Holy Church long frowned upon the translation of the Bible into the common languages of Western Europe; the Latin Vulgate was comprehensible, at least in theory, to the clergy, and that was enough. In the same way the Malikite school of Moslem theologians protest against the translation of the Koran, and the Hanifite and Hanbalite schools consent to it only if the original Arabic be printed side by side with the Turkish, Persian, Urdu, Malay or other modern version. "The formulæ of the *salat* [the five daily prayers of obligation]," says Father Lammens, S. J., in his book on Islam, "must be recited in Arabic — nothing less will do." One of the ostensible purposes of the Protestant Reformation was to carry the Gospels to the people, but the architects of the Authorized Version could not bring themselves to put the text into everyday English, and so resorted to an artificial poetical language, full of deliberate archaisms. Even the most unceremonious Methodist, addressing God directly, does not use the English he would use in addressing another Methodist; he fills his petition with phrases and syntactical forms that are consciously rococo, and reserved for Omnipotence alone.

Mankind has always felt that mere prose, however ornate and esoteric, is not sufficient for such lofty representations; the adornments of verse and of music are commonly added. True enough, there are religions, *e.g.,* Moslemism, that have no hymns, but they are very rare. Practically all the Christian sects lay great stress upon them, and they are sung by barbarous peoples from the Arctic Circle to Tierra del Fuego. Among some of the American Indian tribes the memorizing of certain sacred chants is the principal item in the education of a priest, and any priest who invents a new one becomes a kind of prophet. Among the ancient Sumerians, the first civilized people whose customs are known to us with any precision, as among the Babylonians who followed them, there were rituals comparable to the Catholic Mass, and music entered into all of them. Many of the Babylonian hymns have come down to us, usually in ritualistic Sumerian with Semitic interlineations, for example, this apostrophe to Shamash, the sun-god:

*Shamas in the midst of Heaven, at thy setting*
*May the bolt of the limpid heavens speak thee greeting;*
*May the door of Heaven bless thee;*
*May Misarum, thy beloved minister, direct thee!*

The Egyptians also had Mass-like rituals, invariable in form and very elaborate, and all of them included hymns. The late Dr. J. H. Breasted of the University of Chicago, translated some of these hymns. Here, for example, is part of one to the sun-god from the time of Amen-hotep IV, the great reformer who tried to introduce monotheism into Egypt:

*Thou art he who createst the man-child in woman,*
*Who makest seed in man,*
*Who giveth life to the son in the body of his mother,*
*Who soothest him that he may not weep,*
*A nurse even in the womb.*
*Who giveth breath to animate every one that he maketh.*

Here one may well suspect Dr. Breasted of helping out the dithyrambs of Amen-hotep's temple poet with phrasings borrowed from the Bible, for the ancient Egyptians were surely not poets, nor were the Sumerians before them. Most of their hymns followed well-worn formulæ, and precisely the same gaudy flatteries were addressed indifferently to Rê, to Amen, to Osiris, and to a multitude of lesser gods. There was seldom any direct petition in them, as in the familiar Christian hymn, "Abide With Me," and they never exhorted the worshipper, as the "Adeste Fideles" does; all followed the courtly model of Luther's "Ein feste Burg," but without matching its sonorous eloquence. So over all the ancient East. The early literatures were formal and cold; there was very little feeling in them. It remained for the Jews, long centuries afterward, to discover the fine art of lyrical poetry, and bend it to the uses of religion. They learned something perhaps, from the Babylonians during the Exile, but it was not until their return to Palestine, in the Sixth Century B.C., that they perfected the Psalms. How their magnificent talent for poetry helped to propagate their theology, and finally to fix it indelibly in the consciousness of the Western World — this we shall see later on.

## 2

In addition to hymns, many other formalizations attach themselves to religion, and are found everywhere. They run from various outcries and refrains, sometimes quite unintelligible to the worshipper, to complicated posturings and genuflections, and from the use of elaborate sacred objects, often of great cost, to the employment of homely machines for relieving the devotee of the burden of prayer. In the earliest days of which we have any record the priests were already laying great stress upon the tools of their trade. In their armamentarium were all of the images, relics, holy oils, perfumes, lights and hallowed symbols that are still employed by the clergy of Holy Church. The cross goes back to the Bronze Age, and perhaps even beyond. It was the symbol, in Assyria, of the sun-god, as it was also in ancient South America. Among the early Teutons it was the hammer of Thor; among the Chinese it stood for the earth, with its four corners; among the Egyptians it represented life, as it did among the Aztecs. "The Spanish conquerors of Mexico," says Spence, "were astonished to find among this peculiar people a number of rites which appeared in many respects analogous to some of those practised by Catholics. Such were the use of the cross as a symbol, communion, baptism and confession."

Incense, as everyone knows, is often mentioned in the Old Testament — the word occurs in the Authorized Version thirty-four times, with frankincense ten times and myrrh thirteen times —, though its general use among the Jews probably did not come in until the Seventh Century B.C. But it was in use among the other peoples of the Near East many centuries before that, and so early as the Eleventh Dynasty in Egypt the Pharaoh Sanchkara sent an expedition to the Land of Punt (probably Somaliland) to get a supply. Among the Babylonians, if Herodotus is to be believed, a thousand talents of frankincense (nearly forty tons) was burned on the great altar of Bel at his annual feast. The Greeks burned cedar, myrtle and lemonwood; the Romans burned laurel, saffron, myrrh and crocus. When the Persian magi came to Bethlehem, as Matthew records, and "saw the young child with Mary his mother, . . . they presented unto him gifts: gold, and frankincense, and myrrh."

The first Christians, notwithstanding this example, made no use of incense, and when it came in at last, in the Fourth Century, it was apparently employed mainly as a deodorant, to purge churches and graveyards of the stenches of mortality. Later it seems to have become, as in the ancient religions and in the cults of savages, a means of pleasuring (and hence propitiating) the Unseen. If sweet song was agreeable to God's ear, and gorgeous vestments and temples to His eye, then it followed logically that perfumes would be agreeable to His nose. But with the progress of refinement this notion was put away, and to-day, in the Catholic church, the use of incense is only symbolical. According to Monsignor John Walsh, author of a standard work upon the Mass, it represents "the fire of holy charity that should consume us," "the good odor of Christ that is diffused in our hearts," and "the practice of prayer." But in other religions it continues to have a more literal significance. The Moslems of Morocco burn it during the great fast of Ramadan, the Lent of Islam, to scare off *jinns,* and the Andaman Islanders employ it against the demon who causes epidemics. In China it is used to fumigate the dead, that they may enter Heaven in a state of purity, and to induce sneezing and terror among the evil spirits who hang about open graves, eager to ensnare the mourners.

All peoples, even the lowest savages, approach their gods in attitudes and with gestures that differ materially from those of everyday life. So far as I can determine, this rule has no exceptions. Sometimes, as among the Moslem Mauliwis and Isawis and the Hopi Indians, the thing goes to the length of a frantic leaping and cavorting, but usually it stops with decorous bows and abasements. The Catholic, entering a church, drops upon one knee and makes the sign of the cross; the Protestant prepares for public prayer by rising, throwing back his head, folding his hands and shutting his eyes. The Catholic priest washes his hands before vesting, after the Offertory and after Communion; the Greek priest washes them only once, after vesting. In the Nestorian church the priest says Mass in bare feet; in the Armenian church he wears black slippers, but his attendants are barefooted. In the Catholic church the faithful are expected to kneel during the whole of Low Mass, though those who are infirm may sit after the Credo. At High Mass it is more complicated. I quote Monsignor Walsh:

*All stand during the Asperges. They kneel from the beginning of Mass until the priest intones the Gloria, when they stand. They sit whenever the priest sits, and also when the announcements are made, and during the sermon. They stand during the singing of the prayers, except at a Requiem Mass. They sit during the reading of the Epistle until the missal is carried over to the left of the altar. They stand at the Gospel, also at the Credo, whilst the priest is reciting it at the altar, and sit when he goes to the bench. They kneel when the officiant recites and the choir sings:* Et incarnatus est de Spiritu Sancto ex Maria Virgine: et Homo factus est. *They sit during the Offertory and rise when the priest begins the chant of the Preface. They kneel before the Sanctus until after the Communion. They sit whilst the priest purifies and covers the chalice. They stand during the last prayers, kneel for the Blessing, stand during the last Gospel, genuflect at the* Verbum caro factum est, *and stand until finished.*

The ancient Sumerians, so far as we know, did not kneel at worship, nor did they bow. Their typical gesture was kissing the hand; in their picture-writing the graph for the verb *to pray* shows a priest throwing a kiss to the gods. Later on, in Babylonian days, the kiss was changed into something resembling a modern military salute. The priest stood erect with his right arm raised and its fingers touching his lips, and his left arm folded across his waist. Still later the right arm was thrown forward and the hand turned outward, with the index finger pointing at the image of the god addressed, and the thumb closed over the remaining fingers. Or both hands were thrust in air, with the palms turned inward. Kneeling and prostration seem to have been unknown to the ancient peoples of Mesopotamia; they were apparently invented by the desert Semites, and did not come in until a comparatively late period. They survive among the Moslems to this day. At each of the five *salats* that he must perform every day a Moslem begins by spreading his prayer-rug, turning his face toward Mecca, and raising his open hands to the two sides of his face. Then, while he recites his prayers, he stoops until his hands reach the level of his knees, rises again to his full height, and then drops gently to his knees. After that he puts his hands on the ground a little in front of his knees, and slowly bends forward until his head touches the ground between them. Then he raises his head and body, but continues to kneel until the first *rak'ah* of the *salat* is finished. For each of the succeeding *rak'ahs* he goes through the whole process again. Before he begins he must wash his face and hands, his arms to the elbows, and his feet to the ankles — with water if it is obtainable, and if not then with sand. This puts him into a state of *tahara,* or ritualistic purity. It may be broken by contact with a corpse, a hog, a dog or any other abominable thing. He must take good care that his body is covered, at least from the waist to the knees. He must also wear some sort of head-covering. In the old days in Turkey it was a fez, but since the fez was prohibited by Kemal Pasha it may be anything, including, I suppose, a golf-cap or a plug hat. The Jews, as all know, likewise cover their heads while at prayer.

Everywhere, both in civilized lands and among savages, religion tends to congeal into such forms, many of them quite devoid of visible rationality. Historically, no doubt, they all go back to logical beginnings, but with long-continued repetition their significance becomes vague, or is lost altogether. Not many Catholics of today, I suspect, could explain plausibly why candles are burned in church, or when and how the custom originated, or what it meant when it began; even theologians, in fact, differ in their explanations, as they do in their accounts of the origin of the rosary. Why do the savages of Polynesia (and also of Africa) make a hideous din with bull-roarers before they begin their ceremonies? Is it to attract the attention of the gods, to scare off demons, to alarm and prepare the worshippers, or simply to indicate that something important is afoot? They do not know, though no doubt every one of their priests has his theory. Why do Christian churches commonly have spires? It is not known with any certainty. There are students who relate them to the Tower of Babel, and say that they symbolize the devotee's yearning to get closer to God; there are others who see in them a phallic survival; there are yet others who regard them simply as overgrown bell-towers, signifying no more than the fact that the medieval cathedral builders were ostentatious, and liked to outvie one another.

I have just quoted Monsignor Walsh's explanation of the use of incense. It is full of obvious after-thoughts. certainly myrrh and frankincense were not burned in the early days as symbols of "the fire of holy charity"; there is, indeed, no evidence that charity was then regarded as a fire, whether holy or otherwise. The first Christians, as I have said, probably used incense mainly as a deodorant, for they usually met in highly unsanitary places and the dead were apt to be unpleasantly close. But no doubt they also had some notion of smoking out demons, and that notion has by no means lost its hold upon the faithful today. A Catholic priest, it must be remembered, still devotes a large part of his professional energies to circumventing the machinations of Satan and the infernal host. "At the consecration of a church," says Father William Stang in his instructive treatise on pastoral theology, "the cross is planted at the door and marked repeatedly on the walls to protect the sacred place and the faithful who are to worship in it against the wicked attacks of the Devil. Water, salt and oil, used for sacramental unction, are first exorcised; the same is done at the blessing of bells, crosses, medals and reliquaries." In this exorcism incense often has a place, as it has in the operations of the priests of many other faiths, ancient and modern, near and far.

### 3

This tendency of worship to freeze into formulæ has psychological causes that are anything but recondite. Chief among them lies the plain fact, noted at the beginning of this essay, that relatively few men have any positive talent for religion. They may believe in the gods more or less earnestly, but they lack the address that is needed for approaching them. Thus they prefer to have priests do their praying for them, and the priests, if only from professional ennui, seek to make the labor as little burdensome, spiritually speaking, as possible. The easiest device to that end is formalization. The representations and attitudes that seemed to be effective yesterday, either against the gods or upon the worshippers, are used again today, and by to-morrow they cease to have any immediate significance. Prayer, by then, is no longer a petition for a definite favor; it becomes simply a generalized artifice of propitiation, designed to put the gods in an amiable humor by assuring them of the continued devotion of the faithful. Such things as the Moslem *salats,* the Lord's Prayer, the *Om mani-padme Hum* of the Tibetan *lamas,* the *Ave Maria,* and indeed the whole of the Catholic Mass are thus attempts to strike a common denominator of piety — in the mathematical sense, the lowest attainable. Some of them, notably the Lord's Prayer and the *Om manipadme Hum,* reach down to such elementary strata of religious feeling that they are used in common by sectarians who, on higher and more refined levels, are violent enemies. The thing might go much further than it does. There are prayers in the Moslem *salats* that would fit very neatly into the rituals of the Unitarians and the so-called reformed Jews, and I have no doubt that the ancient Babylon Word from the Abyss, *Muazaga-gu-abzu,* if loosed *sforzando* at a seance of Holy Rollers, would be adopted forthwith.

Even the most private and intimate prayers yield to this inevitable freezing. The worshipper not only gives his ear to canned pleas and remonstrances, many of them unintelligible to him, when he goes to church; he also makes use of them in his secret praying-closet. The rosary, a familiar device to help him in that direction, is used by all the sects of Christians save the Western Protestants, and also by Moslems, Buddhists, Brahmans and Taoists, not to mention innumerable devotees of more primitive cults. The Buddhist rosary, in Tibet, has 108 beads, and getting through it must be a formidable business, for many of the prayers are in Sanskrit and others are in a frank gibberish. Only a *lama* may hope to master the whole ritual, so the ordinary layman confines himself to repeating the Buddhist Paternoster: *Om manipadme Hum, i.e.,* Hail, thou jewel in the lotus! This Paternoster is also printed on long strips of paper, and they are rolled on wheels, and endlessly wound and unwound. The worshipper says nothing: his operation of the wheel is sufficient notice to the gods that he is devout and wants to be remembered. This Paternoster is also printed on flags that flutter in the wind: every flutter is a prayer. In China, for some obscure reason, the Buddhist rosary has 109 beads. In Korea, for some other, it has 110 and in Japan 112. The rosary of the Brahmans usually has 108, but may have some fraction thereof, *e.g.,* 6, 12, 18, 27, 36 or 54. The Moslem rosary has 99, one for each of the awful names of God. To recite these names *seriatim* is an act of high merit, but the devotee who can't remember them may substitute ninety-nine repetitions of *al Hamdu li-'llah!, i.e.,* God be praised! Tradition has it that Mohammed once said: "He who recites the *al Hamdu li-'llah* a hundred times in the morning and a hundred times in the evening shall be like one who has provided a hundred horsemen for a holy war."

The standard Catholic rosary consists of 150 beads divided into 15 decades by beads of larger size, though in practice rosaries of but five decades are common. The devotee begins by making the sign of the cross, and then recites the Apostles' Creed, the Paternoster, three Hail Marys and a Gloria. After that he recites one Paternoster, ten Hail Marys and one Gloria for each decade of beads, at the same time meditating upon one of a series of fifteen mysteries — five joyful, five sorrowful and five glorious, *e.g.,* the Annunciation, the Crucifixion and the Resurrection. This meditation, it may be suspected, is not infrequently somewhat casual. The rosary of fifteen decades is called the Dominican, because it was formerly believed that St. Dominic introduced it in the Thirteenth Century. In 1883, indeed, Pope Leo XIII pronounced this an historical fact. But research by Catholic antiquaries has made it plain that rosaries were in use in the Western Church long before the time of Dominic. They were apparently borrowed from the East, like many another piece of pious furniture. In the Greek church the lay faithful do not say beads, but every priest has a string of them. Of late the rosary has come into fashion among High Church Episcopalians, both in England and America, along with auricular confession and the use of incense, holy water, candles, scapulars and the Gregorian chant. In America certain Methodists of ritualistic tendency have begun to burn candles in their tabernacles, but so far they have not adopted the rosary. Perhaps it will come a bit later.

All such devices — the rosary, the scapular, candles, holy water, holy oils, incense and so on — go back to a remote antiquity and are used by the peoples of many creeds today. The earliest races of whom we have any record recognized certain objects as sacred, and ascribed transcendental powers to them. The Egyptian temples were full of representations of the gods, both in the flat and in the round, and they were given the same veneration which modern Catholics give to holy images and the crucifix. The ritualistic prohibitions which forbid a Catholic to eat meat on Friday or a Jew to eat pork at any time are matched exactly by the taboos of the Polynesians and other savages. The Chinese ring a bell during their devoirs to their ancestors just as it is rung during Mass at the elevation of the Host, and the simple folk of Africa and the South Seas employ bull-roarers precisely as the Salvation Army employs cornets. The Egyptians, in the Fourteenth Century B.C. adorned the altars of their gods with flowers, and the Sumerians of many centuries earlier invented the Recessional, and provided characteristically gay music for it. The halo of the saints was borrowed by the primitive Christians from the Greeks, and has been borrowed in turn by the Buddhists. Fasting is so widespread that it is difficult to find a sect which does not practise it; even the Methodists, in their Book of Discipline, make it obligatory, though most of their pastors seem to be unaware of the fact. The scapular is familiar, in some form or other, to every savage, and the sign of the cross has a thousand analogues.

The sacraments themselves are all hoary with age and worn out by heathen use. Among the Aztecs, says Spence, "penance was apportioned and absolution given much in the same manner as in the Roman Catholic church. There appears to have been more than one kind of communion. At the third festival of Huitzilopochtli they made an image of him in dough kneaded with the blood of infants, and divided the pieces among themselves. . . . In the rite of baptism . . . the midwife . . . touched the mouth and breast of the infant with water in the presence of the assembled relations, and invoked the blessing of the goddess Cihuatcoatl." Among the Incans of Peru, according to the same authority, "bread and wine were distributed at the festival of Raymi in much the same manner as that prescribed in Christian communities. Baptism was practised. Some three months after birth the child was plunged into water after having received its name." Baptism, in fact, apparently goes back to the very infancy of the human race. Primitive man, like his savage heirs of today, regarded a parturient woman as spiritually unclean, and her child with her. Both had to be purified by a ceremony precisely like the Christian ceremony which purges the new-born child of its share of Original Sin. In West Africa baptism by sprinkling is almost universal, and it is accompanied, as among Christians, by the naming of the child. Among the Papuans the child is taken to a spring and immersed. Among the Negritoes of the Philippines its mouth is first filled with salt, and it is then plunged in. Among the Lapps of Finland, as Robert Briffault tells us in "The Mothers," illness in a young infant is accepted as a proof that its baptism was what the Catholic canonists call invalid, and it is baptized again. In Tibet the Buddhist *lama* comes 'round when it is from three to ten days old, lights candles, repeats a Sanskrit formula, collects a fee, and immerses it three times. Among the Buddhists of Ceylon the ceremony is postponed until the fourteenth day, and there is no immersion, but only a ceremonial washing of the child's head, with appropriate remarks. Among the Japanese Buddhists the age for baptism is one month.

When Christian missionaries first penetrated the forests of Central Europe they found that the pagan Teutons had all been baptized by their own rites, and the question arose whether it was necessary to baptize them again. That question, in one form or another, still afflicts the canon lawyers of Holy Church. What of a convert who has been baptized by some other Christian rite? Obviously, baptism by a priest of one of the uniat churches of the East must be presumed to have been valid, but what of baptism by an Episcopalian, a Methodist or a Baptist? In practice it is common to beg the question by resorting to what is called conditional baptism, the priest saying, "If thou art not yet baptized, then I baptize thee," etc. Theoretically, any person, even an atheist, may baptize a child in case it seems in imminent danger of death, but the ceremony is null unless the form indicated in Matthew xxvii, 19, is followed precisely: "I baptize thee in the name of the Father and of the Son and of the Holy Ghost." This stressing of an invariable formula, even to the peril of an immortal soul, is a phenomenon that is encountered in many other religions. It has its parallel in the kindred field of magic, where the word is usually so much more important than the substance that the most potent spells have no rational meaning at all. What lies under all this, of course, is an effort to exalt the office of the priest. He alone can be trusted to engage and persuade the higher powers in serious matters, for he alone speaks their awful and sinister language. Not infrequently, especially among savages, he alone knows their names.

## 4

The Christian Eucharist is the central mystery of the faith, and if it were taken away little that is genuinely mystical would be left. Nevertheless, there is not much in the sacrament that is exclusively Christian. Nearly every idea in it may be found in other religions, *e.g.,* the idea of the Divine Sonship, that of the Atonement or blood sacrifice, that of the *agape* or common meal, and that of what students of comparative theology call theophagy, or god-eating. The last-named is encountered in a great variety of cults, from the highest to the lowest. On the level of the African and Polynesian savages it constitutes the *raison d'être* of sacrificial cannibalism, and among other primitive peoples it accounts for the ceremonial eating of totem animals. Ordinarily a totem animal, on account of its sacred character, is taboo, and eating its flesh is as strictly forbidden to members of its clan as eating pork is forbidden to a Moslem or a Jew, but on occasions of great solemnity, as J. G. Frazer shows by abundant examples in "The Golden Bough," it is slain and devoured. Thus the Todas of India, among whom the buffalo is sacred, nevertheless eat its flesh once a year, and thereby absorb the qualities that they admire in it. Among all primitive peoples this notion prevails: that eating the flesh of an animal transfers its qualities to the consumer. So with gods. It is impossible, of course, to ensnare and butcher them *in propria persona,* but the thing may be accomplished by surrogate. Thus the Aztecs, at the annual feast in honor of Tezcatlipoca, appointed a victim to represent him, and after suitable rites of consecration accepted that victim as identical with the god. When he was slain his arms and legs were eaten by the principal dignitaries of the nation, and the rest of his flesh, chopped fine, was distributed among the people. In other cases the god was incarnated, by priestly magic, in suitable inanimate objects: I have already cited, quoting Spence, the proceedings at the feast of Huitzilopochtli. The image of the god, made of dough mixed with the blood of infants, was of colossal size, and after it was set up it was converted, by a process of transubstantiation, into the god himself. Then it was "killed" with great ceremony, and solemnly devoured. The part corresponding to the heart was reserved for the king; the rest of the "flesh" was given to the priests and warriors. Only men ate it, for it was considered too stimulating to be safe for women.

Huitzilopochtli, the offspring of the sun-god and a human mother, had been originally, it would seem, the divine patron of all growing things — what the anthropologists commonly call a corn-god. "When the god is a corn-god," says Frazer, "the corn is his proper body: when he is a vine-god the juice of the grape is his blood; and so by eating the bread and drinking the wine the worshipper partakes of the real body and blood of the god" — and absorbs thereby the qualities that make him potent and admirable. What the qualities of a satisfactory corn-god are I don't know, but probably generosity is one of them, and no doubt fecundity is another. Huitzilopochtli, in the course of time, moved from the harvest field to the armed camp and became the Aztec Mars, and in consequence the Mexicans began to believe that they gained something else by eating his body and blood, to wit, courage in war. Yet more, he was their hereditary totem — the sacred humming-bird from which they believed themselves to be descended. Thus they also ate him as the Todas eat the buffalo — in order to renew all the high qualities which, in the days of their beginnings, had won them their place in the sun. The historians do not tell us what those qualities were, but no doubt the Mexicans imagined a list identical with the list cherished by all the imperialist peoples of today: an impeccable integrity, a passionate and romantic altruism, and a complete incapacity for error. Here we see the fruits of the Eucharist changing as the worshippers change their view of the god.

The phenomenon is no stranger to Christianity. Dr. Adolf Harnack, in his "Lehrbuch der Dogmengeschichte," says that the early Christians knew nothing about some of the benefits that their heirs and assigns derive from communion today. Their "partaking of the consecrated elements," he says, "had no particular relation to the forgiveness of sins"; its one and only purpose was to obtain "a guarantee of eternal life." The body of Christ was eternal; *ergo*, they would gain immortality by eating it. Fifteen centuries later St. Francis de Sales, summing up the intervening changes in Christian thought, added many other objectives, and today any priest can improvise new ones to fit a hard case. But under all of them lies the primitive idea that consuming the body of the god is both a means of sharing in the benefits that flow from his virtues and a means of transferring those virtues, in however modest a measure, to the worshipper himself. Christians go to communion, not only to earn and enjoy Christ's manifold benevolences, but also to become, within the limits of their vocation, more Christ-like.

The idea of the Atonement embodies a group of concepts that go back to the days of the earliest historical religions. The sacrifice that lies at the bottom of it was ancient, indeed, when recorded history began. Nothing could be more logical or equitable. The god, like any other laborer, is worthy of his hire; more, he is a sort of king, and so deserves attention, politeness, flattery. What more natural, when he has conferred a valuable benefit, than to give him something valuable in return? And what more natural, when a benefit is desired, than to propitiate him with a gift on account? The exchange is so obvious that even children in arms, to whom adults are gods, often think of it: who has not been offered a rubber ball or a spoonful of mush for his watch, with its miraculous and fascinating ticking? The corn-god got the first fruits or the largest ears: the Earth Mother got libations; the sun-god got pretty sea-shells, curious stones, and the first things fashioned of gold. I say the gods got these things, but in reality, of course, they went to the priests, then as now. The fact explains, no doubt, the unbroken popularity, before money was invented, of sacrifices of food. When the Egyptians went to their temples with offerings of bread, geese, beef and wine the priests promptly performed a miracle comparable to transubstantiation. The substance of these victuals, as a Catholic theologian would say, was changed into an ethereal manna fit for the alimentation of the gods, but the species or accidents remained, and so the priests could dine.

Such propitiatory and thank offerings, as everyone knows, continue to be made to this day, to the gratification of the gods and the nourishment of their agents. Save in the backwoods and among savages they are no longer made in kind, but collecting the cash that has taken their place is still one of the chief functions of the priestly craft, and failure or reluctance to bring it in is still a serious offense by the priestly code. It is rare indeed for a Christian to go to church or meet a priest without being dunned for money. In the United States the denominational papers, especially among the evangelical sects, devote far more space to the unhappy subject than they give to any other concern, not excepting dogmatic polemics, ethical expostulation or ecclesiastical politics. Among the Catholics liberal contributors are rewarded with papal titles of nobility and other such semi-celestial honors; among the Protestants benign prodigals of the order of Candler the coco-cola king, Kresge the ten-cent-store king, Heinz the pickle king and Buck Duke the cigarette king are automatically purged of their sins, and take on a character hard to distinguish from that of saints.

But at an early day men began to suspect that the sacrifice of mere food and drink was not enough. It sufficed, to be sure, for such mild and grandmotherly gods as the Earth Mother, and for such roistering good fellows as Bacchus, but there were also gods of harsher and more carnal appetites, and satisfying them was no such facile matter. Some of them plainly craved blood, for that is what they made their devotees shed when they were in bad humor. They were gods of war, gods of the lightning and of fire, storm and wind gods, gods who armed and protected wild beasts, gods of the avalanche, gods who made trees fall, gods who sent broken limbs and bloody noses; in later days they were reinforced by hordes of gods who had begun as totem animals, chosen for their very ferocity — lions, tigers, leopards, buffaloes, crocodiles, snakes, wolves, foxes, eagles, vultures, sharks. It was plainly idle to offer such divinities corn and wine, fruits and nuts; what they craved was red meat, raw and bleeding. So there arose the horrible custom of sacrificing living things to them, and for thousands of years it was a principal rite in all the salient religions of the world, including those of peoples on the highest contemporary plane of civilization.

Traces of it remain to this day, albeit somewhat concealed by rabbinical metaphysics, in the Christian communion cup and the Jewish rituals for slaughtering oxen, sheep and poultry. When a Jewish *schochet* cuts a chicken's throat he lets the blood run on the ground: it is Yahweh's share. The theory that its removal makes the flesh a better victual is only an afterthought: in essence the proceeding is ceremonial, and a true sacrifice. According to Talmudic law, indeed, the prayers and scriptural studies of a pious Jew are no more than transient makeshifts for the old bloody offerings. When the Jews are restored to their ancient glories and the Temple is rebuilt in Jerusalem, its stones will again run red with the gore of sacrificial lambs, as they did in the days of Solomon. The Moslems, whose faith shows strong Jewish influences, cling to similar ideas. When one of them slaughters an animal for his table he faces Mecca and says, "In the name of God!" And when, in the holy month of Dhu'l-Hijjah, he makes his pilgrimage to the sacred city, he takes a sheep with him, and on the tenth of the month he goes to the nearby Mina and there sacrifices it.

## 5

All blood sacrifice, of course, is primarily substitution. The devotee seeks to save his own blood by offering the carnivorous god that of some other creature — another man or one of the lower animals. Sometimes, even more slyly, he tries to substitute a part for the whole, as when the primitive peasants of parts of India draw blood from their arms and sprinkle it on their fields. The practice of circumcision may have had some such origin. But usually the devotee (or the priest) slaughters his offering, and so gives the hungry god all of the blood, though nearly always he keeps the flesh for himself. Whether the first blood sacrifices were of human beings or of dumb creatures is not certain. The ancient Jews seem to have begun by sacrificing their first-born, and no doubt the practice was suggested by their earlier sacrifice of the first fruits to the Earth

Mother. The underlying idea, as one gathers it from the Old Testament, was that the mighty and warlike Yahweh deserved a reward in kind for making their wives fertile and their nation great, just as the gentler Earth Mother or corn-goddess deserved a reward in kind for prospering their fields. But such butcheries must have seemed shocking even to barbarians, and the process of substitution was carried further. First, prisoners of war were sacrificed in place of children of the tribe, and then malefactors, and finally animals. The sheep was the cheapest and therefore came into general use, and in the form of the Paschal lamb it retains a place in Jewish ritual to our own day. It was thus quite natural for the early Christians to think of Jesus as the Lamb of God, for His sacrifice on the Cross suggested a proceeding with which they had been familiar all their lives.

The Old Testament, as everyone who has looked into it is aware, drips with blood; there is, indeed, no more bloody chronicle in all the literature of the world. Half of the hemorrhage is supplied by the *goyim* who angered Yahweh by flouting His Chosen People, and the other half issues from living creatures who went down to death that He might be suitably nourished and kept in good humor. Yahweh's revelations to Moses commanded an almost continuous butchery, as we learn from the Book of Numbers. Every day, year in and year out, "two lambs of the first year without spot" had to be burnt, "for a sweet savor unto me." Flour, oil and wine (the last named, it was provided, had to be "strong") went with the lambs, and on the Sabbath the ration of flour was doubled. Once a month "two young bullocks, one ram, and seven lambs of the first year" were sacrificed, along with a kid and the usual flour, oil and wine. At the Passover this was repeated, with a goat substituted for the kid. And likewise at the Feast of Tabernacles, at the New Year, on the Day of Afflicting Souls (the modern Day of Atonement), and on all the other holy days of the calendar. No doubt other animals were sometimes sacrificed. In Numbers XIX we hear of a red heifer, slaughtered with elaborate hocus-pocus by "Eleazer the priest." The color was significant: it was that of blood. Among many other ancient peoples redness suggested special fitness for the honor of sacrifice. Diodorus Siculus tells us that the Egyptians, when a red-haired stranger wandered among them, sacrificed him to Osiris. Such unfortunates were commonly burnt alive.

The ingenuities shown by the priests in the despatch of victims often did great credit to their professional resourcefulness and imagination. Among the early Scandinavians they immersed the elect in bogs, with the water and muck up to their necks, and there let them starve to death. At other times they broke their backs, and turned them adrift in the forests, to fight it out with the wolves and bears. Cæsar tells us in "De Bello Gallico" that the Gaulish priests encased their victims in close-fitting basketwork armor, not unlike the coffins of the Egyptian kings, and then set fire to them. At other times they impaled them on stakes, or hanged them on trees until their limbs rotted off, or thrust them head-first into vats of water, or flayed them to death with thorns. The Roman writers are full of edifying accounts of such pious transactions. But it was in the New World that the technique of sacrifices reached its highest development. When the Spaniards reached the City of Mexico they found a pyramid of 136,-000 skulls beside the chief *teocalli* (temple), each representing a sacrificial victim. That was in 1519. Thirty-three years before this the great *teocalli* of Huitzilopochtli, son of the sun-god, was dedicated, and no less than 70,000 victims went to death in his honor. The Aztec priests told their Spanish colleagues that the procession stretched for two miles, and that butchering the 70,000 was a job they would not soon forget. Their work required a considerable finesse. The victim was bound to a jasper altar, and his heart was cut out deftly and swiftly with a stone knife. If there was any bungling the officiating priest was severely punished. Once a year a woman was sacrificed to Centeotl, the Aztec Earth Mother. She was first decapitated and then flayed, and the chief priest arrayed himself in her bloody skin and was borne in procession through the city. Later the skin was cut up and buried at the four corners of the empire, to dissuade foes from invasion. When there was a drought hundreds of children were sacrificed to the rain-goddess, Tlaloc. If they wept when the priests bound them to the altar it was taken as a sign that the goddess was pleased and would send the needed rain.

As I have said, such wholesale brutalities shocked even barbarians, and there were probably always skeptics and humanitarians ready to defy the gods by protesting against them. We know very little about skepticism among the ancient peoples, but the chances are that it always existed, and that it was responsible for the gradual disappearance of human sacrifice. Today, men and women are sacrificed to the gods only among savages, though the old idea of immolation persists in the practices of fasting, sacerdotal celibacy, and voluntary poverty and obedience. In the Benin country of Nigeria the natives still seek to propitiate the rain-god by fastening a young woman in a tree and leaving her to be devoured alive by buzzards, and when there is too much rain they club another young woman to death and heave her body into the nearest river. But their English overlords, supported by the more enlightened tribesmen, are seeking to put down the practice, as their colleagues in India put down the practice of throwing babies into the Ganges, and the early American missionaries talked the Chippewas out of placating the gods, in times of epidemic, by tying a young girl in a canoe and setting her adrift to starve or drown.

The Jews, in their early days, were quite familiar with human sacrifice, as we know by the cases of Hiel, who "laid the foundation of Jericho" in Abiram his first-born, and set up the gates thereof in his youngest son Segub; and Ahaz, who "made his son to pass through the fire"; and Manasseh, who did the same. In the days of Jeremiah (*circa* 600 B.C.) a special place, the Ge Ben-Himmom, was set aside for the burning of children. But the practice was denounced by Isaiah, Micah, Ezekiel, Jeremiah and other reformers, and by the time the great code we know as Leviticus was drawn up it was specifically prohibited. The sacrifices of Hiel, Ahaz and Manasseh, described in the Book of Kings, are there ascribed to heathen influences and are said to have provoked Yahweh to anger. Long before the beginning of the Christian era the Jews had substituted bullocks, sheep and goats for children, and in the course of time, as they declined in wealth, even these were sacrificed seldomer and seldomer. The other nations of antiquity went the same way, notably the Egyptians and Greeks. The Egyptians, in the end, tried to convince the somewhat gullible Herodotus (*circa* 450 B.C.) that human sacrifice had never been known among them. In

137

Greece itself, though Socrates could still call for the sacrifice of a cock in the age of Pericles, many of the priests boasted proudly that their altars were innocent of blood, whether human or animal. Among such clean altars were those of Apollo at Delos and Zeus at Athens.

Two influences, both of them still operating among savages, worked against the abandonment of human sacrifice among the ancient peoples, and caused it to survive to relatively recent times. One of them, paradoxically enough, was the gradual growth and refinement of the belief in immortality. Primitive man, as we have seen, probably had only the vaguest sort of concept of life beyond the grave. He could imagine ghosts, for he had seen them, but he believed that they walked for only a short while; after that the dead were finally and irrevocably dead. But with the rise of theology the priests gradually extended the period of existence after death, partly on purely speculative and metaphysical grounds and partly to give greater dignity and authority to their scheme of *post mortem* punishments, and finally it began to be believed that ghosts went on living indefinitely. Obviously, this made it necessary to consider their subsistence and comfort, for it was already well known that they were likely, when unhappy, to afflict the living. Thus the custom arose of providing them with clothes to wear, weapons for their defense among the shades, meat to eat, and, in case they were of high rank, wives and servants to attend to their other wants. All of the ancient graves were full of evidences thereof, ranging from the stone hatchets and fragments of animal carcasses that are found with the bones of Neolithic men to the elaborate and costly trappings that fill the tombs of the Egyptian pharaohs. The safest way to make sure that a deceased dignity would be suitably cared for in the place of the dead would be to butcher his attendants at his grave, and so send their ghosts after him. In the royal tombs at Ur, in what was once Sumer, archeologists have found the bones of an unidentified king surrounded by those of twelve women in court dress, a number of soldiers fully armed, and various grooms and body servants. At the same place the bones of Queen Shub-ad's harpist, ladies in waiting and grooms lie in the shaft outside the chamber wherein her own bones have rested for five thousand years.

Basically, of course, sacrifices such as these were not made to feed and appease the gods, but simply to give the dead company beyond the grave. But it is very probable that notions of propitiation usually became superimposed upon them. For example, it appears that the king's servants were sometimes killed, not after his death but before it, in an apparent effort to fill the maws of the gods with blood, and thereby turn them from the greater victim. In precisely the same way the Samoans, when a chief was dying, used to wound themselves with stones, thinking thus to satiate the transcendental sharks, eels, cuttle-fish, owls, lizards, flies, turtles and snakes which served them as gods. Also, there was probably some notion that sending an important personage to the shades with a formidable retinue would impress and maybe even terrify the gods, and so induce them to treat him politely. If that idea was entertained logic must have suggested the corollary that priests, considering their special influence with the gods, would be more useful than harpists, grooms and soldiers, but the records show that they were very seldom sacrificed. No doubt the science of theology came to their rescue with proofs that it was safer to keep them on earth, where they could note the daily needs of the people and take measures accordingly. Finally, it must have been felt that making an elaborate sacrifice after one calamity would tend to stave off another: the same concept appeared later among the Jews, who tore their beards and rent their garments when they had suffered misfortune, and drenched their altars with the blood of sheep and goats. Thus I suppose that a crown prince sometimes filled his late father's tomb with slaughtered attendants in order to postpone his own inevitable death as long as possible.

## 6

The second consideration that kept human sacrifice among the sacraments, long after the best thought of mankind had begun to view it with shame and loathing, was the consideration that, in times of extraordinary exigency, extraordinary devices were necessary to placate the raging gods. It appears likely that some such notion was in Abraham's mind when he attempted to sacrifice his son Isaac, as recorded in Genesis xx. Abraham, as a theologian, must have been well aware that human sacrifice was forbidden by Jewish law, but he was also well aware that he had tried the patience of Yahweh very severely by marrying his step-sister Sarah, and by turning Hagar the Egyptian, his bondwoman, into the wilderness with her baby. So he decided to square his account by making the most precious sacrifice imaginable, and accordingly he lured poor Isaac into the land of Moriah, bound him to an altar heaped with firewood, and prepared to cut his throat and burn him.

This bloody expiation, fortunately enough, turned out to be unnecessary, for Yahweh, taking the will for the deed, sent down an angel with the message: "Lay not thine hand upon the lad, neither do thou anything unto him, for now I know that thou fearest God, seeing thou has not withheld thy son, thine only son, from me." Abraham thereupon looked about for a ram to serve as a substitute, and at once discovered that the now mollified and amiable Yahweh had conveniently provided one, "caught in a thicket by his horns." In a few moments the ram was burning and all was well. It seems likely that many another ancient Jew, following Abraham's example in times of extraordinary fear and woe, actually sacrificed his first-born. The practice would not have been so violently denounced by the prophets and reformers if it had not been more or less common. In India it survived the growth of the moral sentiments in the same way. It was stringently prohibited by Asoka, the Constantine of Buddhism, in the Third Century B.C., but children continued to be sacrificed until, in our own time, the British police finally put an end to the practice.

All the ancient peoples seem to have believed thus that the ordinary offerings to the gods were not sufficient in times of overwhelming calamity. A few lambs or heifers might be enough to bring rain or give luck to a hunting party, as a couple of malefactors or prisoners of war might be enough to save a sick king, but when really serious trouble fell upon the land it was necessary to propitiate the gods with tender meat. Thus arose the custom of sacrificing eminent warriors and wiseacres, handsome young princes and princesses, and even kings. The story of the three Decii, *père, fils et petit-fils,* is familiar to readers of Roman history. In 320 B.C., during the Latin War, the first of them, a general of high rank, deliberately invited death in order to appease the angry gods and insure a Roman victory. The fact that the victory was duly won inspired his son, at Sentinum in 295, to do the same thing, and at Asculum in 279 his grandson is said to have tried it a third time. In Egypt, before the days of the first pharaohs, the local kings seem to have been ritually slain whenever misfortunes overwhelmed the people; the practice survives to this day among the Shillucks of the upper Nile, who appear to be direct descendants of the primitive Egyptians, isolated and forgotten in their swampy retreat for thousands of years.

The Dinka of the same region sacrifice a volunteer, always of high rank. The Tchuktchi of far Northeastern Asia, until the practice was forbidden by the Russians, sacrificed a chief whenever they were beset by pestilence. The Aztecs and their neighbors, the Tlaxcaltecs, slew an albino whenever there was an eclipse of the sun, for albinos were rare among them and much esteemed, and inducing the sun to come back demanded strong medicine. In the Ch'un Ch'iu or Spring and Autumn Annals of Confucius there are accounts of various similar doings among the Chinese of the Sixth and Seventh Centuries B.C. Once a high official was sacrificed by the people of Chu in order to induce the gods to turn back a wild tribe that was threatening invasion, and another time the heir to the throne of Ts'ai, after his realm had been conquered by the people of Tso, was taken to Tso and there slain as a thank offering to their divinities. The Roman custom of putting enemy commanders to death after the triumph of a victorious general seems to have originated as a similar thank offering. In Greek mythology the story of Iphigenia is familiar

— a princess summoned by her father to placate the angry Artemis with her life, but let go by the humane god at the last moment.

In the course of time it began to be felt that, when emergencies of the first calibre presented themselves, even princes and generals were not enough, and the priests began to toy with the notion of sacrificing actual gods. At first, no doubt, the lesser were sacrificed to the greater. There were always plenty of the former lying about, and the loss of a few of them would not be calamitous. I suppose that the sun-god, as he gradually rose in eminence, saw scores of petty local gods butchered in his honor. It was not possible, of course, to lay physical hands upon these celestial victims, but the business could always be achieved symbolically, either by burning images of them or by slaying human beings chosen to represent them. To die for a god in this way seems to have been a high honor, much sought by men of piety. Among the Aztecs a youth was chosen annually to represent Tezcatlipoca, who was sacrificed every Autumn, apparently to his father, the sun-god. At each sacrifice next year's representative was chosen, and during the ensuing twelvemonth he led a life of voluptuous ease, attended by multitudes of priests, musicians and body-servants, arrayed in gorgeous garments from the priestly wardrobe, and with four wives to soothe and divert him. The Aztec priests told the Spaniards that it was never difficult to find a volunteer for the office. On the contrary, there was considerable competition for it, for the successful aspirant, after he had been butchered on the jasper altar, became a sort of god himself, and his family took on a high dignity, comparable to that of a Catholic family that has given the church a pope or a saint.

Eventually the thing went a step further and gods began to be thought of as sacrificing themselves. Hitherto they had been, in the main, powers of uncertain temper that had to be propitiated; now they began to be benign, philanthropic, altruistic, taking the burdens of the faith-ful upon their own shoulders and viewing the sinfulness of man more in sorrow than in anger. Some of them, thinking thus to shock and stimulate lazy consciences, committed suicide; others incarnated themselves in vari-ous semi-divine creatures, and then let these creatures turn upon and devour them. Thus Adonis was slain by a boar, who was Adonis himself. Contrariwise, Mithra was incarnated in a bull, and the bull was then sacrificed to him. So with Dionysos, who became a bull and a goat, and Artemis, the twin sister of Apollo, who became a bear. Attis castrated himself and died. Odin, the ancient Teu-tonic god, hung on a tree for nine days and nine nights, wounded with a spear — "dedicated to Odin, myself to myself."

This notion that gods could die went back to the early fertility cults, and was probably suggested by the daily disappearance of the sun, and, in the North, by its wasting away in Autumn. The priests, it may be assumed, saw an advantage to themselves in its general acceptance. On the one hand, it offered a powerful reinforcement to their moral scheme, for they could depict the god as driven to death by despair over the sins of man. On the other hand, it enabled them to exhibit their professional prowess by resurrecting him. For the dead god, of course, always came back, just as the sun, after sinking in the evening, rose the next morning. Tammuz, the Babylonian precursor of the Greek Adonis, died every year, but returned almost instanter. Rê, the Egyptian sun-god, passed to the land of dead gods every night, but was restored to life with the dawn. One of the chief aims of Egyptian theology, as a science, was his daily restoration. All over the ancient East the death and resurrection of gods was believed in, and everywhere it gave birth to elaborate symbolic rituals. Thus in early Sumer, more than five thousand years ago, priests and people engaged in ceremonials suggesting those of Holy Week in Rome today, and to music that was the faraway grandfather of the two grand Passions of Johann Sebastian Bach.

To the idea that gods could die, driven to melancholia and suicide by the sins of man, there was early attached another: that they could also become the fathers of mortal children, or, at all events, of children by mortal mothers. This second idea, in fact, probably preceded the first, for it must have been almost universal in the days before the physiological rôle of the father was discovered. At the beginning of the historical period it was very widely accepted. The Sumerian gods all had official human consorts, and so had those of Egypt: the office was not uncommonly filled by the wives of the priests. In other cases it fell to queens: thus every pharaoh of Egypt was assumed to be the son of Rê, the sun-god. "The Mahabharata, the great epic of India," says W. J. Perry in "The Origin of Magic and Religion," "is full of instances in which the sun-god, in one of his many forms, becomes the father of heroes. In San Cristoval of the Solomons . . . it is believed that a woman can have a child by the sun. The stories of old Samoa likewise tell of times when the sun caused a woman to have a child. A like belief was held in old Fiji, where a chief shut up his daughter so that the sun could not see

her. . . . The Incas of Peru kept their virgin daughters
in convents, away from men, under the charge of one of
the royal princesses. If one of them was found with child
she was condemned to death. But if she said that the sun
was the father of the child, she was released, and the child
was included in the royal family. . . . Danaë, although
shut up in a tower by her parents, was approached by Zeus,
himself originally a sun-god, in the form of a shower of
gold, and became by him the mother of Perseus."

It was, indeed, not unusual in those days for a female
devotee to fall in love with a god, and to be inspired
thereby to parade her charms before his shrine, seeking to
seduce him. Sometimes, succumbing, he took a pleasantly
human form, perhaps that of a handsome young priest,
and achieved his adultery in the normal manner of mortals, but more often he appeared as a wisp of smoke, a great
light, a loud and lovely voice, or a vague shape in a dream.
Now and then he came in the guise of a stallion, a bull, a
ram, a he-goat, an eagle, a vulture or a swan: it will be recalled how Leda, wife of Tyndareus, King of Sparta, was
undone by Zeus incarnate in a swan, and how she brought
forth two eggs, one of which hatched Castor and Pollux
and the other Helen of Troy. Sometimes, as in this case,
the partner of the god was a married woman, but usually
she was a virgin. The issue of the union, if not downright
divine, was always a personage of high dignity and importance — an emperor, a great conqueror, or a law-giver
who saved his people from sin and woe.

## 7

This idea, throughout the East, tended to become confused with another idea that was also widely prevalent, namely, that of the coming of a messiah, but the two, though analogous, were by no means identical, and the Jews of the period just before the birth of Jesus seem to have kept them apart. What was looked for in the days of Herod was the appearance of a purely human messiah, the heir and successor to David, the great king, not of an incarnate god, or of the son of one by a human mother. The Old Testament, to be sure, taught the Jews that Yahweh himself might one day walk the earth again, as He did in the Garden of Eden, but they had pretty well given up hope of seeing that, and were content to welcome a human hero, half prophet and half king, who should deliver them from their oppressors, restore them as a free nation, and perhaps reign over them as the bearer of the Davidian torch, now smoking so sadly.

His function, of course, would be largely religious, for like most other peoples of the time, they laid all their troubles to the wrath of their god, and believed that only an inspired prophet, a "teacher of righteousness," could save them. Such teachers had come among them in the past — Isaiah, Micah, Hosea, Ezekiel and many another; what they looked for now was simply one who should be greater than all the rest, and hence more potent to save them from sin, error and wretchedness. But he would necessarily have a political character also, for they were the Chosen of Yahweh, and the deliverance that they dreamed of would not only strike off their bondage but give them dominion. Thus the expected messiah would be of "the seed of David" — that is, he would be a scion of the Old Jewish royal line, and hence fit to reign. Jesus Himself seems to have deprecated this idea, perhaps on prudential grounds, for He was well aware that it would be highly unappetizing to the Romans, who cared little what religions their subject peoples practised but were alert for every sign of political rebellion. He also avoided giving any hint that He was a divine Personage, and it is very probable that the Disciples, while He lived, had no belief that He was. He was more successful in this second direction than in the first, for when He was crucified the derisive placard that the Roman soldiers hung on the Cross did not read "This is Jesus, the Son of God," but "This is Jesus, the King of the Jews."

There is no reason, indeed, to believe that He was ever regarded as a god before His death, save maybe by a few extremely fanciful followers, or that He had ever heard anything about the Virgin Birth. The earliest Christian documents, the epistles of Paul, do not mention it, nor is it mentioned in the gospels of Mark and John or in Revelation. The references to it in Matthew and Luke are probably interpolations, for, as everyone knows, they conflict with the genealogies in the same gospels, showing that Jesus descended from Abraham through Joseph. All of the Gospels, as we now have them, were written years after Jesus's death, and by men who had never seen Him. They show an assimilation of myths that were old before Jesus was born — some essentially Jewish, but others belonging to the common stock of religious ideas in the Near East. The Temptation in the Wilderness offers an example. It was so common a legend in those days that it was related of practically all prophets, not only Jewish, but also Persian, Indian and even Greek. So with the miracles. They were the common accomplishments of all great preachers, whether Jewish or pagan, and certainly would not have struck a contemporary theologian, in themselves, as evidences of divinity. The miracle of the loaves and fishes was simply a repetition of what every Jew knew had been done by Elisha. The raising of Lazarus was so little surprising, in that day of signs and wonders, that a record of it got into but one of the Gospels — that of John. Jesus Himself made light of these doings. When the woman "with an issue of blood twelve years" touched "the hem of His garment" and "was made whole," He said to her, "Daughter, thy faith [*i.e.*, in Yahweh] hath made thee whole." In His own home, where, like most prophets, He was without honor, "He could do no mighty work," for His lack of honor was due to unbelief in the powers and mercies of Yahweh. Given that faith, and anything was possible, not only to prophets, but to anyone, even unto the moving of mountains, as we learn from Mark xi, 22-3.

But once He was dead and the news got about that He had risen from the grave, a belief in His supernatural character began to be entertained, and soon it was enriched and reinforced by ideas borrowed from a hundred other hero cults. The idea of the Virgin Birth, as I have said, was widely dispersed in the East, and it was thus quite natural that it should be attached, soon or late, to the story of Jesus. And it was just as natural that His mother should have the name of Mary, for that was the name borne by the mothers of a long line of other prophets and heroes with divine fathers, among them, Myrrha the mother of Adonis, Maya the mother of Buddha, Maia the mother of Hermes, and Maritala the mother of Krishma. Other prophets of the time went through a precisely similar process of deification, for example, Apollonius of Tyana, whose life was written by Philostratus. Apollonius, too, came to be thought of as the son of a god, and there arose a legend of an Annunciation which warned his mother of his impending birth. He, too, came into conflict with the Roman administration, and he, too, like Jesus again, was acquitted of treason, but there were no Jews to insist upon his death willy nilly, so he lived to be a centenarian and died in bed.

The very Crucifixion itself, according to some scholars, was no more than a repetition of what had often happened before. Once a year, at the Passover, the Jews chose a malefactor to put to death, apparently as a refined form of the ancient blood sacrifice to Yahweh. This malefactor was called Bar Abbas, the Son of the Father, and seems to have been a surrogate for a royal prince. The rite, indeed, was not exclusively Jewish, but went back to the Babylonians, and had its analogues in many places, including (as Arthur Weigall observes in "The Paganism in Our Christianity") the island of Rhodes, where a criminal was sacrificed annually to commemorate the sacrifice of Ieoud by his royal father, Kronos. When Jesus was arrested a Bar Abbas already lay in prison, waiting to be crucified at the Passover, for as Caiaphas the high priest said, speaking (as John is careful to note) *ex cathedra,* "it is expedient for us that one man should die for the people," *i.e.,* that the wrath of Yahweh should be thus diverted from the rest. The appearance of a palpably nobler victim (for Jesus was not only of aristocratic blood but a man of learning to boot) caused the priests and Pharisees to lose interest in

Bar Abbas, but the Romans, being good policemen, released him very reluctantly, for he was guilty of secular
crimes and had been condemned to death for them.

Jesus, though much superior to any such common felon,
was still essentially a criminal in the eyes of the Jewish
authorities, and there is not the slightest evidence that they
suspected Him of being the Son of Yahweh, or that anyone else, save maybe one or two of the more naïve Disciples, so thought of Him. His deification came after His
death. In the immediate circle of His followers, made up
mainly of simple-minded peasants, its conflict with the
monotheism that He had preached probably passed unnoticed, but among theologians of greater sophistication
that conflict made a serious difficulty. Was he truly and
fully a god, like Yahweh Himself? If so, were there then
two gods instead of one? The question soon got itself
complicated further, for the prevailing taste of the time
was not for dual gods but for trinities, and so there was a
demand from the fringes of the crowd for a Third Person.
Next to the competition of Mithraism, the most formidable competition that the new cult had to face was probably
that of the Osiris-Isis-Horus trinity; moveover, there were
many other contenders of the same sort, for the taste of the
time, under the influence of Greek metaphysics, ran to
complex and mystical godheads. Thus the Fathers were
impelled to round out their Duality into a Trinity, and
they solved the problem by assimilating the Holy Spirit,
which to Jesus Himself had been no more than the pervasive presence and benevolence of Yahweh, with the Greek
Logos or Word. The issue of that miscegenation was the
Holy Ghost.

But the concept of a god who was also three gods and

of three who were also one was essentially and incurably irrational, and it did not take long for critics to attack it. Some of them were Jews and Greeks outside the pale of the new faith, but others were perfectly good Christians. For many centuries the debate went on, ranging far afield and awakening rancors of the most violent and implacable sort. As Christianity spread, exarchs and emperors took a hand in it, and more than once it led to sanguinary conflicts. Strangely enough, the divinity of Jesus seems to have caused even more trouble than the anomalous and incredible position of the Holy Ghost, and toward the end of the Third Century the row over it took the form of a famous three-cornered struggle between the Homoousians, the Homoiousians and the Heterousians. The Homoousians, led by Athanasius, Bishop of Alexandria, held that God and Jesus were of exactly the same substance, and were hence complete equals. The Homoiousians, led by Arius, the learned pastor of a fashionable Alexandria church, held that they were only of similar substances, and that God was the superior. The Heterousians held that they were of distinct substances, and that Jesus was not really divine at all. At the great Council of Nicæa, in the year 325, the Athanasians prevailed, and their doctrine remains orthodox in Christendom to this day, but the Arian heresy has never died out. Not only does it survive formally in such shapes as Unitarianism; it also lurks in the orthodox churches, among believers who cannot quite grasp the idea of the Trinity. That idea, in point of fact, is one of the most difficult ever formulated by theologians, and the chief texts expounding it, whether Catholic or Protestant, are magnificent examples of furious logic-chopping and unconscious humor. It may be made palatable, indeed, only by a resort to pure metaphysics, which is to say, by a deliberate repudiation of all the overt and obvious facts. But more of that anon.

## 8

As we have seen, primitive man probably imagined a sort of Hell before ever he conceived the notion of a Heaven. All he knew with any surety about the dead was that their ghosts occasionally came back to disturb his dreams at night, or to afflict him with sickness, or to annoy him otherwise, and so he naturally concluded that they were more or less uncomfortable in their own abode, whatever and wherever it was, else they would not leave it. Thus the place of departed spirits came to be thought of as an unpleasant domain, and no one wanted to go to it any sooner than he could help. How long the dead remained in it, of course, was unknown, but the available evidence indicated that it was not for long.

The concept of a *post mortem* existence stretching over endless years did not arise until man began to remember his history. Listening around the fire to tales of heroes long dead, he would naturally see them in dreams afterward, if only vaguely, and so he would believe that their spirits still lived, far beyond the span of ordinary ghosts. One may fancy that the notion of a Heaven, in the elemental sense of a place measurably more attractive than the common abode of the dead, flowed out of it. It would be hard to think of dead chiefs and high priests wandering about that common abode, cheek by jowl with proletarian ghosts and sharing their unhappy yearning to come back to earth. Something better was necessary for men of extraordinary merit — and by merit, of course, rank and prowess were understood, not mere virtue. The Teutonic Valhalla was by no means open to the general; it was reserved very strictly for heroes who had died in battle. In the South Seas ideas of the same sort are widespread. The plain people are doomed normally to go to a very cheerless Limbo, but for nobles there is something better, with food in abundance and plenty of wives and servants to wait upon them. If a commoner aspires to this more charming place, he must pay a priest to teach him how to coax and flatter the guardian of its portal. Among the Aztecs, an ordinary man, at death, went to Mictlan, a sombre and inhospitable realm, but nobles and priests went to the Mansion of the Sun, where all was warm and comfortable. Spence suggests that the rapid conversion of the Aztec people to Christianity, following the coming of the Spaniards, was due far less to the zeal and eloquence of the Spanish priests than to the yearning of everyone to escape Mictlan. The Christian Heaven seemed identical with the Mansion of the Sun, and when news got about that anyone who was baptized would go to it, multitudes presented themselves at the font.

The ancients located their Heavens and Hells in widely dispersed places, and according to the dictates of a lush and protean fancy. There were Heavens underground and Heavens in the sky, Hells under rivers and Hells on the tops of mountains. The influence of the sun-cult was potent in this department. On the one hand, it suggested that the blessed deceased dwelt somewhere in the blue empyrean, near or beyond the sun, and on the other hand it suggested that their place was in the vast and mysterious depths below the earth, whither the sun went at night.

When it was daytime on earth, the dead, by this latter theory, shivered in darkness, but while living mortals slept they basked in the smiles of the sun-god. Thus life among them was much like life among the living. It is so, indeed, among many primitive peoples today. When they think of the place of the dead as predominantly pleasant they fill it with all the things they long for on earth: laden fruit trees, tame game, and docile wives; when they think of it as disagreeable they afflict it with drought, darkness, famine, war and pestilence.

Among island peoples it nearly always lies on an enchanted island to westward, where the sun goes down; this is the case all over Oceania. In Central Africa it is in the depths of the jungle, or on a mountain top, or under a river. The American Indians, before Christianity reached them, put it just beyond the sky-rim, in a land swarming with deer and buffalo: the Happy Hunting Grounds. In Haiti it lay in the western valleys of the island, and the dead hid in caves by day, so that no one ever saw them: at night they issued forth to feast upon the fruit of the *mamey* tree. The Patagonian place of the dead was a vast series of caverns underground, and its chief delight was getting drunk. The ancient Celts were transported at death to a blissful island in the British seas, probably to be identified with the Isle of Man. The Greeks, too, believed in Isles of the Blest. The early Teutons, if they were warriors, went to Valhalla, but if they were not they were doomed to Hel, a gloomy region under the world, or to Na-strand or Nifhel, which seem to have been even worse. Later on, probably under Christian influences, a Heaven was added, at first for nobles only and then for everyone.

But such abodes of the dead, in ancient times, were not

believed in universally, any more than they are believed in universally today: there were plenty of peoples to whom the concepts of Heaven and Hell were shadowy or unknown. The early Romans seem to have belonged in that category. Until they began to be influenced by Greek ideas they thought that the spirits of the ordinary dead simply hung about their tombs. These spirits were called *manes,* which meant good people, but that designation was no more than a sign of polite discretion, for they were pretty generally feared. To prevent them roaming the land and annoying the living, it was necessary to propitiate them with offerings of milk, honey, eggs, beans, wine and flowers. When they were especially malignant they were called *larvæ,* and a living man who had been driven crazy by their attentions was called a *larvatus.* They were also called (mainly in secret) *deformes,* or *furiæ,* for many of them were thought to be hideous in aspect and of malignant humor. Once a year, at the festival of Lemuria, every householder went through a ceremony designed to exorcise such ancestral spirits as infested his house: its principal rite consisted in throwing their favorite black beans over his shoulder. At the Feralia, which occupied nine days in February, the whole population turned out to propitiate the dead. In later times the Romans borrowed from the Greeks the idea of an underworld separated from the land of the living by a river, the Acheron or the Styx, but that belief sat upon them very lightly. To the end their ceremonials indicated plainly enough that they thought the spirits of the departed, at least of the undistinguished departed, were nearby, and not gathered at some distant place. Those of men who had not been buried properly had no habitation at all, but wandered about the earth, blighting crops, causing cows to go dry, and scaring the pious on dark nights.

The ancient Jews, as the Old Testament shows plainly, had no very clear idea of a life after death. They called the abode of the dead Sheol, and supposed it to be a pit under the earth, but they had only the vaguest notion of what went on in it, and they showed very little interest in the subject. The dead were certainly not thought of as blessed; the existence they led was, at best, only a miserable half-life, and they were cut off from all communication with Yahweh. They suffered no punishment for the sins they had committed on earth, save the general punishment of being dead, and they got no formal reward for their virtues. Kings and beggars were all one. How and when the belief in immortality was introduced among Jews we do not know, but it was probably cordially welcomed and diligently propagated, as among other peoples, by the priests, for the moment they heard it stated they must have seen how admirably it reinforced their system of divine jurisprudence, the chief stay and glory of their sacerdotal authority. The fact that, in this life, they could sway and condition the will of Yahweh, inducing Him to reward what they regarded as virtue and to punish what they regarded as sin — this fact, at bottom, was their main excuse for being. But how, now, if they could project that scheme of rewards and punishments into infinite time and space, and make it inescapable, even by death?

Obviously, the advantage to them would be enormous. At one stroke, they would make their penology both more terrible and implacable, and more plausible. In the past the problem of evil had dogged them, and in the Book of Job it had been stated by some unknown skeptic with

such devastating clarity that not all their glosses had sufficed to dispose of it. But now they had an answer that was
itself unanswerable. The sorrows of this world would be
compensated in the world to come, and its vanities would
encounter their corresponding rebuke. The man of evil,
contumacious to priests, would spend eternity cut off from
Yahweh's favor and radiance; the pious men, reverent,
docile and keeping the Law to the last letter, would enjoy
endless years of bliss, close by the Throne. Isaiah the son
of Amoz seems to have been the first to spread the glad
news: "The dead men shall live, together with my dead
body shall they rise, Awake and sing, ye that dwell in dust
[*i.e.* that lie in the grave]; for thy dew is as the dew of
herbs, and the earth shall cast out the dead." The acceptance of the idea made a revolution of the first consideration, for it gave the priests a new and vastly greater authority than they had ever had before. No one could now
escape their penal system, for the dead, like the living,
were brought directly under Yahweh's awful eye, and His
Law, interpreted by His priestly agents, now ran for all
eternity.

## 9

As I have said, the history of this great innovation is
vague, and we know very little about its early stages. Many
Jews, it appears, opposed it; the Sadducees, indeed, held
out against it to the end. In Ecclesiastes iii, 19–20, it is
flouted openly: "For what befalleth the sons of men befalleth beasts; . . . as the one dieth, so dieth the other.
. . . All go unto one place; all are of the dust, and all turn
to dust again." And again in Ecclesiastes ix, 2 and 5: "All

things come alike to all: there is one event to the righteous, and to the wicked: to the good and to the clean, and to the unclean; to him that sacrificeth, and to him that sacrificeth not: as is the good, so is the sinner. . . . For the living know that they shall die: but the dead know not anything, neither have they any more reward." But the idea of immortal life was too sweet to be extinguished by any such skepticism, and so it persisted among the Jews, and the scheme of *post mortem* rewards and punishments with it. It got powerful reinforcement from other Eastern religions, notably Zoroastrianism, and in the course of time Sheol divided into a place for the righteous and a place for the wicked, with Yahweh presiding over the one and the Devil over the other. In the apocryphal Book of Enoch, probably written in the Second Century B.C., Sheol has no less than four compartments. The lowermost swarms with the fiends that are characteristic of all Hells, the Christian included, and the damned suffer all the classical burnings, boilings, rackings, disembowelings and other horrors.

But the Jews, having adopted Heaven and Hell somewhat grudgingly, did not waste their normally florid imagination upon limning either the felicities of the blest or the sufferings of the damned. They pictured the former promenading with Yahweh along streets of gold and jasper and the latter hidden from His radiant presence in a dark pit, but beyond that they did not go. There is nothing in the Old Testament, even as the fancy of Christian theologians interprets it, to match the voluptuous precision of Revelation. John's almost photographic vision of a Hell belching fire and brimstone, and peopled by all sorts of appalling monsters, including locusts as large as horses, with human faces, the teeth of lions, and crowns of gold on their heads — this vision was not Jewish, but had its roots in other religions of the time, and some of those roots reached as far as Persia, and even India. The very name of the arch-fiend who reigned over the "great furnace" was suggestive of the fact, for John gave its Greek form as Apollyon, a probable echo, though there are philological considerations to the contrary, of the Apollo cult which raged over the whole Eastern Mediterranean region, and was the offspring of a sun-cult borrowed from the further East.

The real fatherland of apocalypses and eschatologies is India. More Heavens and Hells have been invented there than in all the rest of the world, and their influence is visible in all modern theologies. The early Buddhists showed a magnificent talent for the art, and their masterpieces remain unmatched to this day, even by such Christian virtuosi as Jonathan Edwards. A simple division of the dead into two categories, the blessed and the damned, with maybe a class of probationers waiting between — this typically Western device was not enough for them. Instead they made five categories, and then proceeded to divide each into numerous sub-categories. The best fate after death was naturally reserved for priests, who became gods. Next to them came pious laymen, who were reincarnated as still more pious laymen, and sometimes even as priests, and thus moved a step toward divinity. Next came the middling good, who were turned into *pretas* at death, which is to say, wandering ghosts, and might be rescued from their misery by the prayers of their heirs, supported by proper offerings to holy men. Sinners of the fourth category became animals, mainly of a dirty and degraded type, and those of the fifth went to Hell.

But going to Hell was not the simple matter that it is to a Christian, for there was no single penitentiary for the damned, but eight of them, and each of the eight had sixteen subsidiary Hells, like chapels in a cathedral, making 136 in all. Each cardinal sin had its own Hell, and so a man of many offendings might make a tour of all of them. The first, called Sanjiva, was for robbers and murderers, and in it they were slowly cut to pieces. If they swooned they were permitted to revive, that they might miss none of the pain. The second Hell, Kalasutta, was for liars and slanderers, and its chief punishment was being knocked down with red-hot clubs, apparently of metal. The third, called Samghata, was reserved for those who had taken the lives of living creatures below man in the scale; they were anchored on a burning mountain, and there crushed like sugar-cane. The fourth and fifth, both called Roruva, were for those who tortured animals without killing them, and for those who destroyed the property of the gods, *i.e.,* of the priests. The sixth, Tapana, was for those who set fire to forests: they were impaled on stakes and then burnt. The seventh, Pratapana, was for infidels. The eighth, Avichi, was for those who slew mother, father or priest. Avichi, meaning without rest, was the worst of all. Flames leaped out of its four walls, so powerful that they reached the opposite sides, and others spouted from the roof and floor. A sinner who once got into any of these Hells remained there for a long time. In Sanjiva his sentence was usually for 500 Hell-years, each day of which was equal to 50 human years. In Kalasutta he remained longer, and in Samghata still longer, and so on up to Avichi, in which his stay was commonly 64,000 Hell-years, each day and night of which had now expanded to 6400 human years. Thus the standard sentence for killing a priest was 149,504,000,000 years in Hell. At the end of that time the assassin's evil *karma* was assumed to be exhausted, and he reached *nirvana,* or annihilation.

The chapel Hells were for the expiation of minor offenses, and most of them provided only relatively mild punishments. In Milhakupa violators of decency were immersed in a bog of dung and beset by worms. In Vetarani loafers who went fishing were plunged into a river of bitter water. In one of the other chapels adulterers were set to climbing the thorny *simbali* tree. In Kukkula various classes of culprits were forced to walk barefoot over hot ashes, and in Aspittavana they were incarcerated in a forest whose tree-leaves were all sharp swords. Persons who refused to give alms to priests were not condemned, curiously enough, to any of these Hells, but became *pretas* at death. A *preta,* properly speaking, was a ghost, but nevertheless he seems to have had a human form. At all events, he could suffer from hunger, and that was his chief punishment, for any living being who saw him roaming about would run, and so he had a hard time getting food. Many *pretas,* driven to it by starvation, ate filth, and others became cannibals. Yet others suffered from such deformities and diseases that they could not eat, even when food was before them. The teeth of some, for example, turned into needles, and mastication became impossible. The stomachs of others swelled to immense proportions, making large quanitities of aliment necessary, but at the same time their throats contracted, so that they could not swallow. There were others who suffered principally, not from hunger, but from thirst. They became so dry that their stomachs took fire, and flames issued from their nostrils and mouths.

To offset the woes of such poor souls there was the bliss of the virtuous. They inhabited fourteen separate Heavens, six of which were "of sensual enjoyment." Life therein was extraordinarily delightful. Every inhabitant had a palace of solid gold, studded with rubies, and a cloud to float about on. His food corresponded to the ambrosia of the Greek Olympus, and he had a retinue of lovely maidens to sing and dance for him. Unfortunately, his stay was not for eternity; instead, as in the 136 Hells, he always attained to *nirvana,* or nothingness, in the end. In some of the lower Heavens he remained but a few million years, but if he went to the most exalted one he might linger for 9,344,000,000, "eating huckleberries all day long and learning how to love."

These Indian Heavens and Hells worked their way westward through Persia, and were considerably toned down *en route.* The Persians, indeed, seem to have reduced all Heavens to one so early as the time of Zoroaster, probably eight or ten centuries before the time of Christ. In the sacred poems called the Gathas it is called Garo-demana, which means house of song. Later on it was reinforced with three subsidiary Heavens, through which the virtuous dead passed in order. The first was Humata, the place of good thoughts; the second was Hukhta, the place of good words; and the third was Hvarshta, the place of good deeds. Having survived them all, the elect entered Garo-demana, later called Garonmana or Garotman, and there spent eternity in ineffable bliss. For the wicked there was a Hell called Drujo-demana, the house of lies, or Druji-gereda, the pit of lies, and in the course of time it, too, acquired three ante-chambers: Dushmata, the place of evil thought; Dushukhta, the place of evil words; and Dushvarshta, the place of evil deeds.

The Persians produced a Dante 800 years before the Christian Italians. His name was Arta-i Viraf, and he lived in Sasanian times, probably in the Fifth or Sixth Century of our era. His work is still a favorite among the Parsees. It describes how the soul of the author, by the effects of a drug called *mang,* is separated from his body, and conducted through Heaven and Hell by two angels, Srosh and Ataro, who correspond to Dante's Vergil. At the entrance to the two realms is a river that the dead must cross: it is made up of the tears of those who mourn for them. The more they are mourned for the harder it is for them to cross, for the gods believe that their summons should be welcomed, and an excess of grief is plainly a reflection upon it.

Arta-i Viraf devotes no less than 83 of his 101 chapters to Hell, whereas nine are sufficient for Heaven. By his account, all of the usual sins of mankind are punished in the usual blistering and bloody manner, and in addition there are special penalties for acts which are regarded as felonious only in Persia, for example, feeding a dog hard and uneatable bones, letting the sun shine on a fire, going barefooted, and eating while talking. In Heaven and its three chapels the blest swoon in endless ecstasy, gathered around the gorgeous solar throne of Ahura Mazda, the god of gods. There is also a sort of purgatory, Hamistagan by name, for the dead who were neither virtuous enough when alive to be fit for Heaven nor evil enough to deserve Hell. "Their punishment is cold or heat from the revolution of the atmosphere, and they have no other adversity"

— in other words, they suffer from the weather, but are otherwise unmolested. The Parsees of today do not believe that damned souls will remain in Hell forever. When the world comes to an end, which it is doomed to do eventually in a great deluge of molten metal, they will be set free, and thereafter they will be happy for all eternity.

The Moslem theology, despite the Christian libels upon it, is similarly humane. The mercy of Allah, it teaches, is sufficient to liberate even the worst infidel from Hell; as for the ordinary run of offenders professing the True Faith, they will probably get off with very light sentences at the Last Judgment. But what of their punishment in the meantime? Do they go straight to Hell at death or do they linger in Limbo, awaiting the trump of judgment? Certain passages in the Koran, notably in the twenty-second *sura,* called The Pilgrimage, indicate that they are not judged at death, but simply lie in the tomb against the day of resurrection, when "we [*i.e.,* Allah] will make him [*i.e.,* the sinner] taste the torment of burning." But other passages hint that the pious, on dying, go straight to Heaven, and the conflict has given much concern to Moslem theologians. Some of them resolve it by setting up a theory not unlike the Catholic theory of particular and general judgments. That is to say, the dead go to either Heaven or Hell at death, but at the resurrection they will be judged again, and finally. In the *sura* called Mary, it is explicitly stated that those who go on their knees in Hell, and petition for forgiveness, may be liberated by grace of the All Merciful. Following this promise, however, comes a hint that one sin, at least, can never be forgiven, to wit, the sin of believing that Jesus was the son of Mary by the Holy Ghost. This belief strikes Moslems as libellous and indecent, for, as the Koran says, "it becometh not God to beget children."

The Moslem Hell is of the standard oriental model, and differs from the familiar Christian Hell only in unimportant details. Its tortures are mainly thermal. The damned, when they arrive, will find the smoke from its vast furnaces arising in three columns. That smoke "shall not shade you from the heat, neither shall it be of service against the flames; but it shall cast forth sparks as big as towers, resembling yellow camels in color." There will also be "burning winds and scalding water" and the damned "shall have garments of fire fitted unto them, boiling water shall be poured on their heads, their bowels shall be dissolved thereby, and also their skins, and they shall be beaten with maces of iron. So often as they shall endeavor to get out of Hell, because of the anguish of their torments, they shall be dragged back into the same, and their tormentors shall say unto them, Taste ye the pain of burning." But Hell interests pious Moslems relatively little, for, as I have said, most of them cherish a hope of escaping it. It is a place for infidels rather than for the faithful. The latter all expect to go to Heaven, and so their theological literature is full of eloquent and charming descriptions of it.

The Koran depicts it as a series of "gardens through which rivers flow," and life in it as infinitely peaceful and enchanting. "Its food is perpetual and its shade also." The rivers are of "incorruptible water," and there are also "rivers of milk, the taste whereof changeth not; and rivers of wine, pleasant unto those who drink it; and rivers of clarified honey." The blest, clad in silk, "with bracelets of gold and pearls, . . . shall dwell amidst shades and fountains, and fruits of the kinds which they shall desire; and it shall be said unto them, Eat and drink with easy digestion." The accounts of hostile Christian missionaries have made much of the houris in the Moslem Paradise, but as a matter of fact they are seldom mentioned in the Koran, and then only in the *suras* written before Mohammed's hegira from Mecca to Medina. In the *sura* called The Merciful they are depicted as "beauteous damsels, refraining their eyes from beholding any beside their spouses, whom no man shall have deflowered before them," and in the *sura* cryptically entitled S they are said to be "of equal age with them." In the later, or Medinese *suras,* these houris are converted into lawful wives, of an extraordinary discretion and virtue, eager for the comfort of their lords and full of docility.

Moslem literature has produced no apocalypt comparable to Dante, Arta-i Viraf or St. John; nevertheless, it is full of attempts to expand and fill out the somewhat meagre descriptions of Paradise in the Koran. A typical essay in that direction is to be found in a commentary called Mishkat al-Masabih. By this it appears that the blest dwell in houses made of "gold and silver bricks, with musk for mortar," that the gravel they walk on is of pearls and rubies, and that the earth which produces their food is of saffron. "A tree grows there under which one might ride for a year and come to no end. . . . No one will sleep there, for sleep is death's brother. All men and women are beautiful." In general, this literature promises the faithful everything that dwellers in a hot, dry climate may be supposed to long for most ardently on earth, especially shade, cool and pure waters, and plenty of luscious fruit. If its authors had been born in the North instead of in the

Levant, they would have given Paradise less boskage and
more sunlight. The same wish neurosis shows itself in all
apocalyptic writings. Heaven is always rich in what is
longed for, and Hell has an infinite abundance of what is
already too abundant. The Tibetan Buddhists, inhabiting
the cold and windy roof of the world, reject the 136 hot
Hells of orthodox Buddhism, and substitute eight of their
own, in which the grateful fires are displaced by geysers
of icy glacier water, and the damned are so thoroughly
refrigerated that their jaws freeze tight, their tongues are
so paralyzed that only the exclamations, *Kyi-u* and *Ha-ha*,
are possible, and their bodies are dissolved in horrible
chilblains, with the flesh falling away like the wither-
ing petals of the sacred lotus.

## 10

But all such melodramatic fancies belong to a relatively late stage of theological speculation. Most of the
ancient peoples do not appear to have troubled themselves
greatly about the state of their souls after death; what
engaged them mainly was the harsh business of making
life tolerable on this earth. The sacrifices that they offered
to the gods were not made with an eye to an eternity of
bliss; they were made with an eye to the here and now.
Thus the Earth Mother got her first fruits, not as an
insurance against Hell, but simply as a fair and reasonable payment for the remaining fruits. J. B. Carter, in "The
Religious Life of Ancient Rome," well describes the
scheme. "A prayer," he says, "was a vow (*votum*) in which
man, the party of the first part, agreed to perform certain
acts to the god, the party of the second part, in return

for certain specified services to be rendered. Were these services rendered, man, the party of the first part, was, *compos voti,* bound to perform what he had promised. Were these services not rendered, the contract was void. In the great majority of cases the gods did not receive their payment until their work had been accomplished, for their worshippers were guided by the natural shrewdness of primitive man, and experience showed that in many cases the gods did not fulfil their portion of the contract. . . . There were, however, other occasions when a slightly different set of considerations entered in. In a moment of battle it might not seem sufficient to propose the ordinary contract, and an attempt was sometimes made to compel the god's action by performing the promised return in advance, and thus placing the deity in the delicate position of having received something for which he ought properly to make return." In all this the inability of early man to imagine immortality, or to visualize with any clarity even a limited life after death, was plainly a factor. He wanted the gods to be kind to him on earth, not in some vague beyond, for he could think of that beyond only as a land of shadows, and he harbored no hope or desire to inhabit it forever. Even in India, the very gonad of theology, there was, as we have just seen, no belief in immortal life: the blest and the damned were alike doomed to eventual nothingness. The concept of infinity came in relatively late, even in Egypt, and as I hinted some time back, its first fathers were more likely metaphysicians than theologians.

In looking backward, as in looking forward, early man was quite unable to imagine endless time. Always he concluded that the animal creation, including his own kind, must have had a beginning, and the earth he walked on with it. Sometimes he ascribed the act of creation to the gods, or to one of them, and sometimes he laid it to a potent being of lesser dignity, usually a totem animal. The Athapascan Indians of the Northwest, before they became Methodists, believed that the world was fashioned by a gigantic raven, and that this bird was also their own first ancestor. Where it came from they did not know. Some of the Iroquois tribes believed that the creator was a beaver, and others that he was a muskrat. This beaver or muskrat, navigating the primeval waste of waters, dug up sufficient earth from the bottom to make an island, and the island kept on growing until it was the North American continent. In parts of Melanesia the creator was one Qat, a spirit-being of great potency, but still not a god. In pre-Columbian Peru he was Con, a boneless son of the sun and moon. In Polynesia he was a divinity variously called Tangaloa, Taaroa or Kanaloa, whose left eye was the sun.

Among the ancient Egyptians, at least at one period, he was Rê, the sun-god, who was hatched from an egg that seems to have come into existence spontaneously. Among the early Japanese it was believed that the earth and the first gods appeared simultaneously, and apparently out of nothing: all that was known of a certainty about the business was that the gods, who were three in number, bore the appalling names of Ame-no-mi-naka-nushi-no-kami, Taka-mi-musu-bi-no-kami and Kami-musu-bi-no-kami. The Mayans of Yucatan believed in four separate creations, set off from one another by obliterating deluges. Anthropologists and archeologists, delving into the superstitions of savages and the records of the past, have unearthed almost endless variations and permutations of these naïve cosmogonies. The imagination of the race has played upon the fascinating subject since the beginning of history. The earth has been thought of as emerging from water, from fire, from fog, from air, and from the impalpable mind-stuff of the gods, and the origin of mankind has been ascribed to everything from their adultery to their playing with mud-pies. The question of the creation of the gods themselves has stimulated the same lush and fecund fancy. In no department of theology is there a vaster accumulation of amusing rubbish.

The cosmogony of the Jews, as recorded in Genesis, was mainly borrowed from the Babylonians. According to A. H. Sayce, the creation myth that it embodies arose at Eridu, a town on the Persian Gulf. "Here," he says, in Hastings' Encyclopedia of Religion and Ethics, " the land was constantly growing through the deposition of silt, and the belief consequently arose that the earth had originated in the same way. The water of the great deep accordingly came to be regarded as the primordial element out of which the universe was generated. The deep was identified with the Persian Gulf, which was conceived as encircling the earth." In Genesis 1, 2, the Spirit of God moves "upon the face of the waters" before there is anything else, even light. Not only are fish precipitated from their substance, but also "fowl that fly above the earth" and "great whales," i.e., mammals. Man himself appears to be watery, too, for, though in the next chapter he is represented as formed "of the dust of the ground," it is explained that just previously "there went up a mist from the earth, and watered the whole face of the ground." This is a palpable echo of the Babylonian Gilgamesh legend, wherein Eabani, the first man, is fashioned of clay by the Goddess Ishtar.

171

The Garden of Eden is also plainly Babylonian, for one of its rivers, the Euphrates, bears a Babylonish name, and another, the Hiddekel (no doubt the Tigris) is said to run "toward the east of Assyria." The Babylonians, whose notions of a life after death were of the vaguest, believed that there was an earthly Paradise somewhere to the northward of their country. In it those mortals who were lucky enough to obtain entrance dwelt with the gods, just as Adam dwelt with Yahweh in Eden, and from it flowed the four rivers that watered the earth. The very name of Eden seems to have been Babylonian, for in that language *edinu* signified a pleasant plain. The Jews also got the Flood legend from the Babylonians, though in one form or another it was common throughout the East. Catastrophic floods were familiar in the Euphrates and Tigris valleys, but they must have been very rare in Palestine, and the lay of the land was such that even the greatest of them could not have been very destructive. Noah's landing, it will be recalled, was not made in Palestine at all, but "upon the mountains of Ararat" in the Caucasus, at least 750 miles from Jerusalem as the crow flies. The prodigious ages of the patriarchs, as given in Genesis v, likewise show Babylonian influence, though here the Jews seem to have tempered imitation with a considerable moderation. To match Methusaleh, who lived 969 years, there were kings of Ur who reigned for 28,800, 36,000 and even 43,200 years!

The Flood legend is common to all parts of the world save only Africa, and even there it is occasionally encountered. Nearly always a chosen few escape in a canoe or on a raft or by fleeing into a high mountain, but sometimes the whole human race is exterminated, and another creation is necessary in order to continue it. The gods usually send the obliterating waters because man has become hopelessly wicked, but occasionally they do so for a trivial reason — an accidental insult or something of the sort. In one of the legends prevalent in the South Seas a careless fisherman, fishing in sacred waters, arouses the sea-god from a nap by catching his hair, and the angry god straightway drowns the whole race. In most of the stories in which there are survivors, they are succored by ravens, pigeons, parrots or other birds, and it is not uncommon for these birds to reveal their mission by appearing with something corresponding to the Biblical olive leaf. The fable of the Fall of Man is also widespread, and nearly always, as in Genesis, it is based upon a violation of taboo. The first man, forbidden by the gods to eat of the fruit of this or that tree, or to go into some area reserved for their pleasure, or to bathe in a certain pool, or to kill a certain animal or catch a certain fish, does so notwithstanding, and is immediately doomed to suffer disease, famine and death.

The problem of evil is something that all religions, however primitive, have to wrestle with. How did pain and misery come into the world? Why must man mourn all his days, and then pass into darkness at the end? The answer still waits, but theologians have surely made gallant efforts to formulate it. On the one hand they have tackled the business with all the more subtle devices of metaphysics, but on the other hand they have sought to soothe the lowly with an endless series of facile tales about evil apples, tempting serpents and angry gods.

# IV     Its Christian Form

In the world that we moderns know Christianity is the prevailing religion among the most enlightened peoples, but that is not saying that the evidences supporting its theology meet all the tests of enlightened men or that they are more persuasive than those supporting other civilized religions. It might be argued very plausibly, indeed, that the contrary is the case, for Christianity leans upon supernaturalism more heavily than any of its principal rivals, and there is in it, even in its more refined forms, a great deal that is irrational and incredible.

As it exists today it shows few elements that may be traced with any probability to its Founder. There is no reason to believe that He ever heard of the Virgin Birth, or of the mystical and unintelligible dogma of the Trinity, or even of Original Sin. The notion of the Apostolic Succession, with some appearance of historical probability, may be traced to Him, but certainly it is hard to imagine Him, after His bitter onslaughts upon the Jewish hierarchy, countenancing the pretensions of the bishops who now adorn and astound the earth, or believing in the infallibility of the pope. He knew nothing about saints and it never occurred to Him that men should ever worship His Mother. Inasmuch as He is said, on occasion, to have turned water into wine, we may assume that the miracle of transubstantiation might have struck Him as not absurd,

but there is no evidence that He ever charged His followers to perform it, or that those He knew in the flesh ever
undertook to do so. His ethical teachings, like His theology, have been vastly modified by priestly embellish-
ment, and in certain fields they have been turned completely upside down. If He could come back to earth today
it would probably shock Him profoundly to find Catholics
doomed to Hell for neglecting their Easter duty and Protestants damned for drinking wine, for He held a cynical
opinion of all priestly jurisprudence and wine to Him was
a more natural drink than water.

Unfortunately, it is hard to determine just what He
taught, even on capital matters, for the written records are
scanty and in large part they are palpably undependable.
The collection of tracts called the New Testament is so
full of inconsistencies and other absurdities that even children in Sunday-school notice them. There is, for example,
the familiar discrepancy between the accounts of the Virgin Birth in Matthew and Luke and the genealogies of
Jesus in the same Gospels, tracing His descent through
Joseph. Again, there is the difference between Matthew
and Luke in the matter of the Flight into Egypt. Matthew
says that Joseph, warned in a dream, made off with mother
and child as soon as the wise men from the East had departed, and remained in Egypt until after the death of
Herod; Luke says categorically that the three stayed in
Bethlehem until Mary's "purification according to the
law of Moses was accomplished" — a period of seven plus
thirty-three days — and then went to Jerusalem, and
thence to Nazareth. There is, yet again, the gross contra-
diction between the flat statement credited to Jesus in Matthew xvii, that John the Baptist was a reincarnation of

175

Elias the prophet, and John's own explicit denial, in John 1. There is, once more, the wide variation between the accounts of the calling of the Twelve Apostles in the four Gospels — a variation so wide that to this day the precise personnel of the little band is uncertain. A hundred other conflicts, some of them in matters of the first importance, will reward the diligent searcher of the Scriptures. The reports of the Sermon on the Mount, in Matthew and Luke, are contradictory and, in part, irreconcilable. Matthew, Luke and John differ hopelessly about the anointing of Jesus, both as to the time and as to the place. Matthew differs from Mark, Luke and John about the betrayal of Judas. Each of the four has a different account of the denial of Peter. Matthew and Mark tell one story of the trial of Jesus; Luke tells a second; John tells a third. Even when they come to such colossal events as the Crucifixion and the Resurrection they do not agree. It is all immensely confusing, and the resolution of the dilemma is surely not helped by the theological doctrine that each and every one of the four, having been divinely inspired, must be accepted as infallible.

The simple fact is that the New Testament, as we know it, is a helter-skelter accumulation of more or less discordant documents, some of them probably of respectable origin but others palpably apocryphal, and that most of them, the good along with the bad, show unmistakable signs of having been tampered with. "No Biblical scholar of any standing today," says Weigall, "whether he be a clergyman or a layman, accepts the entire New Testament as authentic; all admit that many errors, misunderstandings and absurdities have crept into the story of Christ's life and other matters." The earliest parts of the canon, in the opinion of all competent authorities, are the Epistles of Paul, and of these I Thessalonians seems to be the most ancient. It was apparently written at Corinth during Paul's second missionary journey, which fixes its date as 51 A.D., or about twenty years after the Crucifixion. In it, as in all the other Pauline Epistles, there is a complete lack of any reference, whether direct or indirect, to the four Gospels, and so it is a fair inference that they did not exist in Paul's lifetime, else he would have mentioned them. He was put to death in Rome, according to the most plausible guess, in the year 64. At some time during the next ten years, and probably before the year 70, the Gospel of Mark was written. Who the author was we do not know with any certainty, but there is internal evidence that he was a Christian of Jewish birth and good education, more or less familiar with Greek, Latin and Aramaic, and a reference at the end of I Peter, supported by an ancient tradition, makes him the companion and amanuensis of Peter, one of the Apostles. Peter is thought to have been martyred at Rome in 64, along with Paul, but Mark's record of his master's recollections does not seem to have been set down until afterward: at all events, it was not generally circulated. Mark himself, if he ever saw Jesus at all, saw him only as a boy. What he sets forth is what Peter told him.

The other Gospels are plainly later. Those of Matthew and Luke lean heavily upon Mark, and almost as heavily upon a lost Gospel, to which the German critics long ago gave the designation of Q, from the German word *Quelle* = source. Of the two, the Gospel of Luke seems to be the older. It was probably written after the year 70, for there are passages in it which are generally taken to refer to the destruction of Jerusalem in that year, and it may have been written before the year 80; further than that sound historical criticism cannot venture to go. The Gospel is in the form of a letter to one Theophilus, reputed by tradition to have been a rich convert of Antioch, and Luke begins his narrative by saying that many other Gospels were in circulation at the time he wrote. "It seems good to me also," he goes on, "having had perfect understanding of all things from the very first, to write to thee in order . . . that thou mightest know the certainty of those things, wherein thou hast been instructed." But despite this claim to a "perfect understanding of all things from the very first," there is no reason to believe that Luke ever saw Jesus. All the evidence indicates that he was converted to the new faith by Paul, who made a companion of him, was fond of him, and took him on various missionary journeys. He was a Gentile by birth, a physician by profession, and a man of rather more education than was common among the first Christians. His Greek is better than Mark's. He also wrote the Acts of the Apostles, again in the form of a letter to Theophilus, and apparently immediately after he wrote his Gospel.

The Gospel of Matthew belongs to a somewhat later date — possibly to the closing years of the First Century. That it was written by the Apostle Matthew is next to impossible, for he must have been older than Jesus, and by the year 90 he would have been a centenarian. But it is not unlikely that the author, whoever he was, made use of memoranda left by the Apostle, and these memoranda may have constituted the Q document which Luke also drew from. For that theory there is support in a statement by one Papias, Bishop of Hierapolis (*circa* 140), that "Matthew composed *logia* in Hebrew, and everyone interpreted them as he was able." These *logia,* which seem to have consisted mainly of the sayings of Jesus, may have been in general circulation in the East, and the author of Matthew may have written them into his Gospel, just as he wrote in much of Mark. If so, perhaps the faithful mistook the whole work for the Apostle's and so gave it its present name. All we know of a surety is that it already bore that name about the year 185, when it was mentioned by Irenæus, Bishop of Lugdunum (the modern Lyons, in Southern France), in his celebrated tract, "Adversus Hæreses." Who the actual author was is completely unknown, though he seems to have been a Jew.

The Gospel of John is still later: it was probably not written until the end of the First Century. But the ideas in it were widespread by the middle of the century following, and so we may put its date at not later than the year 125. The identity of the author remains in doubt. He was apparently the same who wrote the two Epistles of John, which belong to the same period, but not the John who wrote the Revelation, which is earlier. Internal evidence indicates that he was a Jew, and though he wrote in Greek it is probable that he did his thinking in Aramaic. The remaining books of the New Testament are of varying dates, and show varying degrees of authenticity. The first Epistle of Peter, for example, may have been actually written by the Apostle, though its Greek seems too good for him, or for his amanuensis Mark. If so, it belongs to some time before the year 64. But the second Epistle of Peter is plainly by another hand, and must have been written in the Second Century, years after the Apostle's death.

## 2

Such is the New Testament — a miscellaneous collection of historical records, theological speculations, pontifical bulls and moral homilies, often in sharp conflict, one with another, and never in complete harmony. The thing one chiefly notices, reading them in the order of their probable composition, is the gradual development of a complicated theology, most of it having only the most remote sort of relation to what seems to have been the teaching of Jesus. The precise nature of that teaching, indeed, we shall never know, for no one appears to have set it down during His lifetime, and by the time Mark, Luke and the pseudo-Matthew began to record the recollections of such ear-witnesses as Matthew and Peter the latter were already aged men, and what they remembered had begun to be corrupted by the vaporings of theologians, including especially Paul and the apocalyptic John. We are by no means sure that the basic Gospel, that of Mark, now stands as he wrote it; on the contrary, there is every reason to believe that it is full of the sophistications of editors and copyists. For example, no competent scholar believes that its last twelve verses, beginning with xvi, 9, were written by Mark. They are missing from most of the early MSS. that have survived, whether Greek, Latin, Syriac or Armenian; they were not cited by any of the early fathers save Irenæus, who did not quote them until the year 185 or thereabout; and they were apparently unknown to Luke and Matthew, who made heavy use of all the rest of Mark's Gospel.

It was in Gaul that they seem to have originated; Ire-

næus himself was a bishop there. Not until the beginning
of the Fourth Century were they accepted in the East, and
even then they were still held suspect by the celebrated
Eusebius of Cæsarea (c. 260–340), who had access to the
great library of Pamphilus and was the first critic to give
the text of what is now the New Testament anything approaching scientific study. The importance of the disputed verses will be realized when it is recalled that they
ascribe to Jesus the words "Go ye into the world, and
preach the gospel to every creature" — the most forceful
form of the mandate that animates all Christian missionary effort to this day, and has cost, in its time, the lives of
millions of poor heathen. It is not hard to believe that the
whole passage originated in the enthusiasm of some missionary to the Gauls, eager to have at them gloriously in
their sinister forests. No doubt he embodied in it an actual
saying by Jesus, but he almost certainly added embellishments of his own, for following the mandate comes a
plainly preposterous promise that "them that believe" shall
have the power to cast out devils, to speak in the tongues,
to take up serpents and "drink any deadly thing" without
hurt, and to cure the sick by laying on hands.

There are several other passages in Mark that hint
broadly at uninspired tampering — for example, the lame
retelling, in the eighth chapter, of the story of the feeding
of the multitude, already told better in the sixth —, but of
very much more importance, as showing the effort of early
theologians to improve the original narrative, are the wide
discrepancies between Mark on the one hand and Matthew
and Luke on the other. By the time the latter two began to
write, Christian theology had already departed considerably from the simple teaching of the Founder, and there

were bitter disputes over important points of doctrine, as the Pauline Epistles sufficiently show. Naturally enough, each theologian in active practice tried to prove that what he himself taught was the only true orthodoxy, and so a great multitude of expository and polemical writings, sometimes in the form of gospels but more often in that of epistles, got into circulation, each designed to that end. Some of them were quickly rejected, by a sort of general consent, as spurious, but others gained wide acceptance in this or that area, and became formidable rivals to the present books of the New Testament. A number survive to this day, though usually only as fragments, and more are being discovered from time to time, mainly in Christian graves in Egypt.

They all deserve harder study than they have got, for if they do not show what actually happened during Jesus's ministry, they at least show what large numbers of earnest Christians believed during the century following. But it is not necessary to resort to them to prove that in that century there were great fluctuations in Christian dogma, with a general movement in the direction of supernaturalism, for plenty of evidence is to be found in Matthew and Luke. Both evangelists, writing after Mark, made very obvious efforts to introduce refinements into his somewhat bald and naïve narrative. Where he was content to set forth the overt facts as Peter remembered them, they were eager to give those facts a profound and transcendental significance. Sometimes it sufficed them to heighten the colors a bit or to suppress a few inconvenient details, but at other times — and this was especially true of Matthew — they went to the length of adding episodes that Mark

182

apparently never heard of, and appending interpretations that would have probably greatly surprised him.

Their chief aim, it is easy to see, was to augment and glorify the personality of Jesus — to lift Him out of His merely prophetical character and make Him a veritable divinity. In Mark there is no hint of the Virgin Birth (nor indeed in John); in Matthew and Luke it has first place and is of the utmost importance. In Mark Jesus is essentially human; He yields to emotion; He wonders and asks questions; He is fallible. In Matthew and Luke He passes into a godlike calm and becomes omniscient. Mark, describing the healing of the man with the withered arm, makes Jesus fly into a rage against the Pharisees who objected to miracles on the Sabbath; Matthew and Luke discreetly pass over His anger. In Mark we are told that, visiting His "own country," He was so daunted by the unbelief of His people that "He could there do *no* mighty work," and that He "marvelled because of their unbelief"; in Matthew *"no* mighty work" is toned down to *"not many* mighty works," and there is no mention at all of His human wonderment. In Matthew (and usually in Luke) the miracles are always a shade more splendid than in Mark. The man whose "unclean spirit" is put into the Gadarene swine becomes two men; blind Bartimeus, the son of Timeus, becomes two men likewise, and the modest saying, "Go thy way; thy faith hath made thee whole," is supplanted by "Jesus had compassion on them, and touched their eyes: and immediately their eyes received sight, and they followed Him."

So in many other instances. In Mark 1, 32–34, *all* the sick are brought in, and he heals *many;* in Matthew VIII, 16, *many* are brought in, and He heals *all*. Always there is that pointing up, that increase of emphasis, that augmentation of the wonder. The purpose, plainly enough, is not merely to make the story more marvellous, but also and more especially to give it a greater theological coherence and significance — to bring it into harmony with the developing theology of the infant church, by Paul out of the *Zeitgeist*. Even the Apostles take on a new dignity and decorum. In Mark we see James and John demanding raucously that they may have the best places in glory; in Matthew the demand is put discreetly into the mouth of their mother, and in Luke it is not recorded at all.

Matthew is more Jewish than the other two, and at the same time more Christian in the modern sense. His dealings with the Jewish Law and Jewish prophecies show an easy familiarity with them and he is not above embellishing Mark's narrative in order to bring it into harmony with the Old Testament, as when, for example, he converts the colt of the entry into Jerusalem into an ass and a colt, thus meeting the terms of Zechariah ix, 9. On occasion, indeed, he does not hesitate to make radical changes in the very words of Jesus, as when he interpolates the important reservation, "saving for the cause of fornication," in the sweeping prohibition of divorce. That reservation is in strict accord with Jewish law, but the principal branch of the Christian church has chosen to disregard it completely, though still insisting that every word of the New Testament is inspired and infallible. In another salient case, however, the church prefers Matthew to the others. I allude to the celebrated passage at the end of his Gospel: "Go ye therefore, and teach all nations, baptizing them in the name of the Father, and of the Son, and of the

Holy Ghost." Here is a square and unequivocal statement of Trinitarian doctrine — but Mark knows nothing of it and neither does Luke, and in the Acts of the Apostles baptism is invariably in the name of Jesus alone. Obviously, the passage is quite as dubious as the verses at the end of Mark; we may safely assume, indeed, that it was not written by the original pseudo-Matthew at all, but by some later theologian, and at some time after the church had begun to accept the dogma of the Trinity — a dogma of which Jesus Himself was as completely unaware as He was of the nine symphonies of Beethoven.

But such passages, though plainly interpolations in the original narrative, at least have ancient acceptance behind them, for they are found in very early manuscripts, dating at the latest from the Fourth Century. The case is different when we come to certain other parts of the present text, notably the account of the appearance of an angel and of Jesus's bloody sweat in Luke xxii, 43–44, the *Pericope Adulteræ,* or story of the woman taken in adultery, in John viii, 1–11, the doxology at the end of Matthew's version of the Lord's Prayer, and the clear statement of Trinitarian dogma in I John v, 7–8. For these there is no authority whatever in the early manuscripts: they first appear relatively late and under very shady auspices. The essential words of the last-named — "For there are three that bear record in Heaven, the Father, the Word and the Holy Ghost: *and these three are one"* — are not found in any Greek manuscript of earlier date than the Fourteenth Century, and do not appear in Jerome's translation of the New Testament into Latin. They seem to have got into subsequent Latin translations in the Sixth Century or thereabout, though they may have originated earlier. Even orthodox Catholic scholars question them seriously, and so recently as 1897 the Congregation of the Holy Office at Rome was asked to decide formally whether they could be "safely denied." It answered no, but when, twenty-three years later, the eminent Catholic theologian, Heinrich Vogels of Bonn, printed a new critical edition of the Greek Testament he quietly relegated them to the margin. The doxology at the end of the Lord's Prayer in Matthew vi, 13, is equally dubious: it does not appear in any of the early manuscripts. So with the beautiful *Pericope Adulteræ* and the passage about the bloody sweat in Luke xxii.

### 3

It is hard to discover any rational purpose in some of these interpolations; they probably got in, indeed, by accident rather than by design, for the early scribes were notoriously of little professional conscience, and a study of the surviving manuscripts of the New Testament reveals nearly 175,000 discrepancies, mainly of a minor kind. But in other cases it is plain enough that the aim was to give support to this or that dogma — usually, no doubt, a dogma that happened to be under fire. The early church rocked with debates and disputes, and was exposed, in addition, to constant bombardment from theologians outside the fold. Some of the apocryphal gospels, now rejected but once in high esteem, seem to have been written for the precise purpose of meeting such attacks. This was probably true, for example, of the so-called Gospel According to the Hebrews, which was quoted as authoritative by Jerome, who translated it into both Greek and Hebrew; it also had the confidence of Origen and Clement of Alexandria. Its composition was commonly credited, in the early days, to no less a personage that the Apostle Matthew, and there are critics today who believe that it was made use of by the pseudo-Matthew in writing the Matthew that we know. One of its characteristic passages shows the effort of the early Christians to explain away certain difficulties in the other Gospels. Many of them must have asked themselves the question (or had it put to them by skeptics), Why did Jesus, the Son of God and hence without sin, accept baptism at the hands of John the Baptist, who viewed the rite as a sign of "repentance for the remission of sins?" The answer of the Gospel According to the Hebrews is that Jesus, though He felt that He was sinless, was yet sufficiently humble to admit that He might be mistaken, and to act accordingly. Here is the passage: "Behold, the mother of the Lord and His brethren said to Him, John the Baptist baptizeth for remission of sins; let us go and be baptized by him. But He saith to them, Wherein have I sinned, that I should go and be baptized by him? *unless perchance this very thing that I have said is ignorance.*"

Similar efforts to get around difficulties are visible in many other of the rejected gospels. In the one, for example, called the Book of James, or the Protoevangelium, which survives in Greek and Syriac texts, there is an attempt to answer the argument, common among Gnostics and other critics of Christianity in the First and Second Centuries, that so poor and obscure a woman as Mary could not have been the Mother of God. The answer takes the form of a long and romantic account of Mary's ancestry, birth and youth, showing that she came into the world by a sort of miracle. Her mother, Anna, was childless for many years, and her father, Ioacim, was so displeased thereat that he "betook himself to the wilderness, and pitched his tent there, and fasted forty days and forty nights." Meanwhile, Anna sat at home and prayed, until one day "an angel of the Lord appeared, saying unto her: Anna, Anna, the Lord hath hearkened unto thy prayer, and thou shalt conceive and bear, and thy seed shall be spoken of in the whole world."

To the average decent-minded Jewish woman of the time this assurance could have meant but one thing: that she would bear a son. But Anna, it appears, was superior to the common ideas of her race and sex, and so she said: "As the Lord my God liveth, if I bring forth *either male or female,* I will bring it for a gift unto the Lord my God, and it shall be ministering unto Him all the days of its life." And when the child was born and "she said unto the midwife, What have I brought forth?" and the midwife answered, "A female," she did not mourn, but cried proudly, "My soul is magnified this day." Here, in a false gospel of the Second Century, we have the beginnings of mariolatry and perhaps also of the dogma of the Immaculate Conception, which was not to come to official statement until December 8, 1854. In some of the other gospels the new ideas introduced are not so much theological as political: they represent efforts to protect the infant church against the suspicion of treason to Rome, or to shame and flabbergast the opponents who were always trying to induce the police to put it down as a public nuisance. Thus in the Gospel of Peter (*c.* 150), the whole blame for the Crucifixion is laid upon the Jews, and Pilate is completely exonerated, and even represented as believing, more or less, in Jesus's divinity.

Despite the competition of these rivals, the four Gospels that we know today gradually gained in authority, and by

the middle of the Second Century they were pretty generally accepted as superior to all the rest. Irenæus, in his
tract against heretics (c. 185), spoke of them as the Tetramorph, and corectly named them, and even before that
they seem to have been recognized by Justin Martyr (c. 100–
165) and the heretical Basilides of Alexandria (c. 140).
Irenæus, in the manner of the time, sought to explain their
number on mystical grounds. "It is not possible," he said,
"that the Gospels should be either more or fewer than
they are. For since there are four zones of the world in
which we live, and four principal winds, . . . it is fitting
that we should have four pillars. . . . The living creatures
are quadriform, and so the Gospel is also quadriform."
Harnack, the great German critic, believes that Matthew,
Mark, Luke and John came to this canonical dignity at
some time between the years 140 and 175. The rest of the
New Testament as we now know it had harder sledding,
and parts of it were under suspicion for many centuries.

The thirteen Pauline Epistles seem to have been the
first to get a firm lodgment. Acts followed them, and then
I Peter, and then the three Epistles of John. Hebrews,
James, Jude and II Peter lingered in the twilight a bit
longer, and Revelation came near being excluded altogether. Origen was in favor of letting it in, but his disciple,
the learned Eusebius, was violently opposed to it, apparently on the ground that its gaudy nonsensicality made
it a favorite with amateur theologians, then as now, and
hence tended to nurture heresy. At the behest of Constantine, Eusebius had fifty copies of the New Testament as he
understood it made for the churches of Asia. Revelation
was excluded from them, as were Jude, II Peter, and II
and III John. He also threw his influence against various

other books, now vanished from the canon, that Origen had regarded with a friendly eye — among them, Barnabas, the Shepherd of Hermes, the so-called Didach, or Teaching of the Twelve Apostles (an early church manual, probably dating from the middle of the Second Century), and the aforesaid Gospel According to the Hebrews. These were all accepted by the Alexandrine church, and it also added the Apocalypse of Peter and the Acts of Paul. But when, in the year 326, the mighty Athanasius, chief defender of the Trinity, became Bishop of Alexandria, he heaved them out, and they have been below the salt ever since, though some of them still have partisans, especially in the Eastern churches.

The great Council of Nicæa, which met in 325, does not seem to have considered the canon of the New Testament, but on Easter Day, 367, Athanasius brought the matter forward at last by sending out an *epistola festalis* from Alexandria, proposing to the bishops of the whole church that a text substantially like the one we now have be adopted universally. Various provincial synods gave their assent, but meanwhile Pope Damasus decided to take a hand in the matter, so he summoned a council for the purpose, to meet at Rome. It began its deliberations in 382, and one of its shining lights was St. Jerome, who was later to translate the whole Bible into Latin. The result was the Damasan canon, which has remained substantially unchanged ever since, at least in the Roman and Greek churches. There was, indeed, no serious challenge to it anywhere until the Reformation, when Luther excluded Hebrews, James, Jude and Revelation, and several other reformers raised doubts about II Peter and II and III John. This assault caused some uneasiness in Holy Church, for there were Catholic scholars who inclined, more or less cautiously, in the same direction. Moreover, there was a rising dissatisfaction with certain passages that Luther had not attacked, notably the last twelve verses of Mark. To put an end to this disaffection and to the numerous other difficulties raised by the Reformation Pope Paul III summoned a great council at Trent, and it deliberated from 1545 to 1563, thus surviving Paul himself and three of his successors. On April 8, 1546, it decided formally and solemnly that the Damasan canon, in the Vulgate translation, should be binding upon all Catholics as inspired and impeccable, and it remains so to this day. Most Protestants accept it also, including even the German Lutherans, though the latter still make some changes in the order of the books.

The Higher Criticism has done relatively little damage to this canon. It rejects Revelation, of course, as a statement of fact, and it points to the glaring sophistications in Matthew and Luke, but on the whole it accepts the New Testament as a reasonably accurate record of what certain pious men of Jesus's time saw and heard or thought they saw and heard. The historicity of Jesus is no longer questioned seriously by anyone, whether Christian or unbeliever. The main facts about Him seem to be beyond dispute: that He lived in Palestine during the reigns of the Roman Emperors Augustus and Tiberius, that He was a pious Jew and a man of great personal dignity and virtue, that He believed the end of the world was at hand and sought to induce His fellow Jews to prepare for it, that He aroused thereby the enmity of the Jewish priests and was put to death at their behest, that certain of His followers after His death believed that He had arisen from the tomb, and that this belief, appealing powerfully to the imagination of the time, carried His ideas from end to end of the Roman world, and so founded what is now called Christianity. The New Testament is thus an historical document of very tolerable authority, needing only to be read with due circumspection. If there are some palpable stretchers in it, then stretchers of the same sort are to be found in most of the secular histories of its remote and innocent age. If it is sometimes contradictory, puerile and absurd, then so are they. One might hesitate to liken it to any modern work of the first credibility, such as Boswell's "Johnson" or Eckermann's "Gespräche Mit Goethe," but it is certainly quite as sound as Parson Weems' "Life of Washington" or "Uncle Tom's Cabin."

## 4

The Old Testament, as history, is on a much lower level, though as poetry it has never been surpassed in the world. It is partly the product, in the form with which we are familiar, of Jews who had been touched by the Greek enlightenment, but the essential parts of it are purely Asiatic in origin, and so they show a great deal more florid fancy than historical conscience. It is at once a book of laws, a collection of chronicles and genealogies, and a series of prophetical tracts, hymn books, erotic rhapsodies, and primitive novels. Parallels to the New Testament, and especially to the Epistles, are to be found in the *belles lettres* of both Greece and Rome, but to find anything resembling the Old Testament one must go to such completely oriental documents as the Code of Manu, the Persian Avesta, the Indian Vedas, and the Egyptian Book of the Dead.

All through the ancient East similar Bibles flourished, and nearly every important people produced one, large or small. And they were all pretty much alike, for each sought to account for the origin of the world and the creation of man, each set down very minutely the wishes of the gods, in matters of private conduct and public devotion, as they had been revealed to inspired sages, and each became overladen, in the course of time, with more or less unintelligible theological niceties. An ordinary man could not hope to understand these books by simply reading them; they had to be interpreted by specialists, which is to say, by priests. Thus they gradually accumulated formidable glosses, and sometimes these glosses became parts of the canon, and even swallowed up what had been written in the first place.

The Old Testament is just such a fabric. From end to end, but especially in the first five books, the so-called Pentateuch, it reeks with irreconcilable contradictions and patent imbecilities. There are two accounts of the Creation, two of the Flood, two of Joseph's combat with his brethren, and two of many another transaction, equally important. Sometimes, passing from one part to another, one finds essential facts and figures changed; at other times, suggesting what we have seen in the New Testament, the facts are substantially unmolested, but they are given an entirely new theological significance. Such things must have been noticed by sensible men at a very early time; we know, indeed, that there were bitter controversies over this passage or that many centuries ago. But it was not until the Twelfth Century of our era that the Pentateuch as a whole was subjected to rational scrutiny. The man who undertook that ungrateful task was a learned Spanish rabbi, Abraham ben Meir ibn Esra. He unearthed many absurdities, but he had to be very careful about discussing them, and it was not until five hundred years later than anything properly describable as scientific criticism of the Old Testament came into being.

Its earliest shining lights were the English philosopher, Thomas Hobbes, and the Amsterdam Jew, Baruch Spinoza. Spinoza's "Tractatus Theologico-politicus," published in 1670, made the first really formidable onslaught upon the inspired inerrancy of the Pentateuch. It called attention to scores of transparent imbecilities in the five books, and especially in Genesis, including a dozen or more palpable geographical and historical impossibilities, and a placid and circumstantial account of Moses' death and burial, together with a highly favorable estimate of his career, comparing him with later prophets, in a book he was supposed to have written himself. The answer of the constituted authorities was to suppress the "Tractatus," but enough copies got out to reach the proper persons, and ever since then the Old Testament has been under searching and devastating examination. The first conspicuous contributor to that work was a French priest, Richard Simon, but since then the Germans have had more to do with it than any other people, and so it is common for American Christians to think of the so-called Higher Criticism as a German invention, and to lay a good deal of the blame for it upon Hitler and the Kaiser.

These scholars have brought forth overwhelming proof that the Pentateuch (or, more accurately, the Hexateuch, for Joshua seems to show the same hands that wrote Genesis, Exodus, Leviticus, Numbers and Deuteronomy) is made up in the main of three distinct parts, often in direct conflict on major points of fact and almost always at sharp variance in points of view. The first, because the name of God appears in it as Elohim, has been designated the Elohistic document and is commonly referred to as E for short. The second, because it calls Him Yahweh (Jehovah), is known as the Yahwistic document, or J. The third, which shows the adept hand of professional theologians and seems to be much later, is called D, from Deuteronomy. E is usually divided further into two documents, one of which is called P, and there have been many efforts to carry the division even further, but such critical hairsplitting need not concern us here.

The Yahwistic document is apparently the oldest, and by far. It goes back to the days of King David at least (*c.* 1000 B.C.), and parts of it, plainly taken from Babylonian sources, are a great deal older. It is full of a primitive and charming naïveté. The Jews, at that time, had just swarmed in from the deserts to occupy Jerusalem, and their religion was that of simple Bedouins. They themselves had but one God, but they did not think of Him as ruling over other tribes and peoples, each of which, in their view, had its own. They imagined Him as a sort of glorified desert *sheik,* a veritable father of His tribe, full of very human whims and caprices, eager for flattery, sociable in His more amiable moments, but quick to punish contumacy, or even mere impoliteness. It is in this character that He appears in J. "He gets about," says E. R. Trattner, in "Unravelling the Book of Books," "without too much dignity, and accomplishes His desires in His own natural and homely way. . . . He brings all the animals to Adam to see what he will call them. He walks in the Garden of Eden in the cool of the day, calling to Adam

and Eve to ask where they are. . . . He closes the door on
Noah when he goes into the ark. He is jealous and appre-
hensive of the men who build the Tower of Babel and
goes down from Heaven to investigate the enterprise and
confound their speech. He appears in human form to
Abraham and eats butter, milk and veal. He goes to make
inquiry about the iniquity of Sodom, to see for Himself
whether it is as bad as represented. He wrestles with Jacob.
He meets Moses and comes close to the point of killing
him." This primitive Yahweh survives as one of the many
forms of the Christian God, and has always been a favorite
among the more simple varieties of Christians. It is easy
for them to understand Him, for His childlike moods are
their own, and they can smell His sweat. He it is what
bucolic Methodists and Baptists think of when their
thoughts turn to the Most High. There is no metaphysical
nonsense about Him; His yea comes with a roar and His
nay is accompanied by a blow of the fist. In His jurisprudence there are no ethical subtleties, but only whites
and blacks. He is preeminently the God of all the gloomy
Little Bethels behind the railroad tracks, of all the fantastic sects which rage where life is drab, of the Salvation
Army, the Seventh Day Adventists, the Holy Rollers, the
Pillar of Fire Brethren, the Dunkards and Amish, the
Baptists.

Elohim, as the Pentateuch reveals Him, is a far more
refined and seemly God. He apparently originated in the
North of Palestine, after the revolt of the Israelites under
Jeroboam had divided the Jews into two nations, North
and South. The Northerners lived mainly in cities and
were thus more cultured than the people of the South.
Moreover, they were closer to the sea, and so came into

better contact with the ideas that were beginning to radiate from Greece. Yet more, they were on the main caravan routes from the East, and thus picked up what was being said in Babylon, the old reservoir of Jewish theology. Fed by the two streams, the religious ideology of the Northern priests made rapid progress, and soon the rough and bucolic Yahweh of the J document was converted into the more urbane and philosophical divinity who confronts us in Genesis i. As He stands today, with the marks of the Greek Logos plainly upon Him, he belongs to a somewhat later time, but even in His first and simpler days He must have been rather too high-toned for comfort, for the lower orders of the Northern Jews frequently turned to other gods, and the local prophets spent a great deal of energy trying to haul them back. Elohim rather than Yahweh is the God of the New Testament. In His capacity of Logos He is therein transformed into the Word, and later on, manipulated by the early Christian Fathers, He was to throw off two more gods and become the Trinity. It was not, however, Jews who achieved that final refinement, but Greeks. The poorer and more pious Jews, always in the South and in the end also in the North, continued to prefer Yahweh to Elohim, and He remains the god of their descendants to this day.

But even Yahweh, in the days of wars and turmoils, failed to hold His adherents, and they sometimes turned to other gods, mainly out of Babylonia but now and then from places nearer home. The prophets denounced these strange gods with great ferocity, but they continued to prosper more or less, and under the heretical King Manasseh (c. 650 B.C.) they came near driving out Yahweh altogether. Manasseh inclined to Babylonish ideas in theology, and so set up an altar to Baal, and sacrificed his own son upon it, and "used enchantments, and dealt with familiar spirits and wizards," and even desecrated the temple itself with his "abominations." The prophets made a great uproar, but all in vain. However, Manasseh could not last forever, and when, in the year 642, he died, a better day dawned. His son and successor, Amon, was quickly slain, and the throne fell to his grandson, Josiah, a boy of eight. At once the prophets began intensive operations upon him, and eighteen years later they were ready for a coup in the grand manner.

The tale is told at length in II Kings xxii. One day the young king sent a servant to the Temple with an order for the payment of workmen repairing it, and the servant came running back with startling news. Hilkiah, the high priest, had made a colossal discovery in the holy archives: no less than a complete Book of the Law, written down by Moses at the dictation of Yahweh Himself. When Josiah heard this book read it scared him almost to death. For it set forth that the "abominations" practised under his grandfather and father were dooming all Judah to a swift and horrible end — that Yahweh was angry beyond endurance, and ready to strike. Josiah, prepared by the prophets, believed at once, and next day he set out to clean up the land, upsetting the altars of Baal, jailing the heathen priests, and even digging up and burning the bones of dead idolaters. It was probably the swiftest reform recorded in human history, and it was one of the most lasting. From that day to this the Jews have never wavered in their devotion to their own God.

The Law that Hilkiah thus discovered so conveniently constitutes what Biblical critics call the D document, and makes up most of Deuteronomy. The Jewish priests ascribed its authorship to Moses, the great myth-hero of their people, but there is no reason to believe that it was more than a few months old when Hilkiah sent it to the king. Who wrote it we do not know, but it seems very likely that Hilkiah himself had a principal hand in it, and that many priests and prophets, including the celebrated Jeremiah, helped. It shows, in places, a Babylonian influence, but in essence it is strictly Jewish, and it remains today one of the most remarkable codes of laws ever promulgated in the world. Its first effects were somewhat unhappy, for it sought to prevent a revival of idolatry by concentrating all sacrifice at Jerusalem, and this threw many country priests out of work, and they flocked to the capital and demanded succor. But eventually they were all provided for, and the new Law began to work smoothly enough. It was, for its time, singularly enlightened. It codified and rationalized the penal legislation of the Jews, it brought a new amenity into social relations, and it frowned upon all the "abominations" that had come in with the heathen cults. That the Deuteronomy which appears in the Old Testament today is without later sophistication is most unlikely, but on the whole the original seems to have been preserved pretty well, and the essential parts are probably much as they were when Josiah heard them read for the first time, and "rent his clothes" in terror.

## 5

The rest of the Old Testament varies in interest and dignity, whether as history, as theology or as literature, and much of it shows evidence of priestly tampering. There are many conflicts in fact between the different books, and even between different parts of the same book. Now and then one encounters a stretch of narrative that is reasonably sober and accurate, considering the easy historical conscience of the place and time of its writing, but more often the record of actual events is bedizened with marvels and wonders, just as the record of Jesus's ministry is adorned in the New Testament. The successive prophets preach theologies that it is impossible to reconcile, and sometimes the naïve demonology of the primitive Jews is combined absurdly with the highly rarified pseudo-Greek speculations of a later day. Some of the books, it is plain, represent amalgamations of two or more discordant texts, often with the addition of complicated and obfuscating glosses. The case of Isaiah is typical. It is so distressing a hash that the commentators have had to sort it out chapter by chapter, and in some places even verse by verse. That a prophet named Isaiah wrote parts of it is very likely, but that he wrote all of it is completely impossible. In several chapters he is actually spoken of in the third person. Three main documents have been separated from the book, but there are also other lesser ones, and two whole chapters appear to be lifted bodily from II Kings. Isaiah has strained Biblical scholarship very uncomfortably, and many of the problems that it presents are still under furious discussion. The literature upon the subject is almost endless, and makes very hard reading.

How the Old Testament came to take its present form is quite unknown. The ancient Jews seem to have started with the Pentateuch, and to have added the other books one by one, just as the early Christians added book after book to the first Pauline Epistles. The principle on which they proceeded can only be guessed, for its rationality is not apparent. How, for example, did the Book of Ruth get in — a sentimental and very charming novelette quite devoid of religious significance, whose only moral seems to be that the reward of a dutiful daughter-in-law is a rich second husband? And how the Song of Solomon — a lascivious lay of carnal love, with no more piety in it than you will find in the sonnets of Shakespeare? For many centuries Jewish rabbis have tried to prove that the Song of Solomon is really a hymn to the Jewish nation as the bride of Yahweh, and for almost as long Christian commentators have sought to make it out a hymn to the Christian church as the bride of Christ, but a simple reading of it is sufficient to reduce all such efforts to absurdity. Consider, for example, this passage, printed in the Authorized Version of the English Bible under the heading, "Christ setteth forth the graces of the church":

*Behold, thou are fair, my love; behold, thou art fair; thou hast doves' eyes within thy locks: thy hair is as a flock of goats, that appear from Mount Gilead.*

*Thy teeth are like a flock of sheep that are even shorn, which came up from the washing; whereof every one bear twins, and none is barren among them.*

*Thy lips are like a thread of scarlet, and thy speech is comely; thy temples are like a piece of pomegranate within thy locks.*

*Thy two breasts are like two young roes that are twins, which feed among the lilies.*

And this, headed "A further description of the church's graces":

*How beautiful are thy feet with shoes, O prince's daugh-*
*ter! The joints of thy thighs are like jewels, the work of the*
*hands of a cunning workman.*
*..Thy navel is like a round goblet, which wanteth not*
*liquor: thy belly is like a heap of wheat set about with*
*lilies.*
*Thy two breasts are like two young roes that are twins.*

And so on, and so on. Try to imagine Yahweh addressing the Jews in any such terms, or Jesus the church! The
truth is that the Song of Solomon probably got into the
canon of the Old Testament simply because the ancient
rabbis could not resist its lush and overwhelming beauty.
It is, in fact, the most gorgeous love-song ever written, and
no doubt even the dourest Methodists and Presbyterians
of today, reading it in their gloomy conventicles, are somehow conscious of that warm and comforting fact, though
they try to convince themselves that it is an exercise in
theology. No direct reference to things spiritual is in it
from end to end, and even such passages as may be forced
to slant in that direction seem to point, not to the cult of
Yahweh, but to that of the god known to the Babylonians
as Tammuz and to the Greeks as Adonis. The rudiments of
the poem, in fact, probably go back to a very early day,
long before either Tammuz or Yahweh was heard of,
and it may have originated in some rustic festival in
honour of the primitive Earth Mother, who, toward the
end of her reign in the Near East, took on lovers and became far more gay than motherly. But now it is intoned
in Sunday-schools from end to end of Christendom, and
according to the Vatican Council of 1870 it was "written

by inspiration of the Holy Ghost" and has "God for its author."

It seems likely that the Jews of different places, in the two or three centuries before our era, had different Bibles — each based, to be sure, on the five books of the Law, but otherwise varying considerably. In those days all books were inscribed on scrolls, and the Law was about as much as one scroll would hold. The lesser writings were on smaller scrolls, and it is likely that poor synagogues had very few of them. In Palestine all such writings were in Hebrew, a language which, at the time of Jesus's birth, had become archaic and unintelligible, save only to priests and a few other learned men. It is possible that Jesus spoke and read it, but if so it was as a foreign language, as Catholic priests read and recite Latin today. His ordinary speech was Aramaic, though He probably also knew more or less Greek. Outside the Jewish homeland Hebrew had been completely forgotten, and the Law and the Prophets had to be translated into other languages. The best known translation was that into Greek, made by the Hellenized Jews of Alexandria during the Third Century B.C. This was the so-called Septuagint. The Alexandrine Jews were rich and so could afford a big Bible. They put into it not only all the books that were generally accepted as authentic in Palestine, but also a number that were under suspicion there. Their Greek Old Testament circulated throughout the Eastern Mediterranean region, and even gained a certain acceptance in Palestine itself, for as yet there was no translation into Aramaic. Of the 350 references to the Old Testament in the New, no less than 300 point to the Septuagint rather than to the Hebrew text.

203

That Hebrew text, in fact, was not brought to order until two generations after Jesus's death, when all the chief theologians of Jewry held a synod at Jamnia, in Southern Palestine, and drew up a canon which expunged certain books of the Septuagint as spurious, and made some changes in those accepted. This canon was approved by Origen, Athanasius, Jerome and other learned Fathers of the early Christian church, but the Septuagint continued to have partisans, and they eventually prevailed at Rome, though only after a long and unhappy debate. With the Reformation came a reopening of the controversy, for the cantankerous Luther was hotly against all of the disputed books, as he was against the disputed books of the New Testament. Finally, at the Council of Trent in 1546, the Catholic church decided that the whole canon of the Septuagint was inspired and infallible. But the Protestants refused to accept what Luther had banned, and to this day Ecclesiasticus, the Wisdom of Solomon, Baruch, Tobit, Judith, and I and II Maccabees are barred from the Protestant Bible. They continue, however, to have a certain pale and surreptitious authority, and are sometimes printed between the two Testaments, under the name of the Apocrypha. In the Church of England they have sufficient credit, though they remain uncanonical, to be quoted in the Book of Common Prayer. To balance this Protestant concession, there is some lingering doubt about them among Catholic theologians, despite their formal approval by the Council of Trent, and they are often spoken of, with delicate discretion, as deuterocanonical. The Greek church, by one of the pleasant ironies of history, has followed the Protestant church in rejecting them, though their whole authority rests upon the Greek Septuagint. In the early days there were many other apocrypha, but they survive today only as curiosities. Some of them would fit into the Old Testament far more decorously than Ruth and the Song of Solomon.

No text of the New Testament earlier than the Fourth Century has ever been found, nor any of the Septuagint. Of the Hebrew text of the Old Testament we have no manuscript earlier than the Ninth Century, and that is incomplete. The Jews did not preserve their old Bibles. When a scroll began to wear out they destroyed it, thus preventing its desecration by profane hands. There were translations of the whole Bible into Latin before the end of the Second Century and into Syriac soon after, and by the year 383 St. Jerome was already at work upon the Latin Vulgate. In English the Authorized Version of King James has been in use among Protestants since 1611. It is based upon earlier versions, and is full of intentional archaisms. It is the most beautiful of all the translations of the Bible; indeed, it is probably the most beautiful piece of writing in all the literature of the world. Many attempts have been made to purge it of its errors and obscurities. An English Revised Version was published in 1885 and an American Revised Version in 1901, and since then many learned but misguided men have sought to produce translations that should be mathematically accurate, and in the plain speech of everyday. But the Authorized Version has never yielded to any of them, for it is palpably and overwhelmingly better than they are, just as it is better than the Greek New Testament, or the Vulgate, or the Septuagint. Its English is extraordinarily simple, pure, eloquent and lovely. It is a mine of lordly and incomparable poetry, at once the most stirring and the most touching ever heard of. That there are gross absurdities in it is apparent to everyone, but absurdities do no damage to poetry. In any case, most of them are the fault, not of the translators, but of the early Fathers. The worst tampering with the Bible, indeed, was done long before the Book that we now know was put together.

## 6

But though the sophistications of the early theologians thus leave it unscathed as literature, and perhaps no less as a practical rule of life and guide to aspiration, they have made it somewhat unsatisfactory as theology. Reading it attentively, one is left in unpleasant doubt about many things, and some of them are of the first importance. For example, there is the question as to Jesus's view of His own mission. Did He regard Himself as a mere man, or as a god, or as half of each? It is not possible to answer categorically. All the evidence indicates that, in the first days of His ministry at least, He had no suspicion that He was anything save an ordinary country evangelist, like His cousin John the Baptist or any other. For many years, indeed, He had been even less than that, for it seems to have taken John's preaching to awaken Him to anything properly describable as a lively interest in religion. He was pious, but no more. If, once a year, He abandoned His work as a carpenter and went up to Jerusalem for the holy days, then He did only what thousands of other good Jews did. He was familiar with the Law and the Prophets, but so were they. He saw the evils of the time and hoped for a better day, but so did all of them. When He went to hear John it was not in the mood of a teacher but in that of a hearer. Great multitudes of other folk were going, too, and after they had heard John many of them confessed their sins and he baptized them in the Jordan, for baptism at that time and place was a common symbol of good resolutions. Jesus went into the water with the rest, and it was not until He came out and sat down to meditate that He showed any sign of wanting to preach Himself. Even so, He waited for forty days, torn by doubts — or, as Mark puts it, urged one way by God and the other by Satan. Would these doubts have beset Him if He had been conscious of His divine mission? Would He have hesitated a moment if He had ever heard of the Virgin Birth, or of the Star of Bethlehem, or of the coming of the magi? To ask these questions is to answer them.

If we knew more about the evangel preached by John we'd know more about the ideas and attitudes of Jesus. As it is, we know next to nothing, for though John made many converts, and they organized themselves into an active sect, and it survives in Mesopotamia to this day, its doctrines, like those of Christianity, have been so greatly corrupted by theologians that we can't make out what they were at the start. In the New Testament John is depicted as a rustic prophet of a very common sort, descending in a straight line from Daniel. Like all the rest he grounded his solemn warnings and remonstrances upon the plain fact that the Jews, as a nation, were in a very uncomfortable and unsatisfactory state, with even worse trouble looming ahead. On the one hand there was the dogmatic assurance that they were the favorites of Yahweh, and predestined to rule the world; on the other hand everyone knew that they had been in bondage, off and on, for centuries, and that the Romans were even now squeezing the life out of them. How was that paradox to be explained?

John probably explained it, like all his fellow prophets, by arguing that the Jews had offended Yahweh — by denouncing them for forgetting the Law and urging them to return to it with their whole hearts. That, in fact, was the meaning of repentance at the time: it simply signified a return.

The reward that John offered for this return was very brilliant, but it did not seem too brilliant to the Jews, for all their prophetical books spoke of it and they had been brought up to believe in it. It was that Yahweh, seeing them once more faithful and humble, would come down from His place in Heaven, blast their enemies with His terrible swift sword, set them in dominion over all the nations, and bring in a new era of peace and plenty, with every Jew fat, rich, powerful and happy. Some of the prophets said that, when the time came, He would appear without preliminary — save, of course, a gaudy fanfare, suitable to so vast an occasion, of fires, earthquakes, floods, pestilences and wars. But other prophets said that He would first send a trusted agent, a messiah, who would round up the Jews for the great day, separate the good ones from the bad, and then, when the millennium had begun, reign over them as king. This messiah, though sent from Heaven, was usually thought of as only human, and very frequently he was called the Son of David, for only descendants of David could legitimately occupy the Jewish throne.

It is possible that Jesus, toward the end of His ministry, began to think of Himself as this Messiah, but it does not seem very probable. Certainly He had no such thought at the start: what He preached was not His own Messiahship but the coming of another and greater — in brief, of the messiah that John and the other prophets had been talking of through so many dark years. He besought His followers to be ready for the great day, for John had convinced Him that it was near. He told them that the one way to grace was the way of a contrite heart — that the poor and humble would be better off, when the awful time of judgment came, than the rich and proud. He denounced the scribes and Pharisees for the hollow formalism, the pedantic mumbo-jumbo, which hid that primary and capital fact. He protested that the Law was not a mere code of ceremonies, but a guide for the heart. And always His preaching was grounded on the assumption, not that the appalling events of the last days had already begun, but that they were a little while ahead — not that the messiah was already on earth, but that he was soon to come.

It is impossible to get any other meaning out of the narrative in Mark, Matthew and Luke. The passages that point otherwise are so plainly in conflict with the general tone of the story that their apocryphal character is apparent at a glance. They have no more authority than the flat statement of Jesus's divinity which stands at the head of Mark, or the account of the Annunciation in Luke 1, 26–38 — an event of which Jesus, so far as we know or can judge, was completely ignorant all His life. Only too plainly they represent, not what the Disciples really saw and heard while He lived, but what they were induced to believe they had seen or heard in the electric days after His death, when their capacity for sober recollection and reflection, never noticeably good, was surely not at its best. The early Christian Fathers, seeking by their bold and often obvious editing of the sacred texts to make a weak case better, only succeeded in making it worse — they and their heirs in theology down to our own day. To them, no doubt, must be laid the grotesque theory that Jesus claimed divinity when He referred to Himself as the Son of Man — in point of historical fact, an everyday Aramaic phrase for man, and so used by all the prophets from Ezekiel onward. True, Jesus also applied it on occasion to the coming messiah, but that seems to have been no more than an earnest that, like most other Jews, He believed that the messiah would be a mere man and not a god.

The evidence as to the Disciples, taking it at its face value, shows them, at the start, following Jesus in the simple, innocent way in which swarms of other pious folk were already following John. He was, to them, a prophet preaching the long-awaited messiah, and that was all. Later on, when He began to work wonders, some of them apparently began to suspect, a bit furtively, that He might be the Messiah Himself. It was, indeed, a not unnatural surmise, considering the uneasy, expectant state of Jewish popular thought at the time, and it seems to have been shared by various other persons, including the man (or men, for here Luke and Matthew differ) whose demons were thrust into the Gadarene swine, the blind man whom He healed at Jericho, and the woman who came to see Him in the Pharisee's house and solemnly anointed Him — a ceremony that the Jews always thought of in connection with the messiah, whose very name meant "the anointed." The Disciples must have discussed the matter among themselves, and perhaps there was a difference of opinion among them, with some far more ready to believe than others. In Mark x, 35-45, we find two of the most forward, James and John, disputing for the best places by His side "in thy glory." But Jesus turned them off without admitting anything, and He was equally reticent on two other salient occasions — first, when some of the Disciples, sailing with Him on the Lake of Galilee, saw Him walk on the water and cried out, "Of a truth thou art the Son of God!" and again when at Cæsarea, He asked the Disciples, "Whom say ye that I am?" and Peter answered boldly, "Thou art the Christ."

7

This last episode, incidentally, offers a shining example of the way in which the New Testament contradicts itself and thus fails as history. In Luke the only answer of Jesus is the peremptory command to "tell no man that thing," and in Mark, the earliest of the three Synoptic Gospels, He replies in substantially the same terms, but in Matthew, the latest and most dubious, He is made to accept the assumption of His divinity categorically, and even to say that it was revealed to Peter by "my Father which is in Heaven!" If He ever actually made so colossal an admission is it possible to imagine Mark and Luke neglecting to record it? Or Peter, the patron of Mark, forgetting or concealing it? The whole passage in Matthew, indeed, is plainly not to be trusted. It smells strongly of post-Petrine sophistication, especially the part immediately following the colloquy, wherein Jesus is made to say, "Thou art Peter, and upon this rock [Gr. *petros*] I will build my church." On this saying, of which Mark and Luke know nothing, the Catholic church founds its claim to universal dominion and doctrinal infallibility, for Peter, according to legend, was the first Bishop of Rome. By a curious irony, not without its consolations to Protestants, the passage leads directly to one in which Jesus turns upon Peter, and denounces him in the bitter words: "Get thee behind me, Satan: thou art an offense unto me: for thou savorest not the things that be of God, but those that be of man." Mark records the same devasting condemnation. How and when the inconsistent and highly improbable nomination of Peter as head of the church got into Matthew we do not know, but there is every reason for guessing that it was inserted at the time the first Bishops of Rome were beginning their long struggle for supreme authority — and their free and ingenious use of forgery and worse to support their claim.

The Disciples, it is apparent, harbored certain doubts to the very end; perhaps, indeed, those doubts tended to increase in the last days, after it began to be evident that Jesus could not save Himself. One of the Twelve denied Him, another betrayed Him, and the rest seem to have cleared out. Even after the Crucifixion most of them were *non est* and to this day no one knows what became of them. Is it possible to imagine them turning their backs upon their Master if they really believed that He was the Messiah, and that His return to Heaven would be followed by the descent of Yahweh in person, breathing fire and lightning, with crowns of glory for the faithful and a rod for skeptics and recusants? Jesus Himself seems to have done nothing to resolve their doubts. At the Last Supper He was still speaking of Himself, equivocally, as the Son of Man, and even when He was brought before the high priest He seems to have maintained a mystifying reticence. The version of Mark that we have today makes Him answer the question, "Art thou the Christ, the Son of the Blessed?" with a straightforward "I am," but that is grossly inconsistent with what stands immediately before it, for there Mark speaks of all the witnesses who testified to His messianic claims as "false." Luke, with far greater plausibility, changes the "I am" to "Ye say that I am," and Matthew makes it "Thou hast said." In his reply there is surely no confession, but only a refusal to plead. The priests accepted it as an admission, not because it was so in fact, but for the obvious reason that they were frantically eager to get rid of a dangerous critic and heretic, and quite willing, like their professional colleagues at all times and everywhere, to accomplish it by foul means when fair means had failed. The whole scene smacks of the third degree in a back room at police headquarters, not of an orderly trial at law. When, the next day, Jesus came before the Roman court for a confirmation of the council's sentence of death, the judge, Pontius Pilate, was doubtful about the whole proceeding, and showed an inclination to liberate Him. But Jesus once more refused to plead, and so the sentence stood.

There is no evidence whatever that He regarded His death as part of a divine plan, foreordained since the beginning of time. On the contrary, the Synoptic Gospels make it plain that He was hopeful of escaping the cross to the last, for He went into Gethsemane in the very hour before His arrest, and there prayed piteously, "O my Father, if it be possible, let this cup pass from me!" There is no hint in the record that He discerned beyond death any glory or reward greater than that which was the portion of every good Jew. He would come back when Yahweh descended to earth, but so would all the other prophets before Him. Why, then, did He die at all? Why didn't He accept the escape that Pilate was so palpably eager to open for Him? Why didn't He simply retreat into the desert, beyond the reach of the priests and their catch-polls? The answer, it seems to me, is plain enough. He was in despair and desperation over the failure of His preaching. Certain humble folk had heard and believed Him, but all the Jews in high places were against Him, and the general reform and repentance that He dreamed of appeared to be far off and almost hopeless. Even among His own Disciples there was heartbreaking questioning and falling away. They doubted not only that He was the Messiah Himself, but also that any messiah was coming at all. There remained for Him but one way to break down the almost universal indifference and worse, and that was the way of spectacular sacrifice. He could testify to the truth of what He taught by dying for it, publicly and brilliantly.

In the device there was nothing new. All the peoples of antiquity were familiar with it, and especially the Jews. Prophets were expected to bear witness to their inspiration by braving torment and death, and there were records of many who had gone down to glorious martyrdoms, hurling their warnings from the stake and the lion's den. Only a year before John the Baptist had so died, reviling and defying Herod to the last, and now people were talking about it everywhere and even Herod himself was notoriously uneasy. Perhaps one more ordeal of blood would be enough to strike the hardest hearts and bring in the radiant faith and splendor of the New Day. So Jesus, very deliberately, very solemnly, went to death on the cross, just as many another earnest man was to go to death in the dark years to come, just as a heathen Nogi was to die in far-away Japan nearly two millenniums afterward. The comparison is not inept, for Nogi too was a good man, grieving for the evils of his time and willing to give his life in sombre warning to his countrymen. The test of a sacrifice does not lie in the cause behind it. Thousands of men have laid down their lives as bravely as Jesus did, for causes infinitely less lofty and lustrous. All martyrs, indeed, believe that they will shake the world, though no other has ever shaken it as He did.

## 8

It is not easy to account for His singular and stupendous success. How did it come about that One who, in this life, had only the bitter cup of contumely to drink should lift Himself, in death, to such vast esteem and circumstance, such incomparable and world-shaking power and renown? As I say, it is not easy to answer, but it is certainly not impossible. Jesus, like all the rest of us, was molded and conditioned by His time, and out of the circumstances of that time arose the great movement that was destined, perhaps with more irony than accuracy, to bear His name.

It was a day of disintegrating institutions and changing ideas, and *per corollary* of deep and pervasive uneasiness. Men felt that some sort of direful catastrophe was ahead, but they could not make out what it would be. The great empires of the East, for three thousand years the citadels of civilization, were all broken down and going to pieces, and the empires that had arisen in the West were apparently headed the same way. Greece was already in full collapse, not only politically but also spiritually. Her incomparable philosophers and sages were all dead, and they had no successors. Her builders built no more Parthenons; her dramatists wrote no more masterpieces; her heirs to Homer were all puerile poetasters. Her old leadership had passed to Rome, but Rome was plainly no Greece. To call that huge congeries of satrapies an empire, indeed, was to change the contemporary meaning of the word; it was rather an overblown trading corporation, run by cynical and mainly ignoble men, and almost as dishonest and disreputable as the modern empires of England, Russia and the United States. The Romans had no philosophers worthy of attention, and no real poets, and few makers of beautiful things. Their religion, to such accomplished theologians as the Jews, seemed childish and degrading; they cared nothing for it, in fact, themselves. In statesmanship they were completely bankrupt, for their politics had reduced itself to a brawl between rival banditti, and the weaknesses that devoured the state from within were no less apparent than the dangers menacing it from without. The Romans had still some time to go in the world, and they were yet to wreak their brutal fury upon the Jews, but it was manifest to all thoughtful men that the structure they had erected by such arduous labors was an artificiality, and hence doomed. Already, on the horizon, there was the flicker of barbarian campfires.

It was an unhappy time, and men were miserable everywhere, from the gloomy bogs of Britain to the failing fields of Mesopotamia. Above all, they were unhappy in what is now called the Near East, for the old civilizations once flourished there, and now they had perished without throwing off new ones. Those old civilizations, whatever their defects, had at least given human life a certain stability, and so men looked back upon them with something akin to nostalgia. Their central idea was that of authority, for it was generally held that authority was indispensable to security. No one, in secular matters, ever challenged the king; his divine right to rule was accepted as unquestioningly as the right of the sun to shine. And in religion the fount of all wisdom and righteousness was the priest. This was, no doubt, an unthinking position to take, but it had the virtue of making life simple and safe. All the great Eastern empires, despite almost continuous wars, endured for many centuries, and while they survived in their splendor the majority of people living under them seem to have been contented, and there was steady progress in all the arts of civilization. Even the Jews, a naturally rebellious and contentious people, were happy enough during their Babylonian captivity, and when Cyrus the Persian liberated them thousands refused to return to their homeland.

We of today, blinded by our somewhat exaggerated sense of what we owe to Greece and Rome, forget that we owe the Ancient Orient even more. "It gave the world," says Dr. James H. Breasted in "The Conquest of Civilization," "the first highly developed practical arts, including metal work, weaving, glass-making, paper-making, and many other similar industries. To distribute the products of these industries among other peoples and carry on commerce it built the first seagoing ships and made the first roads and bridges. It was first able to move great weights and undertake large building enterprises — large even for us of today. . . . It gave us the earliest architecture in stone masonry, the colonnade, the arch, and the tower or spire. It produced the earliest refined sculpture. . . . It gave us writing and the earliest alphabet. In literature it brought forth the earliest known tales in narrative prose, poems, historical works, social discussions, and even a drama. It gave us the calendar we still use. It made a beginning in mathematics, astronomy and medicine. It first devised the administrative machinery of government, with paid officials efficiently organized. . . . It first produced government on a large scale, whether of a single great nation or of an empire made up of a group of nations."

But one thing it did not invent, and that was the idea of individual autonomy and right, of the essential and inalienable dignity of man. To the East anything of that sort would have been unintelligible. It could be kindly and humane, but in the last analysis it subordinated every right to duty — the duty to obey the constituted authorities, to labor unquestioningly for the common weal, to act right and, above all, to think right. There must have been plenty of skeptics in Babylon from the days of the primitive sun-god onward, but history knows next to nothing about them, for the penalty of all heresy was death, and they kept their doubts to themselves. It was not in the East but in Greece that the free speculation we are now familiar with was born. The Greeks were not the first philosophers, but they were the first to make philosophy a dominant concern of man; they were the first to make any concerted attempt to liberate the human mind. That effort, as we know by the death of Socrates and the guile of Plato, was not wholly successful, but neither was it wholly a failure. Men began to think about things as they had never thought before — frankly, boldly, rationally. All the prevailing ideas of government were exposed to a new and candid examination, and with them all the prevailing ideas about the nature of the physical world, the qualities and powers of the gods, and the character of the thinking process itself. Naturally enough, many of these ideas had to be rejected as palpably false, and though philosophy was the monopoly, properly speaking, of a very small class of men, the doubts that they came to harbor soon began to be more or less general. Jesus Himself, as a well-educated young Jew, fell under their influence, and we see proof of it in His audacious defiance of the priests at Jerusalem — a defiance comparable, in the America of today, to heaving the Constitution into the fire, and the Bible and the Revised Statutes after it.

Thus a sense of the dignity of the individual man began to spread at the precise time that the old empires, with their exaltation of authority, were going to pieces, and a violent new interest in the nature and exactions of the gods arose just as the old religions were following the empires into decay and discredit. The result was a great unrest throughout the civilized world. All sorts of political reformers began to rant and roar, and all sorts of religious prophets. Not infrequently they appeared in the same man. The cynical Romans took very little interest in the prophets, but they were very alert for political heresy, and put it down with great vigor. It was, indeed, on the theory that He was an aspirant to the Jewish throne and thus an enemy of the Roman state that they executed Jesus. This was partly true, but mainly false. There seems to be no doubt that Jesus expected the Messiah whose coming He preached to be a Jew, and that He thought this Messiah would liberate the Jewish nation, and probably give it wide dominion. But there is no evidence that He dreamed of any assault upon the Roman power, at least outside Judea. His interest was in the Jews alone, and He made the fact plain enough when he encountered the Syrophenician woman (Mark VII, 26–29) and when he called and charged the Twelve Apostles (Matthew x, 5–6). He made it plain again when the Pharisees tried to trip Him into treason and He confuted and confused them with "Render unto Cæsar the things that are Cæsar's," and He purged Himself wholly of treason when He said to Pilate (if John is to be believed), "My kingdom is not of this world."

9

But any man who afflicts the human race with ideas must be prepared to see them misunderstood, and that is what happened to those of Jesus. The egalitarianism that He preached was anything but the political egalitarianism that we know today, and it is thus absurd to call Him, as so many do, the father of Socialism. What He had in mind was not political or economic equality, but simply the equality of men before God. Believing that the end of the world was at hand — or, at all events, a vast catastrophe and a new beginning — He denounced all human ranks and dignities as vain and blasphemous, and argued that they could only provoke God's wrath. The safest man on the Day of Days would be that one who was poor and humble, and lay under no burden of accusation from his fellow men. It is not safe to assume that He believed in poverty *per se,* though it may have been so; all we are sure of is that He believed it was the way of discretion in the few days that remained. But when He went to His death on the cross, and the few days stretched out into months and then into years, it was perhaps only natural for His followers to put a new sense upon His warnings. It was now obvious that the end of the world was not at hand — though the Disciples and their successors, for a long while, continued to believe that it was. But His words were still cherished, and so they began to take on a new meaning, especially to those who, on other and purely political grounds, were glad to see the old ideal of authority disintegrating and the new ideal of equality coming in.

There was plenty in what was remembered of His preaching, and no less in what was told of His conduct, to give that change of significance a reasonable support. He had been, though a man of gentle birth, notably humble in spirit, and His chosen companions, with few exceptions, were of the lower classes. He disliked the rich, and was an avowed enemy of those priests and publicans (that is, public functionaries) who represented what remained of the old Asiatic order. And in His preaching of the fatherhood of God there was ground enough for any egalitarianism imaginable, for a divine Father could hardly be thought of as making some of His children the slaves of the rest. Thus the teachings of Jesus fell upon soil that had been long preparing for them, and perhaps it would not be unfair to add that they took vigorous root there largely because they were misunderstood. To poor and miserable men, so misunderstanding them, they must have come as revelations of a new and enormously happier world order — as tidings of such stupendous joyousness that the ears of man had never heard the like. Nor was it only the poor who hearkened to them, and hearkening, rejoiced and gave thanks to God, for among the first to accept them were certain persons of rank and fortune, and especially certain women, who had long dreamed of a better day. As I have said, Jesus Himself was a man of some rank in Judea, though he followed an humble trade; He was, as a member of the clan of David, even a sort of noble. But He was by no means the first friend of the lowly to appear from above, nor was He to be the last. Nearly all the liberties and dignities that common men have today were won for them by reformers and revolutionaries who pitied them without being quite of them, and only too often those liberties and dignities had to be won against the bitter opposition of their beneficiaries.

The influence of the Resurrection upon the early spread of Jesus's teachings must have been very great. The time thirsted for wonders quite as much as it thirsted for light and leading. At every street corner from Gaul to Babylon stood an itinerant evangelist, preaching some new and bizarre faith, and almost all of them mingled familiar marvels with their novel schemes of salvation. They cured the sick just as Jesus did; they walked on water without sinking and through fire without burning; some of them even professed to raise the dead. But one wonder, at least, they could not perform, and that was precisely the one that people most waited to see: put to death, they could not raise themselves. Nevertheless, no one seems to have thought that it was intrinsically impossible; people stood ready to believe it without too much urging; more, they were willing to accept it as proof positive of the risen prophet's doctrine, for such was the simple logic of the time. Thus we behold even so enlightened a man as Herod made uneasy by the sudden suspicion that Jesus might be the headless John come back again, and thus we hear the chief priests and Pharisees demand of Pilate that he put a guard at Jesus's sepulchre, "lest his disciples come by night, and steal him away, and say unto the people, He is risen from the dead." The Pharisees, it is plain, had no doubt that the people would believe. They knew that Jesus had been prophesying His own return — if not as the actual

Messiah, then at least as one of the forerunners of the Messiah — and they knew that many poor folk looked for that marvel more or less hopefully and confidently.

The Disciples, it appears, were not among them; they retained their doubts to the last. Instead of following the body of their lost Leader to the sepulchre, they left that office to Joseph of Arimathea, a stranger, and to Mary Magdalene, "the other Mary," and a small band of lesser pious women. Even when, the next day, the news was brought to them that He had actually arisen from the dead they were still disinclined to believe it, and Luke tells us that Jesus had to convince them by tracking them down and confronting them, and that He upbraided them bitterly for "their unbelief and hardness of heart." What actually happened? Unless the whole New Testament is to be rejected as moonshine it seems to be certain that many persons saw Him after His supposed death on the cross, including not a few who were violently disinclined to believe in His Resurrection. Matthew tells us, indeed, that even His arch enemies, the chief priests, were forced to admit the fact of His appearance, and that they sought to account for it, going back to their warning to Pilate, by saying that "his disciples came by night, and stole him away." It seems to be equally certain that many persons spoke to Him and heard Him speak, and that He assured them once more that the end of things was at hand.

But what actually happened — on the cross and in the sepulchre? The question has been threshed out between the faithful and the skeptical for many a year, without bringing any answer satisfactory to all parties, or any hope of one hereafter. Fortunately enough, we need not wrestle with it here. The important thing, and the undisputed

223

thing, is that when Jesus was taken from the cross and put into the sepulchre the crowd that looked on, including both His own followers and the Roman soldiers, believed He was truly dead, and that He Himself, when He came to His senses in the sepulchre, believed He was coming back from death. Upon that theory, though it wars upon every rationality that enlightened men cherish, the most civilized section of the human race has erected a structure of ideas and practices so vast in scope and so powerful in effect that the whole range of history showeth nothing the like.

## 10

What followed immediately is somewhat obscure. It is to be gathered from Acts, written by Luke long afterward, that the Disciples, convinced at last, prepared for the end of the world. To take the place of Judas the traitor they elected one Matthias, and a while later they increased their little band to a hundred and twenty. When, in obedience to Jesus's mandate, they began to preach to the people, their inflammatory warnings and exhortations caused many to believe that they were drunk, but on the day of Pentecost they converted three thousand. Thereafter the new faith was a going concern, but the Disciples themselves faded out of the picture, and soon we find Paul of Tarsus, a convert, at the head of things, and tramping the whole Roman world on missionary journeys. Of the ultimate fate of the original Twelve we know little. One of them, James, was put to death by Herod Agrippa (not to be confused with the Herod who feared that John might return from the dead), and another, Peter, made his way to Rome, and died there under Nero, along with Paul. The rest, according to an ancient tradition, went on preaching trips to eastward, apparently among the Jews of the Diaspora. Where they ended is a mystery. A great many legends about them survive, but not many of those legends show any probability.

The new religion, at the start, was for Jews only; they alone would be "caught up in the clouds" when Yahweh came down in His clouds of fire and smoke, with Jesus at His side. But soon various Gentiles began to enroll themselves, and though at the start some effort was made to keep them out, and the question whether they ought to be circumcised was long under bitter debate, they eventually demanded baptism in such numbers that they could not be stayed. In the course of time, in fact, they vastly outnumbered the Jews, and there arose theologians who argued that they alone could be saved. But it was as a Jewish sect that Christianity really began, and it was as a Jewish sect, in its first days, that it escaped suppression at the hands of the Romans. The Roman law was very tolerant of the religions that flourished in the provinces, but it demanded, as a condition of that tolerance, that each be organized in a seemly maner, with responsible heads. In order to dispose of them conveniently the Christians, at the beginning, were set down as Jewish sectaries, and the Jewish authorities at Jerusalem were held accountable for their conduct.

Those authorities, for a while at least, do not seem to have objected. They had been opposed to Jesus, but His first followers, being mainly humble folk, did not make much disturbance, and so they were not molested. But when Gentiles in large number came flocking to the new faith, and it began to spread to the westward, the chief priests at Jerusalem grew uneasy, and presently they washed their hands of it and suggested to the Romans that the time had come to take measures against it. The Romans, however, always moved slowly in such matters, and thus it was some time before anything properly describable as a persecution began. By that time Christianity had got a firm lodgment in Rome itself, and the local Christians, in order to have a quasi-legal standing, had organized themselves as burial clubs. As such, they could maintain cemeteries, and in those cemeteries, on the pretense of honoring the dead, which was always lawful in Rome, they could carry on their rites, even in the face of a general proscription. If they took to burying the dead in catacombs, like the devotees of Mithra, it was mainly for greater freedom in that direction. It seems probable that Peter, the so-called first Bishop of Rome, was really the president of such a burial club. Actual bishops came later, after Christianity had acquired a theology.

The beginnings of that theology are dark and devious. Who introduced such things as the dogmas of the Trinity, the Virgin Birth, and the Atonement we do not know with any certainty. Jesus Himself was unaware of any of them, and His Disciples were apparently little the wiser. Most of them were not new, but had been heard of in other religions, in one form or another, for years. The impact of Greek philosophy, with its appeal to pure reason, had broken down many of the old barbaric faiths, with their doctrinaire certainties, but their fragments survived, and there was everywhere an effort to reconcile them to the new ways of thinking. The result was a general exchange of theological ideas — a great efflorescence of what theologians call syncretism. Thus we find Judaism accepting, on the one hand, a concept of immortality that came from the East, and, on the other hand, a concept of God that gradually became almost more Greek than Jewish.

Christianity, at the start a very feeble faith, theologically speaking, with doctrines far too simple to satisfy men of genuine religious passion, was soon beset by the two streams of influence — the first coming out of the East, where men still craved wonders, and the other out of the West, where they had begun to put reason above revelation and inspiration. The Virgin Birth was a typically Eastern idea: it had been familiar from Egypt to Mesopotamia for at least two thousand years, and nearly all the prophets and wonder-workers who swarmed in that vast and murky region had been sons of the gods. The idea of the Atonement was also Eastern, and so was that of Original Sin, and so was that of the Resurrection of the Body. All such things were commonplaces, in those days, to every man who listened to street preachers, and the most marvellous among them were naturally the most in favor, especially among the lower orders. Gilbert Murray, indeed, says flatly that the Resurrection of the Body was forced into Christianity from below — that it was "a concession to the uneducated, who would not be content with a life everlasting of the soul alone, freed from bodily substance and form." But there was also an infiltration from above — through Mithraism, the Adonis and Osiris cults, and Greek metaphysics, and, a bit later, through Gnosticism and Manichæism. The idea of the Holy Ghost was probably borrowed mainly from the Greek Logos, an invention of metaphysicians rather than of theologians, and so was its offspring, the idea of the Trinity.

The chief professional difficulty that confronted the

227

early Christian theologians was explaining away the failure of the Second Coming. That the Disciples believed it to be imminent, once they had been convinced of the reality of the Resurrection, seems to be beyond question. Jesus Himself had given them plenty of reason for that expectation, as anyone may see by reading Mark ix, 1, or Matthew xiv, 28. But as day followed day without the awaited signs and portents, and many believers, in the face of His clear promise, began to "taste of death" without seeing "the kingdom of God come with power," it became necessary to revise the orthodox doctrine. So the Second Coming was quietly postponed: it would come, not tomorrow, or next day, but in a few months or years — at worst, within a generation. It was upon this theory that Paul began his preaching, and that such works as John and Revelation were written. The promise, though deferred, apparently sufficed to sustain most of the faithful; they were mainly simple folk and their faith was thus naïve and not too critical — in Paul's own phrase, "the substance of things *hoped* for, the evidence of things *not* seen." But as the years lengthened and the troubles of the time piled up there was a revival of impatience, and many converts, including some of influence, left the young church. Worse, those that remained began to cast about for something to take the place of their perishing hope, and the result was a great burst of theological speculation, with the rapid introduction of ideas and practices from other religions.

To Paul these novelties were anything but welcome. He himself seems to have brought in more than one — some from Greek metaphysics and the rest from Judaism — but he was opposed, like any other theologian, to those brought in by others, and he spent a great deal of his time on his missionary journeys trying to put them down. His denunciations of heresy, indeed, show all of the hearty enthusiasm that we associate with the anathemas of the medieval popes, and once, in writing to "the churches of Galatia," he even went to the length of proscribing, in advance and *en bloc,* any errors that he might later fall into himself. He went still further: he solemnly warned the Galatians against heresies spread by "an angel from Heaven." But all this ardor for orthodoxy was in vain, for new ideas forced their way into Christian theology faster than they could be put down — some coming from the so-called pagan religions of the time, and others issuing out of the great reservoir of Judaism. Soon it became the fashion to search the Old Testament for passages in support of this or that doctrine, waiting for admission into the New, and this quest eventually went to such lengths that the former became as authoritative a Christian guide as the latter, and so got into our present Bible. Both Testaments were sadly mauled to make them agree. Thus Zechariah XIII, 6, was converted into a prophecy of the Crucifixion, Psalms XLI, 9, was made to predict the betrayal of Judas, and Hosea XI, 1, came to be accepted as proof of the Flight into Egypt, which probably never took place. This laborious tugging and hauling was under way before Paul died, but its best days came afterward. What is now the New Testament suffered most, for there was behind it no such settled authority as that of the Jewish rabbis, supporting the Old. Every ambitious theologian tried to write his notions into it. By the Fourth Century Jerome was saying sadly that there were "as many readings as texts."

## II

The theological literature of those turbulent days deserves a great deal more reading than it gets today. It is full of amusing and instructive sidelights upon the mentality of the Fathers. Jerome, one of the greatest of them, recorded all sorts of hair-raising marvels. He saw centaurs, fauns, satyrs and incubi, and had speech with them. Augustine, in his African diocese, saw a headless man with eyes in his breast, and in his celebrated "Civitate Dei" argued gravely that demons came of night and worked their wicked will upon women, and cited as proof that the fauns and satyrs of the heathen did it. All of the Fathers gave a great deal of attention to the question why God created the world. Origen was of the opinion that it was set up as a sort of jail for fallen angels: in the original scheme of the universe, he believed, there had been no place for it. Irenæus, Tertullian, Cyprian and Justin taught that the Devil rebelled out of jealousy when it was created. It is Tertullian who is credited with the motto, *Credo, quia absurdum est:* I believe because it is incredible. Needless to say, he began life as a lawyer. But in the end, unable to believe that the Second Coming was indefinitely postponed, he joined a faction that stood against the growing worldliness of the church, and was damned as a heretic. He remains a heretic to this day, but the complicated legal system of the Roman church owes much to him, for he was one of the most intellectual of all the Fathers.

With the vast credulity of the time went a great contempt for ordinary veracity. Says Cardinal Newman in his "Apologia Pro Vita Sua": "The Greek Fathers thought that, when there was a *justa causa,* an untruth need not be a lie." Augustine, though he wrote two tracts, "De Mendacio" and "Contra Mendacium," to warn his fellow theologians against an excess of pious lying, himself freely suppressed inconvenient facts, and so did Eusebius, the father of church history. Eusebius specialized in accounts of martyrdoms, and invented many of the fantastic stories that are still believed. "On some occasions," he once wrote, "the bodies of martyrs devoured by wild beasts, on the carcasses of the beasts being opened, have been found alive in the stomachs." This echo of the Jonah story had many parallels. Every wonder in the Old Testament was dragged out, attached to some Christian worthy, and made more wonderful. Miracles became so common that even women and heretics began to work them. Jerome, one of the most high-minded of the Fathers, was yet convinced that it was perfectly proper to embellish the facts when they seemed insufficient to enforce a godly point, and defended the custom by showing that Origen, Eusebius, Methodius (a significant name!), Cyprian, Minutius and Hilary had followed it. He even added Paul, whose arguments against the Jews had been full of quotations discreetly stretched. All the early Fathers naturally believed that the earth was flat. All believed in visions, prophecies, signs and portents. All believed in angels, demons, dragons and leviathans. The yearning of the time was for easy assurances, facile doctrines, comforting rhetoric, and so the high places in the nascent hierarchy went to theologians of the general calibre of such moderns as Joseph Smith, Mary Baker G. Eddy and John Alexander Dowie. Men of education were rare among them. If they knew Greek it was more often than not only the Greek of

231

schoolboys. Not many of them differentiated clearly between the puerile catch-phrases heard at every street corner
and the solid body of Greek thinking.

Thus Christianity, in its first days, developed on a low
plane, and years had to pass before it would take on intellectual respectability. Paul, addressing the Athenians on
Mars Hill, was heard politely, but it must be obvious that
his confident talk about the resurrection of the dead struck
them as only silly; moreover, their Unknown God was
palpably more plausible than his barbaric Yahweh, but
lately in from the desert and still a bit shaggy and forbidding. When refinement entered the new faith at last it
came in the form of a heresy, Gnosticism, and was violently opposed by all the Fathers. Gnosticism, says Harnack, was "the acute Hellenizing of Christianity." That is
to say, it represented a concerted effort to introduce the
fruits of Greek philosophical speculation into the naïve
theology of the Synoptic Gospels. The Gnostics, who were
mainly of the educated class, were attracted by some of the
elements of Christianity, but found it impossible to endure
others. The anthropomorphic God that had been inherited
from Judaism repelled them. They could not imagine a
divinity with human passions — jealous, cruel, mercurial,
arbitrary and vain. Nor could they imagine a god being
crucified. Nor could they accept the Jewish Law that still
survived in Christianity, with its harsh prohibitions, its
savage pains and penalties, its general irrationality. They
attempted to posit a higher Mind Force behind all the
gods, and that, of course, left Yahweh stripped of His omnipotence. Like all the other heretics of the time, they
gradually disappeared, but again like all the others they
left something behind them. It shows itself today in the

transcendental elements of Christianity, and in the elaborations of Christian ritual. For the early buttonholing of God, now revived in evangelical Protestantism, they substituted the more decorous approach of the Greek and Roman rites. They took the new faith out of the streets, and made it tolerable to men of culture and dignity.

## 12

The ethical teachings of Jesus did not long survive the abandonment of hopes for the Second Coming. Paul continued to preach them, and to some of them he gave an investiture of eloquence that even Jesus never surpassed, but they soon collided, not only with immediate human needs, but also with the eternal nature of man, and so they had to be modified. So long as it was believed that the end of the world was at hand it all was well enough to be poor and humble, but when years of uncertainty began to stretch ahead every man of any prudence had to take thought for his own security, and that of his family. Thus the Beatitudes were discreetly forgotten, and the immemorial game of dog-eat-dog was resumed.

Paul himself was as much to blame for this change as anyone else, despite all his moral rhetoric. He was not naturally a gentle and tolerant man, as Jesus was, but a fighter, full of delight in controversy for its own sake. There is no evidence that he was ever humble before an adversary, or that he was ever consumed by the modest doubts and misgivings that harassed Jesus. Even when, at Athens, he faced the massed philosophers of Greece, he denounced them boldly as superstitious, a proceeding curiously paralleled in our own time by Bishop Wilberforce's denunciation of Huxley as an ignoramus, and again by Cardinal O'Connell's derisive attack upon Einstein. Nor was Paul under any vow of poverty. True enough, he was occasionally upon short commons, and on one occasion he had to revert to his trade of tent-maker in order to maintain himself, but most of the time, like any other travelling evangelist, he lived at his ease upon the country, made much of by pious women and nourished regularly upon what represented, in that far-off day, the fried chickens and fat hog-meat consumed by Methodist parsons today. In the whole history of the world, indeed, there are few records of ecclesiastics going hungry, save, of course, as a willing sacrifice, to curry favor in Heaven. They are often without ready cash, but except when there is dire and unmitigated famine upon the land they seldom lack aliment.

The chief stress of Jesus's teaching, of course, was not laid upon poverty and humility, though they have a high place in the Beatitudes. The thing He taught mainly, first and last, was simple good-will between man and man — simple friendliness, simple decency. First after love of God came love of all humankind: "there is none other commandment greater than these." Paul, in his Epistle to the Romans, put the idea into a passage of incomparable eloquence, and there can be no doubt that he recognized its capital importance in the Christian scheme of things. But in his everyday business as a theological controversialist he had no more room for the Golden Rule than he had for the Beatitudes. When he saw the head of a heretic he cracked it at once, even though the heretic might be a neighbor. The heirs of his mission followed the same habit, and there is little in the actual history of the early church

234

to indicate that it was founded upon a philosophy of renunciation and benevolence. It was full of wars, and they were carried on with savage ferocity. The common decency that Jesus had preached was still impossible to men born of women — as it remains impossible to their descendants in our own day. Perhaps Jesus Himself, had He lived fifty years, would have somewhat ameliorated His admonitions, bearing the incurable frailty of human nature in mind. As it was, He preached a scheme of conduct that was bearable only on the assumption that it would not have to be borne very long — that is, on the assumption that the kingdom of God as at hand. When the hope of seeing that kingdom faded His followers went back to the *lex talionis,* and first among the scratchers and gougers were the holy men who called themselves His ambassadors and pretended to carry His gospel to the world.

In the early church, in truth, several ethical ideas that Jesus had never heard of — or, hearing of, disapproved — came into far higher esteem than any He had actually preached. For example, the idea of celibacy. When, "on the coasts of Judea beyond Jordan," He discoursed to the Disciples on divorce and told them that remarriage afterward was equivalent to adultery, some of them concluded that He regarded all marriage as more or less dubious. But He cautioned them that this was not so, and proceeded to say, in substance, that celibacy was a sort of gift, and hence not possible to all men. This caution, however, was soon forgotten, and in Acts and the Epistles marriage is spoken of with contempt, as if it were a base yielding to the flesh. The ideal is always complete chastity. Such notions came out of the East, where asceticism was already flourishing, and why they took such ready root in Christi-

235

anity is not known. The fact that Jesus Himself was un-
married may have had something to do with it, and no
doubt some influence was exerted, too, by a lingering hope,
clung to desperately, for the Second Coming and the end
of the world. Probably Paul's own special leaning toward
celibacy was induced by the circumstances of his wandering life: a wife would have been as burdensome to him
as to a Jesuit or a soldier on campaign. Whatever the
fact, he preached against marriage with great vehemence,
and the evidence thereof in the New Testament is reinforced by much more massive evidence in the rejected
apocrypha.

In the Acts of Paul, for example, there is a long account
of the uproars he caused in a town in Asia Minor called
Iconium, after his flight from Antioch. There dwelt there
a beautiful maiden named Thecla, betrothed to one Thamyris. But when she heard Paul preach — he is described
as "a man of little stature, thin-haired upon the head,
crooked in the legs, of good state of body, with eyebrows
joining, and nose somewhat hooked" — she refused to go
to the altar, and in consequence Thamyris and his friends
were greatly enraged. Finally, they appealed to the Roman
governor, Castelius, and Castelius ordered Paul to be
scourged and chased out of town and Thecla to be burned
alive. But when "she, making the sign of the cross, went
up upon the wood, and they lighted it, the fire took no
hold on her, for God had compassion on her, and caused
a sound under the earth, and a cloud overshadowed her
above, full of rain and hail, and all the vessel of it was
poured out so that many were in peril of death, and all the
fire was quenched, and Thecla was preserved." Later on,
continuing in her chastity, she was thrown to the lions,

but once more a miracle saved her, and she lived to be ninety, still unwed.

This curious distrust of marriage, like so many other Pauline notions, afflicts Christianity to our own day. There have been many revolts against it — one of the most formidable, as everyone knows, was led by Martin Luther —, but on the whole it keeps a considerable authority, even among Protestants. The elder branch of the church, amalgamating with it an ideal of poverty that may be fairly credited to Jesus and a rule of obedience that He would have most assuredly repudiated, has made it the foundation of a system of asceticism which now seems so thoroughly Christian that its origin among pre-Christian fanatics — mainly Persian and Indian, but more directly Egyptian — tends to be forgotten. More than once, during the Middle Ages, that system threatened the social and economic stability of Europe. In the course of time a concession has been made to Jesus by granting that only a small minority of men and women are fit for strict celibacy, but there remains an unhealthy, drugstorish feeling that even the most lawful kind of sexual intercourse is still somehow low and discreditable, and that any effort to make it dignified and charming — say by evading its more unpleasant physiological consequences — is immoral and against God. Chastity, indeed, remains the Christian virtue *par excellence,* and in common practice it stands far above either of the two commandments that Jesus put in the first place. A true Christian, of whatever rite, distrusts and is ashamed of his hormones. He approaches even his wedded wife with an uneasy feeling that they are engaged upon something naughty, and ought to be punished for it.

237

## 13

There is no need here to rehearse in any detail the long history of the Christian church, for it has to do with religion only in part. The simple, childlike faith that sustained the first believers in the face of contumely and persecution oozed out of their successors, and in its place there arose a complicated dogmatic structure, bristling with metaphysical refinements and logical impossibilities. The Council of Nicæa in 325 established the divinity of Jesus, paved the way for what is now called the Nicene Creed, and set up the church as a going concern. Before it assembled there was chaos, with every bishop defining orthodoxy in his own terms, and half of them damning the other half. But when Constantine gave Christianity the status of an official faith it became plain that this free-for-all would have to stop, and so discreet and diplomatic ecclesiastical gentlemen went among the bishops near and far, and they were induced to send delegates to a general conference or to come themselves. Sylvester I, Bishop of Rome, was too old to go in person, but he sent two very adroit presbyters, Victor and Vincentius, and they stood behind the presiding bishop, Hosius of Cordova, during all the long sessions and favored him with their advice.

There emerged not only a church formally purged of the great Arian heresy and of a multitude of lesser aberrations, but also a church organized in a rational and competent manner, with a well-knit hierarchy in place of the old rabble of independent bishops, and a natural centre in the see of Rome. Its progress from that time forward, down to the cataclysm of the Reformation, was steady and inevitable. As the Roman Empire gradually disintegrated, at first under the impact of the civil wars, then under that of the barbarian invasions, and finally under that of the great Byzantine rebellion, His Holiness of Rome fell heir to most of its authority and all of its prestige. Nor was his estate confined to the Roman world. Already, at Nicæa, bishops from Persia and Gaul had been in attendance, and now he gradually extended his sway over the whole civilized world. There were, to be sure, murmurs against the process, and so early as the end of the Fourth Century they led to an Eastern schism, but the popes, despite everything, managed to maintain and extend their hegemony for five hundred years more, and when, in the end, the schism of 1054 came and the Eastern churches went their own way, the papacy was so firmly established that not even revolt and secession could damage it.

The Holy Roman Empire, by that time, was two hundred years old, and its true ruler was not the heir of Charlemagne but the heir of Peter. The Emperor Henry IV, crawling on his knees in the snows of Canossa, made that fact plain enough. A century or two more, and it was disputed by no one. The popes, starting out as the clients of a Roman emperor, were now monarchs on their own account, and of a dominion far greater than any he had ever ruled. From end to end of Europe it ran, with bulges into Africa and even into Asia, despite the Eastern schism. Founded upon unchallengeable authority, and with the vague and awful figure of the Crucified behind it, it was an empire that harked back to the great days of the Ancient East. The Greek concept of man as the seeker of knowledge, the solver of riddles, the maker of gods, the master

of his fate was now forgotten, and with it the homelier but
none the less stimulating Roman concept of a free citizen
in a free state. The pope became an Asiatic despot, responsible to no one and almost omnipotent. He was the last
Sassanid, the last heir of Sargon and the Hyksos. He could
be reached, perhaps, by poison or the sword, but not by
law. While he sat on his throne he was infallible and irresistible.

The Dark Ages, of course, were not wholly dark. If the
papacy had been hereditary it might have sunk to the level
of some of the later Egyptian dynasties, but being open to
competition it was constantly fertilized by fresh and vigorous blood, sometimes blue and sometimes red. Not many
popes won their way to Peter's throne by piety alone; the
prize commonly went to far more masculine qualities,
some of them anything but ignoble. There were popes
who were statesmen of the first calibre, the best of their
day; there were others who were theologians and moralists of high-minded earnestness; there were yet others who
could even pass for scholars. Europe in general was
plunged into appalling ignorance, but at no time was that
ignorance unmitigated. Always there was an infiltration
of ideas from without, and always there was a stirring of
speculation within. The Crusades, which began with the
Twelfth Century, made a great upheaval. Men began to
realize that there was more in heathendom than mere sin,
that even Hell-bent Saracens had something to teach, that
there was a wisdom outside the Christian revelation. An
era of what we now call progress ensued, with wealth
increasing, life growing more pleasant, and curiosity un-
chained. The old Christian theology, static now for five
hundred years, had to yield with everything else that was

traditional. What with its naïve wonders, its disregard of plain facts, its general intellectual poverty, it began to seem absurd to rational men. So Thomas Aquinas set himself the tremendous task of bringing it into harmony with what was beginning to be remembered of Greek philosophy, and, since he was a man of extraordinary genius, he made so good a job that it endured for six centuries. And simultaneously the government of the church was overhauled, so that abuses which had been rolling up for centuries were got rid of, the pope's authority as chief bishop was put upon a legal basis, and his relations to the secular princes were given some show of regularity and plausibility. These changes naturally provoked resistance from the old-fashioned, and at one time the row threatened to wreck the papacy altogether, but fortune was with it, for in the midst of the worst turmoils it was adorned by some of its greatest men.

The Protestant Reformation was far more political and economic in origin that theological. What inspired it was simply the fact that the church had become too powerful to be endured. It straddled Europe like a colossus, and was already beginning to reach out for the Western world, discovered only a few years before. As wealth increased, it got so much more than its fair share that presently it was richer than any king, richer than the emperor — indeed, almost as rich as kings and emperor together. There was no nook or cranny where its writ did not run; it had armies to enforce its decrees; it punished rebellion as savagely as any Mesopotamian potentate. The kings all hated it because it pitted one against another and was opposed to the national states that they were trying to fashion; the nobles hated it because its ubiquitous priests stood between them and their serfs; the common people hated it because its exactions kept them poor. It had been reformed, but it had not been reformed enough. There was a new economic order in the world and a new political order, and it was out of harmony with both. Knowledge was increasing faster than it could revise its theology: what had seemed indubitable in the time of Thomas Aquinas and at least believable in that of the Council of Constance now began to look absurd to all sensible men. Unfortunately, no Gregory VII or Innocent III arose to steer the bark of Rome through these stormy waters of the Renaissance. It simply plunged on to disaster. The popes, taking refuge behind the ancient maxim, *Extra ecclesiam nulla salus* (Outside the church no one can be saved), roared maledictions in all directions. The Inquisition was revived, heretics were pursued with vast diligence, and whole nations were threatened with the interdict. Hell served their Holinesses as the lions' den had served their predecessors among the Cæsars; they filled it with their critics. But the Reformation surged on, and presently half of Europe was lost to Rome, part of it only for a space but most of it forever.

The Reformers were men of courage, but not many of them were intelligent. The new theology that they brought in was quite as silly as the old. Few of them seem to have noticed that in rejecting the authority of the popes and setting up the Bible as the sole guide to faith and conduct they were setting up something that bore the mark of the popes on almost every page. Perhaps Luther felt a certain uneasiness in that direction, for he proposed, as we have seen, some radical changes in the canon of the New Testament, but what he left was as unmistakably grounded upon Roman authority as what he rejected. Once the faithful began to search the sacred texts there was an efflorescence of theological extravagance unmatched since the days of the early Fathers, and the new church quickly split into a multitude of factions. That process of division and redivision continues to this day, with the result that Protestantism, for all its numerical strength, remains a feeble force in the world, and has very little influence upon the main stream of human thought. Its theology, taking one sect with another, is quite as preposterous as that of the church of Rome, and its practices, save when they furtively imitate the Roman practices, are quite lacking in the Roman dignity. It has produced some of the most appalling theologians ever heard of, either within the bounds of Christendom or without. Compared to their inventions, such Roman confections as the Real Presence and Papal Infallibility seem almost as persuasive as the binomial theorem. Protestantism, when it wrested the locks from the Bible, naturally turned with most curiosity to what Catholicism had kept under cover — that is, to the apocalyptic parts of the New Testament and to the more florid and inflammatory sections of the Old. Today its God bears the name of the New Testament Father, but, as ordinarily encountered, He is far more the Yahweh of the Old — crafty, cruel, jealous, bellicose, irrational, and vain. There is little tenderness in its order of things, as there is little beauty. In its purer forms, it is almost a reversion to the religion of primitive man. It is a scheme for propitiating a divinity who is not quite trustworthy — a faith that never wholly rids itself of a painful uneasiness.

Thus it was not the Reformation that liberated the soul of modern man. Such moderate intellectual decencies as prevail in the world today owe nothing to Luther, and no more to his colleagues and successors. Some of them were men of a certain learning, but they offered little evidence of it in their expositions of the divine mysteries. As for Luther himself, he was the theologian *par excellence* — cocksure, dictatorial, grasping, self-indulgent, vulgar and ignorant. "Demons," he once wrote, "live everywhere, but are especially common in Germany. On a high mountain called the Polterberg there is a pool full of them: they are held captive there by Satan. If a stone is thrown in a great storm arises and the whole countryside is overwhelmed. Many deaf persons and cripples were made so by the Devil's malice. Plagues, fevers and all sorts of other evils come from him. As for the demented, I believe it to be certain that all of them were afflicted by him." Much more of the same general tenor is to be found in Luther's writings. His followers of today, forgetting everything of the sort, remember only his sonorous declarations for a freedom of conscience that, in truth, he never believed in. "Reason," he said in his old age, "is the Devil's harlot, who can do nought but slander and harm whatever God says and does." His greatest successor, John Calvin, was even worse. Forced to flee from his native France, he took refuge at Geneva in Switzerland, and there set up an Asiatic despotism of his own, modelled upon that of the pope. His rule was so harsh that the oppressed citizens soon chased him out, but presently he returned again, and this time he stayed. The high point of his career was the brutal burning of Servetus, one of the most brilliant men of his time. Calvin was the Paul of early Protestantism, and the greatest of all the Protestant theologians. To this day his gloomy and nonsensical ideas remain in high esteem among the faithful, especially in Scotland, Holland and the United States. He was the true father of Puritanism, which is to say, of the worst obscenity of Western civilization.

# V    Its State Today

THE MODERN era was brought in, not by the Reformation, but by the Renaissance, which preceded it in time and greatly exceeded it in scope and dignity. The Renaissance was a reversion to the spacious paganism of Greece and Rome; as someone has well said, it was a *bouleversement* of all the principles of Christianity. Its test for ideas was not the authority behind them but the probability in them. It was immensely curious, ingenious, skeptical and daring — in brief, everything that Christianity was not. Unfortunately, its intuitions ran far ahead of its knowledge, and so, while it left all enlightened men convinced that Christian theology was a farrago of absurdities, all it had to offer in place of that theology was a series of bold surmises. What was needed was a body of exact facts, explaining the cosmos and man's place in it in rational terms. The task of accumulating those facts fell upon the Seventeenth Century, and the light began to dawn toward its close. One by one the basic mysteries yielded to a long line of extraordinarily brilliant and venturesome men — Bacon, Galileo, Newton, Leibniz, Harvey and Leeuwenhoek among them. The universe ceased to be Yahweh's plaything and became a mechanism like any other, responding to the same immutable laws. The world dwindled to the estate of what A. J. Balfour called "one of the meanest of planets." Man became an animal — the noblest of them all, but still an animal. Heaven and Hell sank to the level of old wives' tales, and there was a vast collapse of Trinities, Virgin Births, Atonements and other such pious phantasms. The Seventeenth Century, and especially the latter half thereof, saw greater progress than had been made in the twenty centuries preceding — almost as much, indeed, as was destined to be made in the Nineteenth and Twentieth.

But it had run out before the fact began to be generally understood, and so the century following reaped the harvest. It was in that century, the Eighteenth, that Christian theology finally disappeared from the intellectual baggage of all really civilized men. On both sides of the Reformation fence the Christian church fought for its life, and nearly everywhere it had the support of the universities, which is to say, of official learning, which is to say, of organized ignorance. But the new thing called science was now really free, even from the control of the learned, so it kept on advancing steadily, and presently the reluctant universities had to take it in. By the middle of the century what Nietzsche was later to call a transvaluation of all values was in full blast. Nothing sacred was spared — not even the classical spirit that had been the chief attainment of the Renaissance — , and of the ideas and attitudes that were attacked not many survived. It was no longer necessary to give even lip service to the old preposterous certainties, whether theological or political, æsthetic or philosophical. In France Voltaire, Rousseau and Diderot were making a bonfire of all the ancient Christian superstitions; in England Gibbon was preparing to revive the long dormant art of history and Adam Smith was laying the foundations of the new science of economics; in Germany Kant was pondering an ethical scheme that

247

would give the Great Commandment a rational basis and a new dignity; everywhere knowledge of the visible world was widening day by day.

The Seventeenth Century had made the basic discoveries, but it was in the Eighteenth that they began to have practical effects upon the everyday life of civilized peoples. The old gloomy dread of *post mortem* penalties and retributions was thrown off, and Western man set out to enjoy himself in a world that grew ever more pleasant. It must have been a charming day to live in. For as skepticism spread everywhere, the urbanity that is its hallmark spread with it, the upper classes improved vastly in manners and dignity, and even the lower orders showed a ponderable advance in that direction. Set free from the fears that had been hag-riding it for nearly two thousand years, the race began to give thought to the amenities, to rational comforts and luxuries, to the cultivation of leisure, to the game of ideas. The arts, liberated at last from the dark influence of theology, sought beauty for its own sake, and found it everywhere. The sciences, leaping forward from the bases established during the century preceding, threw off a long series of practical inventions, most of them conducive to the ease and security of mankind, and some of them working revolutions in its daily life. It was in this era, throughout Western Europe and also in America, that man's most useful and durable possession, the house he dwells in, ceased to be a magnified kennel and became a genuine home, beautiful in itself and filled with sightly furniture. Pestilences diminished, the supply of food became more abundant and varied, the transport of men and goods improved, and even war itself was tamed by new decencies. At no time in history, either before or since, have men and women lived more delightfully, or better deserved to be called civilized.

Unhappily, life became more complicated as it grew more refined, and in the end the Golden Age blew up, as Golden Ages always do soon or late. The new inventions were simply too much for the old aristocracy — a race of military banditti sadly deficient in the enterprise and resourcefulness needed to utilize them. They were also, of course, too much for the lower orders, which lacked altogether the qualities needed to master the machine, and so became its slaves. Its control fell to a new category of entrepreneurs, flowing out of the commercial middle class come down from medieval times, but reinforced by occasional recruits from above and below. These entrepreneurs rapidly collared most of the free wealth of Christendom, and were soon reaching out for power. The revolution that followed was too complex to be summarized hurriedly: its causes and events are debated in whole libraries of books, most of them worthless. Suffice it to say here that the midle class got what it set out to get, but at the cost of launching a ferocious — and well grounded — *jacquerie* below it. The lower orders, once promised a fair share in the new comfort and urbanity, had been thrust into a gehenna where they quickly came to resemble dumb brutes, and meanwhile they were tantalized by lofty talk about the inalienable rights of man. The result, as everyone knows, was a cataclysm. The mob, led by political demagogues on the one hand and theological fanatics on the other, rose against the new civilization and tried to destroy it. The control of the state, seized by the middle class, quickly passed to lower and lower levels, and the popular religion surged up from its sewers and polluted every rank of society save the highest. This vast reaction went further in England than anywhere else. The Eighteenth Century, rocking to its gory end there, saw the whole programme of progress challenged by the twin superstitions of democracy and evangelical Christianity, and the Nineteenth took over a burden of stupidity and folly that the so-called Anglo-Saxon race, on both sides of the Atlantic, is still struggling hopelessly to throw off.

2

In the field of religion, however, the reaction was probably a great deal less catastrophic than it looked at the time, even in England and America. Its proportions were exaggerated beyond the reality by the support it got from the new sect of demagogues, eager for office and willing to do anything, say anything and believe anything in order to get it. In the Eighteenth Century the rulers of the Western world, being secure in their places, could afford to comport themselves as relatively civilized men. Specifically, they could afford to give their countenance and support to the skepticism that was its chief hallmark. I point to Frederick the Great in Prussia, to the gay and mocking obligarchies that ruled France and England, and to such scoffers as Franklin and Jefferson in the nascent United States. A statesman in those days was not necessarily a rogue and an ignoramus: he might, if he would, associate openly with philosophers, artists and men of science, and not infrequently he made some show of qualifying under one or another of those headings himself. Frederick, when he craved society at Potsdam, sent for Voltaire and Johann Sebastian Bach, not for the Eighteenth Century equivalents of radio crooners and movie stars. Franklin was himself a scientist of the first contemporary chop, and amused himself, not with Elks and golf-players, but with savants and charming women. Jefferson, like Franklin, would have passed as a civilized man at the courts of Pericles, Lorenzo de' Medici or Pius II. But with the spread of the democratic pestilence all this was changed. The rulers of the peripheral Christian lands, menaced by the rising of the *Chandala,* began to take their orders from below, and their ideas therewith, and it came to be the chief duty of a statesman to find out and carry out the mandates of persons to whom information was a stranger and thought a pain. On the political level this new polity produced a cancerous proliferation of demagogy in all its forms, with the results now visible everywhere on earth. And on the theological level — to confine examples to the American Republic, the envy and despair of all other nations — it gave us such indecencies as comstockery, Prohibition, and the laws against the teaching of evolution as a biological fact.

But these reversions to the childish certainties of the Ages of Faith were, after all, only diseases of civilization, and it is not to be forgotten that they by no means affected all men in Christendom, nor the best men, and that the underlying course of events continues against them, so that we may yet hope that, in the long run, they will be cured. The rise of Methodism, on the American frontier, was accompanied by the rise of Unitarianism in New England, with a collapse of the old Puritan theology. That theology, to be sure, did not vanish altogether: it was simply transferred to the receding West and South, and still survives in their more barbaric enclaves; moreover, what remained of it on its old stamping-ground was taken over eagerly by an invading horde of moron Catholics, swarming in from Ireland and French Canada. But the main current of intellectual progress has left it behind, and if a current president of Harvard were to preach the theology of Increase Mather he would be locked up as a lunatic, though he is still free (and expected) to merchant the prevailing political balderdash. Save among politicians it is no longer necessary for any educated American to profess belief in Thirteenth Century ideas. The rise of biology, the great event of the Nineteenth Century, is responsible for that change, and especially the appearance and acceptance of the Darwinian hypothesis of organic evolution. Darwin, to be sure, did not answer any of the basic riddles of existence, but he at least showed that the theological answers were rubbish, and he thereby completed the revolutionary work of Galileo, Newton, Leibniz, Harvey and Leeuwenhoek. Today no really civilized man or woman believes in the cosmogony of Genesis, nor in the reality of Hell, nor in any of the other ancient imbecilities that still entertain the mob. What survives under the name of Christianity, above the stratum of that mob, is no more than a sort of Humanism, with hardly more supernaturalism in it than you will find in mathematics or political economy.

In other words, civilized man has become his own god. When difficulties confront him he no longer blames them upon the inscrutable enmity of remote and ineffable powers; he blames them upon his own ignorance and incompetence. And when he sets out to remedy that ignorance and to remove that incompetence he does not look to any such powers for light and leading; he puts his whole trust in his own enterprise and ingenuity. Not infrequently he overestimates his capacities and comes to grief, but his failures, at worst, are much fewer than the failures of his fathers. Does pestilence, on occasion, still baffle his medicine? Then it is surely less often than the pestilences of old baffled sacrifice and prayer. Does war remain to shame him before the bees, and wasteful and witless government to make him blush when he contemplates the ants? Then war at its most furious is still less cruel than Hell, and the harshest statutes ever devised by man have more equity and benevolence in them than the irrational and appalling jurisprudence of the Christian God.

Today every such man knows that the laws which prevail in the universe, whatever their origin in some remote and incomprehensible First Purpose, manifest themselves in complete impersonality, and that no representation to any superhuman Power, however imagined, can change their operation in the slightest. He knows that when they seem arbitrary and irrational it is not because omnipotent and inscrutable Presences are playing with them, as a child might play with building blocks; but because the human race is yet too ignorant to penetrate to their true workings. The whole history of progress, as the modern mind sees it, is a history of such penetrations. They have come slowly, and, as time appears to transient and ardent man, at weary intervals, but nevertheless one has followed another pretty regularly, and since the beginning of the Seventeenth Century they have been coming ever faster and faster. Each in its turn has narrowed the dominion and prerogative of the gods. There was a time when a man laid low by disease sent for a priest and made a votive offering; now he goes to a physician who is an agnostic by definition. There was a time when it took a miracle to fling him through the air; now he proceeds by airplane. There was a time when he bore all his burdens with resignation, fearing to offend the gods that sent them; now he rises in indignation and tries to throw them off. There is no longer any resignation among enlightened men; there is only a resolute patience, fortified by almost endless ingenuity. The problems that remain bristle with difficulties, and every time one of them is solved another confronts the seekers, but there is no doubt any more that even the most vexatious of them will probably yield, soon or late, some part of its secret.

This spirit we think of as modern, and among orthodox Christian theologians, in fact, it is commonly denounced under the name of Modernism, but the truth is that it probably goes back to the earliest days of men. There must have been skeptics at the ringside when the first priest performed his hocus-pocus, and no doubt some of them, revolting against its transparent fraudulence, set themselves to finding a better way to deal with flood, fire and famine. They failed, perhaps, far more often than not, but now and then they must have succeeded, and every time that happened the gods lost a bit of ground, and the priests with them. It was no easy struggle, and only men of the highest courage and resourcefulness were fit for it, for against them stood the vast impediment of human folly, the immemorial imbecility of mankind in the mass. Not many other men could grasp what they had to teach, for it tended to transcend the common store of knowledge and the common way of thinking, and even fewer could appreciate the sweep of its iconoclastic significance — the full extent of the damage it did to the fundamental postulates of religion. But the priests knew, and their counter-attack was characteristic; they replied by denouncing the proponents of the new spirit as no more than priests of a new and heathenish cult, spreading superstitions worse than any ever heard of before. That charge echoes down the ages; it is a constant *leit motif* in the truly operatic war between science and religion. At no time has it been heard more often than today. Science, we are told, has become a religion on its own account, with a theology like any other. Its axioms are derided as mere articles of faith, and its leaders as no more than bogus John Baptists, howling in a wilderness of test-tubes.

This attack has been sharper and more violent in the age we live in than ever before, and for two reasons. The first is the extraordinarily rapid accumulation of scientific knowledge since 1859, leaving the primary assumptions of religion more and more untenable, and filling their defenders with more and more dudgeon. The second is the vast proliferation of democratic ideas in all the more volatile nations, giving every enemy of intelligence a new reservoir of power. Just as the medieval kings played the peasants against the nobles, so the reigning theologians and their lay bullies heat up the mob against the enlightened minority. Even so, of course, they are not sufficiently strong to extirpate the scientific spirit altogether, for even the mob, save on its nethermost levels, begins to show a certain suspicion of them, but they are at least strong enough to put up a tremendous fight, and to spread uneasiness among the less resolute sort of educated men. This last fact accounts for a phenomenon that adds a lot to the gayety of life in the democracy-ridden English-speaking countries: the effort of various alarmed and conciliatory scientists to prove that exact knowledge and theological dogma are not actually at odds — in the common phrase, to reconcile science and religion. Ostensibly, that effort is based upon a modest sense of the limitations of the human mind — upon an humble and hence highly laudable readiness to admit that many of the great problems of being and becoming remain unsolved, and may go unsolved forever. But actually there is something else.

3

In part, I suspect, it is simply cowardice — a disinclination to provoke formidable and unscrupulous antagonists too far — a craven yearning for the cheaper sort of peace and popularity. But in part it is also due to inner turmoils, congenital doubts. One must not forget that the free opportunity which prevails in democratic societies carries certain inevitable pains and penalties with it — that the sweet privilege of offering a hand up to the worthy young man from below may be accompanied by the bitter discovery that he is not fitted by nature to live comfortably on the higher level. This difficulty is frequently visible in the field of statecraft: everyone can recall Presidents who carried the appetites and attitudes of the village grocery-store or the small-town lodge of Elks into the White House. What is too often forgotten is that it exists also in the grove of Athene. Even a cursory examination should be sufficient to reveal plenty of evidences of it — eminent economists who have never learned decent table manners, distinguished physicists who turn to spiritualism in their old age, celebrated surgeons who still believe in Prohibition, big-wigs of other faculties who can never quite rid themselves of the Wesleyan balderdash they learned at their mothers' knees. Such prodigies are not uncommon in the more democratic countries, and they are naturally in the forefront of the effort to reconcile science and religion. They must be endured patiently, and with them the damage that they do to the intellectual decencies. It is too much, indeed, to ask a man bred in a backwoods parsonage and educated at a one-building denominational college to get rid of his infantile dreads and superstitions altogether, even after a year at Göttingen and a long career in the laboratory. But to be polite to such unhappy amphibians is one thing, and to take their incurable piety seriously is quite another.

On the other side of the fence there is a far more resolute spirit. One hears of theologians submitting courteously to the advances and concessions of the scientific faithful, but one seldom hears of them making any concessions of their own, save under the direst compulsion. The truth is that every priest who really understands the nature of his business is well aware that science is its natural and implacable enemy. He knows that every time the bounds of exact knowledge are widened, however modestly, the domain of theology is correspondingly narrowed. If Christian divines admit today that the world is round and revolves about the sun, it is only because they can't help themselves — because the fact has been so incontrovertibly proved that even the mob has had to accept it. So long as they could do so safely they denounced it bitterly, and launched their most blistering anathemas upon those who defended it. In precisely the same way they opposed, while they could, every other advance in knowledge, not only in the physical sciences but also in philosophy and mathematics. To this day the works of Locke, Bentham and Mill are on the Roman *Index Expurgatorius,* and only a few years ago an American cardinal was discovering "the ghastly apparition of atheism" in the relativity of Einstein. The theory that the sciences are fostered in schools and colleges carried on under sacerdotal auspices is moonshine. The only sciences that are actually fostered are the safe ones — meteorology, seismography, descriptive astronomy, and so on — and even in these placid fields very little work of any importance is done. No one ever heard of a pious savant contributing anything of solid value to history, economics or political theory, and even in the domain of biology, the chief exercise ground of modern science, what little has been done has been offered timidly, and with saving protestations of orthodoxy. The case of the Augustinian monk, Gregor Mendel, is in point. When he formulated the great law of genetics which now bears his name he did not go with it to his superiors, as an infidel biologist would have done, expecting praise and reward. No; he kept it very prudently to himself, and when it was given to the world at last it was not by his Augustinian brethren but by secular scientificoes who were all, by theological jurisprudence, doomed to Hell. There have been, to be sure, not a few other scientists who professed allegiance to Holy Church, and yet managed to do valuable work — the cases of Pasteur, Ampere, Lavoisier and Schwann are often cited — but these men did that work by taking chances with its catchpolls, and there is no telling what better work they might have done if those catchpolls had not menaced them.

Dr. Andrew D. White, in "A History of the Warfare of Science With Theology in Christendom," establishes beyond any doubt the unyielding hostility of all Christian theologians, whether Catholic or Protestant, to every sort of true progress, and sets forth amusingly the technique of their retreat when defeated. So long as it seems safe they fight in the open, hitting valiantly on both sides of the belt, and trying to gain a quick victory by sheer ferocity. But once it becomes apparent that this quick victory is impossible, they begin to be more discreet. First they try to force some element of conformity into the heresy before them. Then they discover that it is not a heresy at all. And then they proceed to declare that they were never against it. The Copernican system went through all these stages, and the hypothesis of organic evolution is floating between the first and the second today. Many Protestant sects still reject it utterly, and, in such swamps of the intellect as the American Bible Belt, try to have it put down by the secular arm. Other Protestant sects have virtually accepted it, though always with certain reservations. As for the Catholic brethren, they maintain a somewhat uneasy attitude of watchful waiting. On the one hand, they are constrained to admit that the transmutation of species is possible, and even probable, but on the other hand they maintain that the appearance of man in the world was an exceptional event, due to a special creation, *i.e.,* a miracle. Meanwhile, they ease their consciences by belaboring heartily all evolutionists who happen also to be agnostics, and by speaking of evolution in their colleges, not as an established fact, but only as a sort of surmise — and not too respectable. Eventually, of course, they will have to swallow it, as they swallowed the Copernican astronomy by fiat of the Holy Office on September 11, 1822, nearly three centuries after "De Revolutionibus Orbium Cælestium" was published.

259

The truth is that Christian theology, like every other theology, is not only opposed to the scientific spirit; it is also opposed to all other attempts at rational thinking. Not by accident does Genesis III make the father of knowledge a serpent — slimy, sneaking and abominable. Since the earliest days the church as an organization has thrown itself violently against every effort to liberate the body and mind of man. It has been, at all times and everywhere, the habitual and incorrigible defender of bad governments, bad laws, bad social theories, bad institutions. It was, for centuries, an apologist for slavery, as it was apologist for the divine right of kings. The English bishops voted almost unanimously against every proposal to liberalize the laws of the empire, and the popes opposed every effort to establish freedom of thought in free states. In the domain of pure ideas one branch of the church clings to the archaic speculations of Thomas Aquinas and the other labors under the preposterous nonsense of John Calvin. The recurrent effort to reconcile Platonism to the Christian system only serves to show how far the two stand apart. Plato, as a man of science, was surely cautious enough, but the church has never been able, in any true sense, to take him in. Turn to the laborious works of the late Paul Elmer More if you would see how brilliantly modern a Greek of the Fourth Century before Christ must appear when his ideas are ranged beside those which inform even the most Modernistic variety of Christianity. Dr. More constantly confronted a painful choice between Christian theology and the elements of rational thinking, and every time he allowed his congenital piety to make any concession to the former he had to do violence to the latter.

The only real way to reconcile science and religion is to

set up something that is not science and something that is not religion. This has been done with great earnestness by Robert A. Millikan, A. S. Eddington and other such hopeful men — all of them bred so deeply in the faith that they have been unable to shake it off in their later years, despite their training in scientific method and their diligent professional use of it. The thing that Millikan has described as Christianity is simply a vague sort of good will to men: it has little more objective reality in the world than abstract justice or the love of God. And the thing that he has described as science is so halting and timorous that it is quite as unreal. The notion that science does not concern itself with first causes — that it leaves that field to theology or metaphysics, and confines itself to mere effects — this notion has no support in the plain facts. If it could, science would explain the origin of life on earth at once — and there is every reason to believe that it will do so on some not too remote tomorrow. To argue that the gaps in knowledge which still confront the seeker must be filled, not by patient inquiry, but by intuition or revelation, is simply to give ignorance a gratuitous and preposterous dignity. When a man so indulges himself it is only to confess that, to that extent at least, he is not a scientist at all, but a theologian, for he attempts to reconcile science and religion by the sorry device of admitting that the latter is somehow superior to the former, and is thus entitled to all territories that remain unoccupied.

Nor is there any more validity in the position of that other school of reconcilers which teaches that science and religion address themselves to quite different faculties, the former to the intellect and the latter to the emotions, and that they are thus independent, and equally entitled to

261

respect. Here the psychology is obviously dubious, for it must be plain that even the most instinctive of emotions, in adult human beings, owes something to the intellect, and it must be equally plain that no intellectual process can ever be wholly devoid of an emotional element. So much, indeed, is a commonplace to every schoolboy: the Freudian gospel has carried it, along with a great deal of racy nonsense, from end to end of the world. The evidence of the emotions, save in cases where it has strong objective support, is really no evidence at all, for every recognizable emotion has its opposite, and if one points one way then another points the other way. Thus the familiar argument that there is an instinctive desire for immortality, and that this desire proves it to be a fact, becomes puerile when it is recalled that there is also a powerful and widespread fear of annihilation, and that this fear, on the same principle, proves that there is nothing beyond the grave. Such childish "proofs" are typically theological, and they remain theological even when they are adduced by men who like to flatter themselves by believing that they are scientific gents.

## 4

The more intelligent theologians, in truth, are well aware of their logical inadequacy, and try to find reinforcement for them in more respectable facts. In Christendom this business of discovering what are called Christian evidences has gone on for centuries, and even today it enlists the labors of many industrious men. One of its basic postulates is that the whole process of nature is a sort of continuing miracle, and that it thus establishes the existence of an omnipotent and irresponsible God, — in brief, of the chartered libertine who is the hero of the Old Testament. The error here, of course, consists in confusing what is simply marvellous with what is actually miraculous. A miracle is not a mere marvel; it is something quite different, for it flatly violates some known law of nature. A marvel doesn't. It may be, at the moment, inexplicable, but this is only saying that the laws which govern it are yet unknown. The fact that they are unknown, in itself, is of no evidential value; it simply tells us what every enlightened person already knows, to wit, that man's knowledge of the universe is still incomplete. But it is certainly more nearly complete than it was fifty years ago, or a century ago, or a millennium ago, and there is every reason to believe that it will become still more complete hereafter — that all or nearly all the natural processes, in the course of time, will be brought into harmony with invariable laws.

It is the custom of the reconcilers of science and religion to seek a miserable peace with the theologians by putting an arbitrary limit upon this increase in human knowledge. Eager to pass as virtuous, they give assurances that science will stop before it gets into really close quarters with divinity. Some of them even go to the length of hinting that some of the laws already established are probably dubious, and must be subordinated to theological dogma. But this is politics, not sense. There is, in fact, no reason to believe that any given natural phenomenon, however marvellous it may seem today, will remain forever inexplicable. Soon or late the laws governing the production of life itself will be discovered in the laboratory, and man may set up business as a creator on his own account. The thing, indeed, is not only conceivable; it is even highly probable. When it comes to pass the theologians will be staggered, but I do not go so far as to predict that they will be undone. More than once in the past, seeing this miracle or that suddenly transformed into an ordinary marvel, responsive to lowly natural laws, they have edged out of disaster by abandoning it quietly and turning to another. Their art and mystery will be secure so long as the supply holds out, and that, no doubt, will be a long time.

Their effort to occupy all the areas not yet conquered by science — in other words, their bold claim that what no one knows is their special province, that ignorance itself is a superior kind of knowledge, that their most fantastic guess must hold good until it is disproved — all this is certainly absurd enough, but even more absurd is their frequent attempt, just mentioned, to find support for their dogmas in what they allege to be overt facts. What this process comes to in practice may be discovered by anyone who will go to the trouble to examine the common Christian evidences for the Resurrection and the Virgin Birth, or the Catholic proofs of the miracles of the saints, or the Fundamental Protestant demonstration that the solemn promise in Mark xvi, 18 may be relied upon, or the Mormon evidence that the Book of Mormon was written by Yahweh in person, on plates of gold. Theological literature is largely given over to such ridiculous sophistries, and many of them are supported by multitudes of earnest witnesses. But all they really prove is that theologians are well aware, deep down in their hearts, that faith alone is not sufficient to make even half-wits believe in their mumbo-jumbo; they sense a need to sweeten the dose with such testimony as would convince a judge and jury. The result of their labors in that direction, continued through many centuries, has been only to reduce human reason to the quaking and malarious thing that it is today. They have gradually broken down all the natural barriers between fact and fiction, sense and nonsense, and converted logic into a weapon that mauls the truth far more often than it defends it.

In this increasingly discreet but still very pertinacious war upon science the theologians are greatly aided by the fact that its concepts, as knowledge increases, tend to be more and more complex, and hence less and less intelligible to the vulgar. "I have never yet met a man," said Cardinal O'Connell, "who understood in the least what Einstein is driving at." No doubt His Eminence, searching his archi-episcopal province, might have found one in Cambridge, or even on Beacon Hill, but in South Boston, to which he may be presumed to have confined it, he did well to give it up as hopeless. Here I do not sniff at the South Boston mind: it is simply the ordinary mind of the human race. That mind is almost as resistant to knowledge as the most recalcitrant fire-clay. It has taken in, after centuries of agony, the notion that the world is more or less round, but it is still unable to grasp the evidence which establishes the fact. It functions in bodies which profit like all other bodies by what has been found out about malaria, small-pox and yellow fever, but it could no more give a rational account of the causes of any of those diseases than it could square the circle. No sort of learning save the most elemental can penetrate it. What lies above is and always has been the monopoly of a very small minority of men, and in all ages that minority has been disreputable by canon law and generally unpopular.

265

But though the priests have tried heroically to put it down, it has yet managed to survive, even through the darkest of the Ages of Faith. History, to be sure, tells us next to nothing about the details of the process, for history deals mainly with captains and kings, gods and prophets, exploiters and despoilers, not with useful men. Thus we do not know who the revolutionist was who first set a broken leg, nor the first to launch a seaworthy boat, nor the first to calculate the length of a year, nor the first to manure a field. But of two things we may still be sure: that such men have always existed in the world, and that every one of their triumphs over nature was also a priestly Thermopylæ. The astronomy of the Egyptians grew up under the awful shadow of Rê the sun-god, who had to be fetched up from the Underworld every morning by the prayers and abasements of his royal son and high priest, the pharaoh. How many of the forgotten Keplers and Herschels of that day really believed in Rê? How many of the pyramid engineers? How many of the men who harnessed and tamed the Nile? It is not hard to guess. If the theological answer to all questions had ever actually prevailed in the world the progress of the race would have come to an end, and there would be no difference today between a good European and a good pygmy in the African jungles. Everything that we are we owe to Satan and his bootleg apples.

## 5

In these latter days, with skepticism growing ever bolder and more devastating, not a few defenders of religion set up the argument that, even if the body of evidence upon which it is grounded be rejected as insufficient, its social utility and even necessity remain — that its dreadful threats and solemn sanctions are needed to keep frail mankind in order. There is, it must be confessed, a considerable plausibility in this contention; indeed, facts which seem to support it are not far to seek. No one will deny, I take it, that we owe the Rockefeller Institute, at least in part, to certain purely theological tremors in the donor. As a good citizen, no doubt, he desired simply to do something for the human race, but as a good Baptist he must have also given some thought to his own probable fate *post mortem.* Thus the Institute may be viewed as a magnificent sacrifice to the divine author of the Ten Commandments, in propitiatory atonement for some of the ways in which the money that paid for it was amassed. The same motive is visible in many other great public benefactions: perhaps it would not be going too far to say that every considerable donation to the common weal is a contribution to a conscience fund. Contrariwise, when this or that man works evil it may be argued that he would work even worse evil if he were not made a bit uneasy by the common talk of Hell. The case of the Methodist bishops who ran the United States during the thirteen years of Prohibition comes to mind at once. One of them was a confessed gambler, others were accused plausibly of even worse violations of the moral law they undertook to enforce on their customers, and practically all of them, in the matter of Law Enforcement, winked at murder. Some, indeed, actually gloated over it, as their predecessors in ancient days gloated over human sacrifice. It is not easy to figure out how far they might have gone if an occasional whiff of brimstone had not stayed them, but there is probably nothing unreasonable in the surmise that a few of the more advanced might have gone all the way to cannibalism.

The fact, however, that threats of Hell have their social uses is not an argument in favor of the truth of religion; it is simply an argument against the human race. More, it is palpably libellous, for the overwhelming majority of men and women are not nearly so vicious as the fancy of theologians makes them out. Very few men, if Hell were proved to be a fiction tomorrow, would take to the highroad and cut throats, and very few women would turn drabs. There is, perhaps, no categorical imperative impelling them to what is currently regarded as virtue, but there is at least the powerful stimulus of enlightened self-interest: they know it to be a fact that good behavior is safer and more comfortable than its opposite. The concept of this good behavior changes from time to time and from place to place, but that very fluency makes it more responsive to actual human needs, and hence gives it a higher psychological validity, than any concept deducible from theological precept and example. All of us, indeed, who have ever come to close quarters with theologians must have left them with an elated feeling that our sort of decency is a great deal better than theirs. For they are not, as a class, fair men, nor is there any noticeable honesty in them. To find their match in secular life recourse must be had, not to philosophers, but to politicians. Nor is there anything in the Christian sacred books to indicate that even Yahweh Himself is much better. The searcher there discovers Him in moments of charming sentimentality, but far more often He is discovered in transactions that, on this earth, would get Him expelled from any club. As a journalist in active practice I have spent most of my life among scoundrels, but I can recall very few, even in high office, who deserved to be put alongside the Heavenly Father described in II Kings II, 24; Exodus XII, 29; II Samuel XII, 15; Deuteronomy XX, 17, and Matthew XXVII, 46. No wonder Thomas Jefferson pronounced Him "a Being of terrific character — cruel, vindictive, capricious, and unjust"!

Nevertheless, it is the Christian theory that it is only a regard for this Being — partly a trembling fear and partly a kind of conciliation represented to be love — that keeps the human race from roaring downhill to villainy and disaster. Nor are theologians daunted by the obvious fact that many open and even ribald skeptics are not going that way, but, on the contrary, show a considerably higher degree of virtue than the Christian average. Their answer, in the words of Paul Elmer More, is that the moral sense of every such blameless candidate for Hell "is a kind of parasitic growth upon the otherworldliness of the society in which he lives." In other words, Thomas Henry Huxley was a Christian by osmosis, and without being aware of it. He eschewed adultery and committed no murders because he breathed the virtuous exhalations of the Archbishop of Canterbury. Even men who should know better sometimes indulge in this confusion between the religious impulse and common decency — for example, Alfred North Whitehead. "Religion," says Whitehead in "Religion in the Making," "is world loyalty," which he elsewhere defines as "the conception of an essential rightness of things" and "the concept of the goodness of God." But this is surely going beyond the plain facts. A man may be truly religious without imagining God as good at all, and he may be good without believing that there is any moral order in the universe or even that God exists. Religion does not necessarily make men better citizens, whether of their neighborhoods or of the world. Is a Catholic bishop a good citizen when he commands, on penalty of Hell, that poor and miserable women convert themselves into mere brood sows? Dr. Whitehead was on far sounder ground when, in another place, he said that "religion is the last refuge of human savagery." Whenever, in fact, an effort is made to assimilate the concept of the religious man with the concept of the civilized gentleman it quickly develops that the chief mark of the former is that he is quite unable to grasp the ideas which animate the latter.

Unhappily, religion is a time-binding device, and thus tends to preserve, on the ethical side, the ideas of a remote and primitive day. Christianity, even in the most civilized countries, staggers along under a load of moral concepts which go back, along one line, to a Teacher who believed that the end of the world was at hand and had little to offer save the counsel of despair, and, along another line, to the law-givers of a barbarous desert tribe in which parental authority was supreme, even to the extent of inflicting capital punishment, and every sort of dissent was a danger to the community, and hence treason. Thus skepticism remains immoral by the Christian code, despite the experience of civilized man that it is socially very valuable — immensely more valuable, in fact, than any known sort of faith. So late as 1864, Pope Pius IX, in his famous Syllabus of Errors, was condemning as heresy the doctrine that "the Roman pontiff may and ought to reconcile and adapt himself to progress . . . and modern civilization." Nor are the Protestant brethren much behind him.

Religion, in fact, is never an aid to the establishment of

sound ethical ideas, but always an impediment. The priest, realistically considered, is the most immoral of men, for he is always willing to sacrifice every other sort of good to the one good of his arcanum — the vague body of mysteries that he calls the truth. He is thus a poor judge of the morals of other men, and his teachings on the subject are bound to be misleading and dangerous. True enough, he tends to be influenced, like any other man, by the common moral ideas prevailing around him: in C. H. Toy's phrase, "religious faith always approves and utilizes the ethical ideas of its time." But, not content with that common store, he always adds something to it, and his additions are usually highly impolitic, and not infrequently dangerous. When the medieval priests denounced the taking of interest as sinful they retarded the economic development of Europe for centuries. All the Christian churches, by fighting for the retention of essentially theological conceptions in the marriage laws, help to increase human misery. Does syphilis remain a plague in Christendom, whereas smallpox, malaria and typhoid have been obliterated, and all the other great infections diminish year by year? Then it is only because theologians continue to look at syphilis, not as an infection but as a punishment for sin, and so resist the preventive measures that would quickly dispose of it.

This idea of punishment is always in their thoughts; they are hangmen rather than deliverers. The God of love that they preach invariably turns out, on examination, to be a God of harsh and arbitrary penalties and brutalities, just as the brotherhood of man that they preach, brought to the test, turns out to be only a kind of hatred. Hell is still their headquarters; for all their refinements, they have

271

never succeeded in purging religion of its primary motive of fear. Even in mystics that fear is always around the corner. They are eager for access to God, not because they love Him, but because getting into His society is the surest way to escape Hell. The love of God, in truth, is mainly a phantasm. As Toy says, it is quite unknown to primitive peoples. And among civilized peoples it is far more a fancy to be cultivated than a reality to be experienced.

The whole Christian system, like every other similar system, goes to pieces upon the problem of evil. Its most adept theologians, attempting to reconcile the Heavenly Father of their theory with the dreadful agonies of man in His world, can only retreat behind Chrysostom's despairing maxim that "a comprehended God is no God." Perhaps the most plausible resolution of the dilemma is that of Calvinism: it reduces the loving Father to a vast magnification of an oriental *cadi,* imperious, irresponsible, irrational, and beyond all imagining blood-thirsty. Calvinism is thus not only a gaudy *reductio ad absurdum* of Christianity; it is also an attentat upon all the common decencies, even the most elemental. Nevertheless, it has a considerable support in logic. Its God is an appalling monster, but it is still possible to imagine Him. If, reading the expositions of His priests, one is brought up incredulous by the horrors of His Hell, then it is only necessary to remember that He is also the author of cancer, leprosy and war.

## 6

On the upper levels of the human race Christianity is plainly breaking down. Since the Eighteenth Century it has not been necessary for any enlightened man to profess a belief in it. The life, if not the peace, of a skeptic is quite secure today, even in Tennessee, even in Rome. He may be barred, if an American, from the Presidency of the Republic (how completely Jefferson has been forgotten!), but so is every Catholic and every Jew. A degenerated form of Calvinism, going under various labels, is the dominant religion of the United States, but no American of any dignity believes in it. Nor can the other varieties of orthodox Christianity make any better show of eminent names. Ellsworth Huntington and Leon F. Whitney, searching "Who's Who in America," found that, of every 100,000 Unitarians, *i.e.,* heretics, in the population, 1185 were sufficiently distinguished to be listed therein, whereas only 18 professing Methodists qualified, and only 8 Lutherans, and only 7 Catholics. What the science of statistics thus reveals is ratified by everyday experience. One seldom discovers a true believer who is worth knowing. The intelligent "Christian" is quite as doubtful about the theology that he is supposed to have learned at his mother's knee as the intelligent Japanese is doubtful about Shinto, the intelligent Turk about the heavenly authority of the Koran, or the intelligent Jew about Leviticus.

But what intelligent people believe, under democracy, is after all somewhat irrelevant. They are plainly out of the swim of things. The great majority of men and women, now as then, probably do not know precisely what they believe, but the general cast of their thought is still toward something passing under the name of faith. Thus the priest, in his various guises, continues to be an important man in the world, though it is not often that his importance has any foundation in logic or the evidences. His answer to the insoluble riddles of life is far easier to grasp

273

than the answer of science, and more comforting. As James H. Leuba says, religion is "a way of dismissing the worrying complications of this world, of entering into a circle of solacing and elevating thoughts and feelings, of forgetting and surmounting evil." In brief, it is a flight from reality — and it has this plain advantage over all other flights: that it is along familiar and well-worn paths, trodden always in company. The true believer dies in a gang, like a soldier: he escapes that paralyzing sense of aloneness which must inevitably overtake the skeptic in the end, however sturdy his philosophy. This common pattern of religion, like the similar pattern of government, has been impressed upon the human consciousness for uncounted thousands of years, and it is no wonder that erasing it is an inordinately difficult matter, and, in the great majority of cases, impossible.

People in the mass fear to be singular. Their dominant desire is to be put down as safe, correct, reliable; to be let alone; to avoid challenge. Religion is everywhere a gauge of respectability — save perhaps on the very highest levels, where respectability itself, under the pressure of more subtle values, loses all its significance. Thus one may understand that lady of London told of by George Lansbury who, when advocates of secular education began soap-boxing in the East End, rushed out of a public-house brandishing a gin bottle and yelling, "These are the blighters who want to rob us of our bloody religion!" There is yet something else: the sense of sharing in vast mysteries, remote from ordinary experience and only dimly comprehended. If Yahweh were as familiar as the policeman He would get as little devotion, but on His far-off, pearly throne, hidden by gilded and expensive-looking clouds,

He becomes almost as overwhelming as the pope. The right to participate, however humbly, in His august and transcendental operations offers a powerful satisfaction to the will to power; the same privilege, on a smaller scale, is what takes hordes of human blanks into the Freemasons and other such spookish amalgamations of nonentities. But under all, and more important than anything else, is the primary motive of fear. Theology has sought to refine it away, but it remains today, as it was in the beginning, the be-all and end-all of religion. Remove it, and there is nothing left save a few behavior patterns and a series of dubious propositions in metaphysics. What is unknown is incurably terrifying, even to the best of men; to the majority it is unendurable. What they demand is a way out, a road to security, to peace, to such poor happiness as miserable men may hope for in this world. The road that religion offers may not be the most beautiful, but it is at least the widest, and so it is the most trod.

Here, like statecraft, it profits by the fact that men have short memories, and hate to work them. They recall the promise that was kept, and forget the promise that brought only frustration and disaster. The worst losers, after all, are dead, and cannot voice their complaints. Meanwhile, it actually rains, now and then, after prayers against the drought; the pious, quite as often as the damned, guess the winners of horse-races; people get well of terrifying diseases after the doctor has thrown up his hands and the priest has been sent for; in war, even when both sides pray to the same divinity, one is bound to win. There is, moreover, a subjective gain that is quite as gratifying as this scoring of overt bulls-eyes. The devotee somehow feels that he has lifted himself up — that he has established

275

connection with a power that is superior, not only quantitatively but also qualitatively, to those of this world. His ego glows under the thought; he has demonstrated his significance in the cosmic scheme; he has put himself clearly above the brutes, braying there in the meadow against a fate they cannot comprehend and in protest to powers they cannot even imagine. Even though no secular advantage flows out of this self-apotheosis, there is yet consolation in it, for what is bad might have been worse, and the next time the rewards may be better. No failure, indeed, can be quite complete. For even the most crushing carries a promise of compensation to him who bears it with trusting resignation, and if that compensation never comes on this earth it will come beyond, in the dim region where, to the faithful, evil and sorrow are no more, and the gods actually carry out their engagements. Thus the masses of humankind, in accepting the answer that religion offers to the intolerable riddle of existence, have not been wholly lacking in intelligent self-interest, for they have really got something valuable for their devotion.

Are all these fruits of faith illusions? Then let us not forget that illusions also have their uses — even, on occasion, to the most intelligent and self-sufficient of men. It is thus no wonder that the scent of ancient sacrifice lingers in the world. Few men are sturdy enough in spirit to face a hostile cosmos, day after day, year in and year out, without an occasional tremor of trepidation, a sudden overwhelming feeling, ever and anon, of inadequacy, helplessness, forlornness. It is disarmingly easy, at such times, to slip comfortably into the immemorial patterns. It saves wear and tear of the ego; it is a device of mental economy; it sets up a barrier between character and disaster.

## 7

There is yet a something else, already mentioned: the powerful pull of inherited superstition. Here I speak with biological inexactness, but my meaning, I hope, will be sufficiently clear. Man may not inherit his concrete ideas, but he at least inherits his leaning toward them, his capacity for them. It takes time to breed belief out and skepticism in — time, and a great deal of effort and grief. The only really safe skeptic is of the third generation: his grandfather must have taken the Devil's shilling as a bachelor. The rest, however lofty their pretensions, are all more or less unreliable: no sensible man would trust them in the face of an enemy invasion or after forty days and forty nights of rain. "The tradition of all the generations of the past," said Karl Marx, "weighs down like an Alp upon the brain of the living." Especially in the field of religion, where the weight of ancient credulities is reinforced by the even greater weight of decorum and sentimentality. Not many men like to be accused of treason to what they were taught at their mothers' knees. So the tendency is to handle religion in a careful and even gingery manner — to avoid discussing it as much as possible. Thus in most cases, as James Harvey Robinson has shrewdly observed, "it does not tend to mature." Men otherwise highly enlightened cling maudlinly to ideas that go back to the infancy of the human race. Worse, they assume that what they thereby permit themselves to believe, irrationally and against all the known facts, is a kind of knowledge.

Here, as in the case of the lowly, social pressures have

much to do with it. Religion itself, of course, is not necessarily social; on the contrary, it is peculiarly personal. A
man in a vacuum might still pray lustily for a way out. But
its long history gives it a social authority that is none the
less effective because it is factitious. To dissent from the
principal Christian formularies becomes, in Christendom,
as hazardous as to dissent from the prevailing axioms of
politics, as many a Jew has discovered to his sorrow. The
church, as the most august of all going concerns, acquires
vast and complicated interests, an immense prestige, an
almost irresistible power. It seizes a rôle of importance in
every capital event — birth, marriage, death. It penetrates
to the legislative chamber and the court of law. It demands
and gets a *quid pro quo* for its tender solicitude for emperors and presidents, exploiters and despoilers. In times
of peace it takes over charity, and makes it a billboard
for theology. In times of war it drags out its artillery of
anathema and maranatha to harry and damn the hosts of
Satan, and its casuistry to justify lying, banditry and the
atomic bomb. It knows how to put political, social and
economic pressure upon its more open foes, and how to
relax its rigors for those who waver.

In brief, it takes on the characters of a powerful, ambitious and unscrupulous governmental machine, a deliri-
ously imperialistic state. Naturally enough, all this in-
volves a long series of compromises with its own integrity;
it must sacrifice principles in order to achieve effects. There
ensues, within the fold, a brilliant and not unamusing
parade of contrasts — between the convert on his knees
and the parish priests cadging him for money; between
the sisters in the hospitals and the cardinal on his rococo
throne, arrayed like a movie queen; between Father

Damien and Elmer Gantry. But the very readiness to shift the rules as the game proceeds is one of the church's chief sources of strength, for it opens the doors to men who are not religious by nature, and so depletes the ranks of the enemy. For such men certain humane forms are enough. In order to be a tolerable Catholic it is sufficient, in the last analysis, to keep out of the Freemasons and remember one's Easter duty. To be a good Baptist it is sufficient to go into the water bravely, head and all. And to be a sound Methodist it is sufficient to vote dry whenever the chance offers: how one drinks, like how one robs the widow and the orphan, is a matter of private conscience.

At this sort of compromise and connivance the Catholic church shows a much greater limberness than any other Christian church, and so it seems likely to survive all the rest. It avoids the capital mistake of assuming that all Christians are actually Christians: even the pope himself is under formal suspicion, and must confess his sins like anyone else. Its priests have brought the art of casuistry to high perfection, and employ it with a great daring and effectiveness. In the teeth of Pope Pius IX's celebrated Syllabus of Errors, with its violent denunciation of freedom of worship and the separation of church and state, they once backed a candidate for the American Presidency on the ground that, as a good Catholic, he was in favor of both! How, in the course of time, they have got round the necessary implications of the traditional formula, *Extra ecclesiam nulla salus,* is instructively set forth by C. J. Cadoux in his "Catholicism and Christianity." And how they have managed to explain away what they call the plain mandates of Yahweh in the matters of suicide, birth control, heresy and casting out devils — this is known and admired by everyone who has ever opened a manual of moral theology.

Their Protestant brethren are scarcely to be mentioned in the same breath. Protestantism, in fact, started out upon its career nursing two massive errors, each of them sufficient to ruin it. One was the error of assuming that all Christians were really Christians, and the other was the error of assuming that they were intelligent enough to ascertain and embrace the truth. Both were found out very quickly, but not soon enough to get rid of them. Their collision with the veriest elements of human nature has produced an immense proliferation of fantastic sects and a long series of anti-papal popes, beginning with Luther and Calvin. Today Protestantism is either a banal imitation of Catholicism or a cruel burlesque upon it. It is almost too incoherent to be discussed seriously. I could invent new forms of it almost *ad infinitum,* as a mathematician invents new algebras, and all of them would be ten times as plausible as Swedenborgianism, Seventh Day Adventism, Christian Science, Holy Rollerism, or the imbecile cults of the Mormons, the Mennonites, the Two-Seed-in-the-Spirit Predestinarian Baptists, or the Salvation Army. In such regions bibliolatry turns upon and devours itself. Any half-wit, searching Holy Writ, is free to found a sect of his own — and if not upon the actual text, then upon the interpolations, mistranslations and typographical errors. Thousands of such half-wits, as everyone knows, have made use of that franchise, and the result is chaos. The Roman church has escaped the same disaster by keeping the Bible in its place. What the Bible says, however it may clash with common knowledge and common sense, is inspired and infallible

— but Holy Church reserves the right to determine precisely what it says. In that reservation there is a wisdom beyond the highest flight of philosophers.

Once a Frenchman announced to an American friend that he was leaving the church of his fathers. The American asked what variety of Protestantism he proposed to patronize. "I have lost my faith," answered the Frenchman icily, "but not my reason." The distinction, it seems to me, is quite sound. One might easily imagine an intelligent man yielding himself to the voluptuous Roman lure — if only cynically, as he might marry a rich and not too dreadful widow. But there is surely nothing to seduce him in Protestantism — not even beauty, not even the charm of romantic devotion, not even the dignity of the ancient and honorable. So far as I am aware, no man of any genuine distinction in the world today is a Methodist; if I am in error, I apologize most humbly. The news that a poet had been converted to Presbyterianism would be first-page stuff anywhere — as much so as the news that he had been converted to monogamy. Protestantism, in truth, save in those borderlands where Roman altar-fires perfume and denature it, is endurable only to hinds. It spoils the most lovely poetry in the world by reducing it to harsh and illiterate prose. It turns its back upon the God of Love and embraces the frightful Yahweh of the Old Testament, dripping with blood. It converts the gentle and despairing Jesus into a Y.M.C.A. secretary, brisk, gladsome and obscene. It is, on the ethical side, no more than a machine for enabling the blotched and ignoble to wreak their envy upon their betters. In Fundamentalism it reaches the nadir of theology. What is worst in Fundamentalism is common, perhaps, to all forms of Christianity, but it is only in the imprecations of the backwoods Wesleys that it is stated plainly. No more shocking nonsense has ever been put into words by theoretically civilized men.

## 8

One hears anon and anon of schemes of a reconciliation of all the warring Christian sects, and now and then two or more on the lower levels actually make peace, or, at all events, sign a truce. But it is highly improbable that this movement will ever overcome altogether the centrifugal forces that have been in operation since the day of the Apostles. There were battling factions while Paul still made his missionary journeys, as the exhortations and anathemas in his Epistles show only too plainly, and the young church was already torn by civil war in the grand manner in the Third Century. Since then it has faced schism after schism, including two that cost it large segments of Christendom. All great religions go the same way, and many that are not great at all. No theology is ever static. As refinements are introduced into it, dissent and division naturally follow. Theologians, despite the operations of the Holy Ghost upon them, remain exactly like the rest of us: they prefer their own ideas to the ideas of other men. Thus, even within the fold of Holy Church, there are endless struggles, with one side prevailing this time and some other side the next time. The theory is that the revealed truth never changes, but that is only a theory. The faithful, no doubt, are made sufficiently content when a novelty is represented to be a mere statement of what has always been believed, but that pretense cannot deceive the skeptic outside the fold, especially if he be familiar with the minutes of the Councils of Nicæa and Trent and with the proceedings anterior to the solemn pronunciamentoes of 1854 and 1870. At any time such a reform in doctrine, under whatever name it goes, may launch a new schism.

There is also, of course, a centripetal tendency: every religion, when it comes into contact with another, influences it and is influenced by it. In an earlier chapter I described some of the borrowings that early Christianity made from the other cults of the time, most of which, by its standards, were hopelessly pagan. The same thing is still going on. The American form of Catholicism has not only embraced certain purely political ideas that are excessively obnoxious to Rome; it has also picked up no little Puritanism, which is to say, Calvinism. There is already a ponderable faction of Catholic wowsers and uplifters, allied with Protestant mountebanks in the name of Social Justice. Also, there is a band of street evangelists barking the Only True Faith from soap-boxes — some of them laymen, though by canon law expounding doctrine is the strict monopoly of the clergy. Not a few of these Catholic Billy Sundays are recent converts, with a great deal more zeal in them than knowledge, and more than once I have listened to one of them preaching unwitting heresies that made my blood run cold. Meanwhile, the High Church Episcopalians, forsaking the Order for Morning Prayer in the Book of Common Prayer, turn to denaturized imitations of the Roman Mass, and the less anthropoid Methodists, as they shin up the ladder to social dignity, abandon their shouting, put candles in their tabernacles and vestments on their choirs, and even retire to what they venture to call retreats. The same process goes on everywhere. Buddhism once influenced Shinto so greatly in Japan that it almost ruined it, and a general reform became necessary. In Tibet Buddhism itself shows plain traces of Christianity, and in India both it and Mohammedanism have responded to the proselyting zeal of the Sikhs, whose religion is but four centuries old. But all this play of influence and counter-influence is mainly on the surface. Deep down there is always an implacable antagonism. Almost everywhere in the world the other fellow's religion is as odious as his table manners. More, he tends to become odious himself, and on all counts. The slowness with which the Arab learning spread in Europe was due quite as much to religious prejudice as to simple stupidity. What Christianity has taken from Judaism it has taken grudgingly, leaving the best behind, and what Judaism has taken from Christianity, at least in America, does not go back to Jesus, but to Rotary and the Y.M.C.A secretary. These stealings seldom affect fundamentals. Every religion of any consequence teaches that all the rest are insane, immoral and against God. It is seldom hard to prove it.

Christianity, as religions run in the world, is scarcely to be described as belonging to the first rank. It is full of vestiges of the barbaric cults that entered into it, and some of them are shocking to common sense, as to common decency. The old polytheism lingers on in the preposterous concept of the Trinity, defectively concealed by metaphysical swathings that are worse, if anything, than the idea itself. The Atonement is a reminder of blood sacrifice and the Eucharist of the pharmacology of cannibals. Judaism, in its theology, is far simpler and more plausible. So is Parseeism. A Parsee is not doomed to Hell for neglecting a sacrament, like a Catholic or a Baptist, nor is the Hell ahead of him, supposing he lands there on other counts, the savage and incredible chamber of horrors that Christians fear. He believes vaguely that his soul will go marching on after death, but he doesn't believe that it will go marching on forever; soon or late, he is taught, the whole cosmos must come to an end and start all over again. Buddhism leans the same way; it rejects immortality as not only unimaginable, but also as unendurable. Confucianism evades the question as unanswerable. It teaches that the dead survive, but doesn't pretend to say how long. On the ethical side it is much more rational than Christianity, and very much more humane, for its chief prophets and law-givers have not been ignorant fanatics but highly civilized men, some of them philosophers comparable to Plato or Aristotle. Even Moslemism, in this department, is superior to Christianity, if only because its ethical system forms a connected and consistent whole. In Christianity the problem of evil, a serious difficulty in all religions that pretend to be logical, is enormously complicated by the plain conflict between the ethical teaching of the Old Testament and that of the New. Is God jealous or tolerant, vengeful or forgiving, a harsh and haughty monarch or a loving father? It is possible to answer these questions any way you choose, and to find revelation to support you. Christian theologians have been trying to dispose of them for nineteen centuries, but they still afflict every believer with any capacity, however slight, for anything reasonably describable as reflection.

9

But in one respect, at least, Christianity is vastly superior to every other religion in being today, and, indeed, to all save one of the past: it is full of a lush and lovely poetry. The Bible is unquestionably the most beautiful book in the world. Allow everything you please for the barbaric history in the Old Testament and the silly Little Bethel theology in the New, and there remains a series of poems so overwhelmingly voluptuous and disarming that no other literature, old or new, can offer a match for it. Nearly all of it comes from the Jews, and their making of it constitutes one of the most astounding phenomena in human history. Save for a small minority of superior individuals, nearly unanimously agnostic, there is not much in their character, as the modern world knows them, to suggest a genius for exalted thinking. Even Ernest Renan, who was very friendly to them, once sneered at the *esprit sémitique* as *sans étendu, sans diversité,* and *sans philosophie.* As commonly encountered, they strike other peoples as predominantly unpleasant, and everywhere on earth they seem to be disliked. This dislike, despite their own belief to the contrary, has nothing to do with their religion: it is founded, rather, on their bad manners, their curious lack of tact. They have an extraordinary capacity for offending and alarming the *Goyim,* and not infrequently, from the earliest days down to our own time, it has engendered brutal wars upon them. Yet these same rude, unpopular and often unintelligent folk, from time almost immemorial, have been the chief dreamers of the Western world, and beyond all comparison its greatest poets. It was Jews who wrote the magnificent poems called the Psalms, the Song of Solomon, and the Books of Job and Ruth; it was Jews who set platitudes to deathless music in Proverbs; and it was Jews who gave us the Beatitudes, the Sermon on the Mount, the incomparable ballad of the Christ Child, and the twelfth chapter of Romans. I incline to believe that the scene recounted in John viii, 3–11, is the most poignant drama ever written in the world, as the Song of Solomon is unquestionably the most moving love song, and the Twenty-third Psalm the greatest of hymns. All these transcendent riches Christianity inherits from a little tribe of sedentary Bedouins, so obscure and unimportant that secular history scarcely knows them. No heritage of modern man is richer and none has made a more brilliant mark upon human thought, not even the legacy of the Greeks.

All this, of course, may prove either one of two things: that the Jews, in their heyday, were actually superior to all the great peoples who disdained them, or that poetry is only an inferior art. My private inclination is to embrace the latter hypothesis, but I do not pause to argue the point. The main thing is that Christianity, alone among the modern world religions, has inherited an opulent æsthetic content, and is thus itself a work of art. Its external habiliments, of course, are not unique. There are Buddhist temples that are quite as glorious as the Gothic cathedrals, and in Shinto there is a dramatic liturgy that is at least as impressive as the Roman Mass. But no other religion is so beautiful in its very substance — none other can show anything to match the great strophes of flaming poetry which enter into every Christian gesture of ceremonial and give an august inner dignity to Christian sacred music. Nor does any other, not even the parent Judaism, rest upon so noble a mythology. The story of Jesus, as it is told in the Synoptic Gospels, and especially in Luke, is touching beyond compare. It is, indeed, the most lovely story that the human fancy has ever devised, and the fact that large parts of it cannot be accepted as true surely does no violence to its effectiveness, for it is of the very essence of poetry that it is not true: its aim is not to record facts but to conjure up entrancing impossibilities. The story of Jesus is the sempiternal Cinderella story, lifted to cosmic dimensions. Beside it the best that you will find in the sacred literature of Moslem and Brahman, Parsee and Buddhist, seems flat, stale and unprofitable.

Moreover, it has the power, like all truly great myths, of throwing off lesser ones, apparently in an endless stream. The innumerable legends of the saints, many of them of great beauty, are mainly no more than variations of one detail or another of the fable of Jesus, and so are many of the stories that Christianity has concocted out of what were, in the first place, pagan materials — for example, that of Santa Claus. The human appeal of all this poetry is so extraordinarily potent that it promises to survive the decay of Christianity. Everyone has observed how Jews and infidels succumb in Christendom to the spirit of Christmas. What is less noted is the fact that among Christians themselves there is a growing tendency, when they throw off Christian theology, to salvage Christian poetry. This is plainly visible in the organized lovey-dovey that began with the Rotary movement and has since proliferated so enormously in the United States, with tentacles reaching out to not a few foreign lands. Robert S. and Helen M. Lynd tell us, in "Middletown," how, in the typi-

cal American community they describe, Rotary threatens
to become a substitute for Christianity, to the grave damage of churches and clergy. It is not, of course, a theological system; it is simply a poetical system. Starting out in
1905 on a you-tickle-me-and-I'll-tickle-you basis, it quickly
took on overtones of aspiration, and today its main purpose seems to be to convince emulous but unimaginative
men that it offers a way to something resembling salvation
on this earth — that its puerile mumbo-jumbo can convert
stock-brokers, insurance agents and used-car dealers into
passable imitations of Francis Xavier. The grandiose imbecility called Christian Science is tarred with the same
stick. It is certainly not a science, not even in the lame
sense that spiritualism and psychotherapy are, and no
Christian theologian save a hopeless dipsomaniac would
venture to call it Christianity. It is simply a kind of poetry
— an organized and unquestioning belief in the palpably
not true.

The thirst for such poetry, in the long run, may displace
the old fear of the brutal and implacable gods. Something
of the sort, in fact, was once envisaged by H. G. Wells,
who proposed abandoning the Christian Scriptures in
favor of a new Bible made up of extracts from Shakespeare, Shelley, Thomas Jefferson, Abraham Lincoln and
Karl Marx — all of them poets, though some of them
didn't know it. Upton Sinclair, the American Gnostic,
went a step further: he undertook to write a sort of New
Testament of his own, with incidental help from such
thinkers as Frances E. Willard, Henry George, Dr. Albert
Abrams, and Sacco and Vanzetti. The late Hitler had a
somewhat similar scheme, and the lamented New Dealers
played with one in which the Holy Saints were to be dis-

placed by Roosevelt II, Eleanor Roosevelt and a host of lesser semi-divinities, including, I suppose, the go-getting Roosevelt boys. Such efforts to substitute poetry for theology may be expected to multiply in the near future, for the world is plainly entering upon a new stage of myth-making. The two things, indeed, are much alike, for both are based on the doctrine that it is better to believe what is false than to suffer what is true. That was undoubtedly a sound philosophy in the days when the great religions were born and the great poems were written; it may even be sound enough, at least for all save a small minority of men, today. But it is hard to imagine it continuing sound forever. That modern man still needs such consolations is no more than proof that the emancipation of the human mind has just begun — that he is yet much nearer to the ape than he is to the cherubim. Once he attains to anything approaching a genuine mastery of his environment they will become as irrational to him as the old belief in ghosts, witches and demoniacal possession. Religion, in fact, is already a burden to him. It sends fears to haunt him — fears which stalk upon him out of the shadows of the Ages of Faith, the Apostolic Age, the Age of the Great Migrations, the Stone Age. Its time-binding afflicts him with moral ideas born of the needs of primitive and long-forgotten peoples — ideas violently out of harmony with the new conditions of life that his own immense curiosity and ingenuity have set up. It is, in its very nature, a machine for scaring; it must needs fail and break down as man gains more and more knowledge, for knowledge is not only power; it is also courage.

## 10

It may be that, by thus moving away from religion man will be losing something. Perhaps the theologians are right when they argue that, whatever the falsity of their premises, they are at least more or less sound in their conclusions: that religion, taking it by and large, at least makes human beings happier. But that, after all, begs the question, for it is only a romantic delusion that makes happiness the one end of progress. It may be, for all we know, that the *Übermensch* of the future will do without the boozy delusions of well being that we now call by that name. His prophet, Friedrich Nietzsche, has, in fact, hinted as much: his motto, says Nietzsche, will be, "Be hard!" To sentimentalists breathing Christian air this is revolting. They see in it only a counsel of brutality. But, as William James long ago pointed out, there is a hardness of the mind as well as a hardness of the fist, and we probably owe to it every advance that we have made away from the brutes — even the long, tortured advance toward kindness, charity, tolerance, tenderness, common decency. It has won for us, not only the concept of the immutability of natural laws, but also the concept of the mutability of all laws made by man. It has made us wary of our feelings at the same time that it has given us confidence in our growing store of fact. The truly civilized man, it seems to me, has already got away from the old puerile demand for a "meaning in life." It needs no esoteric significance to be interesting to him. His satisfactions come, not out of a childish confidence that some vague and gaseous god, hidden away in some impossible sky, made him for a lofty purpose and will preserve him to fulfill it, but out of a delight in the operations of the universe about him and of his own mind. It delights him to exercise that mind, regardless of the way it takes him, just as it delights the lower animals, including those of his own species, to exercise their muscles. If he really differs qualitatively from those lower animals, as all the theologians agree, then that is the proof of it. It is not a soul that he has acquired; it is a way of thinking, a way of looking at the universe, a way of facing the impenetrable dark that must engulf him in the end, as it engulfs the birds of the air and the protozoa in the sea ooze.

Thus he faces death the inexorable — not, perhaps, with complete serenity, but at least with dignity, calm, a gallant spirit. If he has not proved positively that religion is not true, then he has at least proved that it is not necessary. Men may live decently without it and they may die courageously without it. But not, of course, *all* men. The capacity for that proud imperturbability is still rare in the race — maybe as rare as the capacity for honor. For the rest there must be faith, as there must be morals. It is their fate to live absurdly, flogged by categorical imperatives of their own shallow imagining, and to die insanely, grasping for hands that are not there. Once, in my days as an active journalist, I attended one such poor fellow in his last moments. With the Seventh Commandment in mind, he had butchered his erring wife, and was now about to pay his debt to the Sixth. A devout Baptist, he was attended by a clergyman of his faith, and gave over his last hours to prayers to and praises of the Yahweh who had dealt with him so cruelly. When, finally, the sheriff came to his cell and summoned him to the gallows he broke into a loud, confident recitation of the Twenty-third Psalm. Thus the last scene:

The march begins — first the sheriff, then the condemned with his arms bound, and then the clergyman.

THE CONDEMNED — (*Loudly*) The Lord is my shepherd; I shall not want. He maketh me to lie down in green pastures. (*They reach the foot of the gallows*). He leadeth me beside the still waters. He restoreth my soul. (*They mount the steps*). He leadeth me in the paths of righteousness for His name's sake. Yea, though I walk through the valley of the shadow of death (*The sheriff binds his legs*) I will fear no evil: for thou art with me; thy rod and thy staff they comfort me. (*The sheriff adjusts the noose*). Thou preparest a table before me in the presence of mine enemies; thou anointest my head with oil; my cup runneth over. (*The sheriff signals to the hangman*). Surely goodness and mercy shall follow me all the days of my life: and I will dwell in the house of —

*The drop falls.*

As an American I naturally spend most of my time laughing, but that time I did not laugh.

# Bibliographical Note

THE LITERATURE of religion is so vast that no man can hope to traverse more than its main roads. On the subject of savage religions alone whole libraries have been published, and when one comes to Christian doctrine the accumulation is staggering. Fortunately, there are some summaries that offer the inquirer succor, though even these are often formidably diffuse. The best of them, and by long odds, is James Hastings' Encyclopedia of Religion and Ethics, in thirteen volumes, commonly bound in seven. First published in 1908, it has been since revised and republished, and it remains a monument of scholarship without a peer. Though prepared under the editorshop of a Presbyterian theologian, it is both scientific and impartial, and despite its large scale, it is so well ordered that consulting it is very easy. I have made heavy use of it in the foregoing pages, as every man must who writes upon religion. The American edition is published by Scribner in New York, and may be found in most public libraries. The Schaff-Herzog Encyclopedia of Religious Knowledge, which was first issued in 1884 and has been revised several times since, is far less satisfactory. It shows, in places, a considerable bias, and is far from complete. It is based very largely upon a German Real-Encyclopädie für protestantische Theologie und Kirche, edited by J. J. Herzog, and first issued in 1853–68. The publisher is the Funk and Wagnalls Company, New York. The work runs to

thirteen volumes. The Catholic Encyclopedia, edited by
Dr. Charles G. Herbermann and other Catholic scholars,
is somewhat better. It presents all controversial matters
from the Catholic point of view, but its attitude is generally
civilized, and it by no means conceals the more embarrass-
ing differences among Catholic theologians. In matters of
prevailing Roman doctrine it may be accepted as authoritative. The cheapest edition is that issued by the Encyclopedia Press, New York, under the auspices of the Knights
of Columbus. It is in sixteen volumes. The Jewish Encyclopedia, edited by Isidore Singer, is also useful, though its
scholarship will sometimes carry the average reader beyond
his depth. It is published by the Funk and Wagnalls Company, New York, in twelve volumes. There are other en-
cyclopedias of religion, but those that I have mentioned are
the best, especially Hastings'.

Of late there have been many studies of the psychology
of religion, most of them in English and many from the
pens of American scholars. The first work on the subject
to make a stir was William James's "Varieties of Religious
Experience" (New York, Longmans, 1902). It has gone
through many editions, and is still widely read. The style
of the author is very charming, but what he has to say seldom has much scientific importance. A somewhat more
sober work is James Leuba's "Psychological Study of Religion" (New York, Macmillan, 1912), to which a supple-
mental volume has been added, "The Psychology of Mysticism" (New York, Harcourt, 1925). Other books upon the
same subject are E. D. Starbuck's "Psychology of Religion"
(London, Scott, 1899), J. B. Pratt's "Psychology of Religious Belief" (New York, Macmillan, 1907), E. S. Ames's
"Psychology of Religious Experience" (Boston, Houghton,

1910), G. M. Stratton's "Psychology of the Religious Life" (London, Allen, 1911), and J. Cyril Flower's "Approach to the Psychology of Religion" (New York, Harcourt, 1927). All of these works save Flower's, together with several others of the same sort, are summarized admirably in A. R. Uren's "Recent Religious Psychology" (Edinburgh, Clark, 1928). Unfortunately, a common defect runs through most of them. They assume that any psychological phenomenon, however fantastic, which shows a religious content is religious in origin and character; only too often it is plainly pathological. Thus the cart is put before the horse. The fundamental religious impulses of a healthy man are really far simpler than psychologists usually seem to think. There is nothing mysterious about them. The hallucinations of eremites in their cells and of morons at Appalachian revivals do not belong to religion in any rational sense; they lie within the province of psychiatry.

Of books on the elemental forms of religion the best that I know is "Primitive Religion," by Robert H. Lowie (New York, Liveright, 1924). The author is an anthropologist, and deals with the subject in a clear and sensible manner, supported by his long study of actual savages. Some light is thrown upon the same matter in "Primitive Man as Philosopher," by Paul Radin (New York, Appleton, 1927), and in "The Child's Religion," by Pierre Bovet (London, Dent, 1928). There is much writing upon it in England, and such works as "The Golden Bough" and "The Belief in Immortality," by J. G. Frazer, have become well known, but they are to be read with caution. Frazer's generalizations are based upon the reports of a multitude of observers in the field, and many of them were far from scientific. He changed his conclusions more than once, and it seems likely that they will be further changed by later investigators. Much new (and far better) light upon the ways of thinking of primitive man is to be found in the books of Bronislaw Malinowski, especially in "The Sexual Life of Savages" (New York, Liveright, 1929). The works of such Englishmen as W. H. R. Rivers and W. J. Perry are even more open to doubt than those of Frazer. These men, following G. Elliot Smith, hold that most human ideas of any significance, including most religious ideas, originated in Egypt, and were thence dispersed throughout the world. It is a theory that has little support in the known facts. In the hands of Perry it only too often reduces itself to absurdity, as readers of his "Origin of Magic and Religion" (London, Methuen, 1923) will quickly discern. Nevertheless, that book also offers some acute observations, and is well worth reading.

There are many so-called handbooks of religion, covering the whole field from the simple superstitions of savages to the highly complicated and refined theologies of the Christian sects. Perhaps the best of them is Crawford H. Toy's "Introduction to the History of Religions" (Cambridge, Harvard University Press, 1924). It is impartially written, and contains a great deal of curious and interesting matter. Another useful book, though on a somewhat smaller scale, is E. Washburn Hopkins's "Origin and Evolution of Religion" (New Haven, Yale University Press, 1923), and yet another, still more modest, is "The Birth and Growth of Religion," by George Foot Moore (New York, Scribner, 1923). A discussion of the subject from a strictly Christian point of view is to be found in "The Philosophy of Religion," by George Galloway (New York, Scribner, 1914). In "Religion in the Making," by

A. N. Whitehead (New York, Macmillan, 1926), the approach is philosophical, and there are many interesting and valuable observations. But Dr. Whitehead occasionally indulges himself, like all metaphysicians, in what has a suspicious resemblance to nonsense.

Perhaps the best recent discussion of Christianity is to be found in "The History of Christianity in the Light of Modern Knowledge" (New York, Harcourt, 1929), a cooperative work by twenty-two English and American scholars, including Gilbert Murray. The point of view is very enlightened, and much useful and unfamiliar matter is got into relatively small space. The chapter on the life of Jesus, by Professor F. C. Burkitt of Cambridge, is a little masterpiece. There is more sound learning and penetrating judgment in it than is to be found in the whole array of popular works on the same subject, from that of Renan to that of Papini. An intelligent discussion of the Bible, Christian in approach but sufficiently scientific, is in "A New Commentary on Holy Scripture, Including the Apocrypha," by Dr. Charles Gore, formerly Bishop of Oxford, and various collaborators (London, Society for Promoting Christian Knowledge, 1928). It is a large work, and presents the results of recent philological and archeological research very fairly, though without surrendering the sacred authority of the Bible. In connection with it "The History and Literature of Christianity from Tertullian to Boethius," by Pierre De Labriolle, should be read (New York, Knopf, 1925).

Of books planned to blow up Christianity there are hundreds, but most of them are trash. One of the best is "The Bible From the Standpoint of the Higher Criticism," by Ramsden Balmforth (London, Swan Sonnenschein, 1904).

Another, somewhat more truculent in tone, is "Is It God's Word?", by Joseph Wheless (New York, Knopf, 1927). An excellent historical conspectus of Christian dogma and polity, generally hostile but very learned, is to be found in "Christianity Past and Present," by Charles Guignebert (New York, Macmillan, 1927), and a good account of the dependence of Christianity upon earlier religions, many of them barbaric, is in "The Paganism in Our Christianity," by Arthur Weigall (New York, Putnam, 1928). Other books that are interesting and useful are "Unravelling the Book of Books," by Ernest R. Trattner (New York, Scribner, 1929), an excellent short account of the history of the Bible, and especially of the Old Testament; "Jesus or Christianity," by Kirby Page (New York, Doubleday, 1929), in which the author argues that modern Christianity is greatly damaged by abandoning the ethics of Jesus; "The Twilight of Christianity," by Harry Elmer Barnes (New York, Vanguard Press, 1929), in which exactly the opposite line is taken, and there is much about the failure of Christianity to meet the needs of modern man; "Religion and the Modern World," by John Herman Randall and John Herman Randall, Jr. (New York, Stokes, 1929); "The Christ of the New Testament" and "Christ the Word," by Paul Elmer More (Princeton, University Press, 1924 and 1927), in which an effort is made to reconcile Christianity and Neo-Platonism; "Pagan Christs," by John M. Robertson (London, Watts, 1928); and "Religion in Human Affairs," by Clifford Kirkpatrick (New York, Wiley, 1929). Nor should the reader neglect such classics as "The Development of Christianity," by Otto Pfleiderer (New York, Huebsch, 1910) and "Christian Origins," by the same author (New York, Huebsch,

1916); the various attempts to put the New Testament into modern English, by Edgar J. Goodspeed (Chicago, University Press, 1923), William G. Ballantine (Boston, Houghton, 1923), James Moffatt (London, Hodder-Stoughton, 1913), Richard Francis Weymouth (New York, Baker-Taylor, n.d.) and others; and Montague Rhodes James's scholarly work on "The Apocryphal New Testament" (Oxford, Clarendon Press, 1924).

The story of the long battle between Christian theology and the scientific spirit is magnificently set forth in Andrew D. White's "History of the Warfare of Science with Theology in Christendom" (New York, Appleton, 1896). This work has been attacked vigorously by Christian apologists, chiefly Catholic, but its main facts and contentions remain unshaken. It is one of the noblest monuments of American scholarship, and deserves to be read far more widely than it is. There is correlative reading of high interest and value in "The Conquest of Civilization," by James Henry Breasted (New York, Harper, 1926), and no one, of course, will overlook Thomas Henry Huxley's two series of essays, "Science and Hebrew Tradition" and "Science and Christian Tradition," both obtainable in his Collected Works (New York, Appleton, 1894).

The literature of Christian exegesis and apologetics is immense, but it consists mainly of pious works of small persuasiveness. The best exposition of Catholic doctrine is probably "The Faith of Our Fathers," by the late Cardinal Gibbons (110th ed., New York, Kenedy, 1945). Another excellent book, addressed to rather more sophisticated readers, is "The Spirit of Catholicism," by Karl Adam (New York, Macmillan, 1929). Other works worth reading are "A Manual of Theology for the Laity," by P. Geiermann (New York, Benziger, 1906); "Handbook of the Christian Religion," by W. Wilmers (New York, Benziger, 1891); and, of course, the various official catechisms, of which "Catechism of Christian Doctrine, No. 4" (Philadelphia, McVey, 1918) is one of the best. The reader who desires to go still further into the faith and practices of Holy Church will find much to interest him in "Pastoral Theology," by William Stang (New York, Benziger, 1891); "The Roman Curia," by Michael Martin (New York, Benziger, 1913); "The Mass and Vestments of the Catholic Church," by John Walsh (New York, Benziger, 1916); and "Catechism of the Vows," by Peter Cotel (New York, Benziger, 1924). A learned and devastating attack upon the Catholic position is in "Catholicism and Christianity," by C. J. Cadoux (New York, Dial Press, 1929). Some of the Protestant denominations print official statements of their dogmas. Those of the Methodists, now combined, after long years of hard effort by consecrated theologians, into one body, are set forth in "The Doctrines and Discipline of the Methodist Episcopal Church" (New York, Methodist Book Concern, annually). That of the Baptists is in "The New Directory for Baptist Churches," by E. T. Hiscox (Philadelphia, American Baptist Publication Society, 1928). The other denominations tend to be less explicit, and it is often hard to find out precisely what they teach. Many of them, in fact, frequently change their doctrines. Even such extreme doctrinaires as the Seventh Day Adventists occasionally do so. A spirited defense of the general Protestant position is to be found in "Faith and Its Psychology," by W. R. Inge (New York, Scribner, 1910).

The best account of the older Eastern and Mediterranean

religions is in the first three volumes of Will Durant's admirable series, "The Story of Civilization," to wit, "Our Oriental Heritage" (New York, Simon and Schuster, 1935), "The Life of Greece" (New York, the same, 1939), and "Caesar and Christ" (New York, the same, 1944). This work is a conspectus of cultural history, and pays constant heed to the flux of theologies. It is learned, it is clearly arranged, and it is very skillfully written. Conspectuses of various other non-Christian religions are in the series of little books called "Religions: Ancient and Modern" (Chicago, Open Court, 1909). They include animism, Mohammedanism, and the cults of the Celts, the early Britons, the Teutonic peoples, and the Aztecs, Mayas and Incans. The authors are all recognized authorities. But the articles in the Hastings Encyclopedia often present the same facts in greater detail. A good brief review of the principal religions, ancient and modern, is also in Otto Pfleiderer's "Religion and Historic Faiths" (New York, Huebsch, 1907). On Mohammedanism the most useful special book is "Islam: Beliefs and Institutions," by H. Lammens (London, Methuen, 1929). On Hinduism in its various current forms the most instructive recent authorities are "The Essentials of Eastern Philosophy," by Prabbu Dutt Shastri (New York, Macmillan, 1928), and "Hindu Mysticism," by S. N. Dasgupta (Chicago, Open Court, 1927). I know of no comprehensive book in English on the practices of the modern Jews.

*Soli Deo gloria!*

# Index

Aaronites, 25, 92
Abiram, 137
Abraham, 140, 141, 148, 196
Abraham ben Meir ibn Esra, 193
Abrams, Albert, 289
Absolution, 100, 125
Abstinence, 124
Accidents of Eucharist, 28
Achelous, 85
Acheron, 156
Acts of the Apostles, 178, 185, 189, 224, 235
Adam, 172, 195
Adam, Karl, 300
Adonis, 144, 149, 202, 227
Adultery, 162, 184, 185, 186, 269
Aeschylus, 87
Africans, 39, 105, 126, 128, 155
Agape, 127
Agnosticism, 86. See also Skepticism
Ahaz, 137
Ahura Mazda, 164
Ailbert, St., 107
Akbar, 66
Albinos, 142
Albiorix, 62
Alexander of Macedon, 65, 83
Alexandrine Church, 190
al Hamdu li-'llah, 123
All, the, 88
Allah, 165
Ama-terasu no Ohokami, 67
Amelu, 101
Amen, 114

Amen-Hotep, IV, 63, 114
Ame-no-mi-naka-nushi-no-kami, 170
American Revolution, 26
Ames, E. S., 295
Amish, 196
Amon, 63, 90
Amon-Rê, 63, 68
Ampere, A. M., 258
Anaxagoras, 86, 102
Andaman Islanders, 117
Animism, 7, 302
Anna, St., 187, 188
Annunciation, 124, 150, 209
Apocrypha, 186, 204, 236, 300
Apollo, 138, 160
Apollonius of Tyana, 150
Apollyon, 160
Apostles' Creed, 123
Apostles, Twelve, 176, 184, 219
Apostolic succession, 174
Arabic language, 112, 113
Aramaic language, 177, 179, 203, 210
Ararat, 172
Arcadia, 85
Arcesilaus, 87
Archbishop, 4, 62
Arians, 152, 238
Aristotle, 87, 285
Arius, 152
Armenians, 65, 117
Arta-i Viraf, 164, 167
Artemis, 142
Asculum, 142
Asia Minor, cults of, 83, 86, 92
Asklepios, 85

Asoka, 141
Asperges, 118
Aspittavana, 162
Assisi, Francis, 7
Assyrians, 81, 112, 115
Ataro, 164
Athanasians, 152
Athanasius, 152, 190, 204
Athapascan Indians, 170
Atheists, 39
Athenians, 85, 102, 232
Athens, 85, 88, 138, 233
Atonement, 127, 130 ff, 226, 247, 284
Atonement, Day of, 135
Attila, 81
Attis, 144
Augustine, St., 7, 230, 231
Augustus, Emperor, 191
Australia, 65
Australians, 51
Ave Maria, 107, 122
Avernus, 96
Avesta, 65, 192
Avichi, 161
Aztecs, 59, 64, 79, 92, 100, 105, 115, 125, 128, 135, 136, 142, 143, 154, 302

Baal, 197, 198
Babel, Tower of, 120, 196
Babylonia, 61, 62, 64, 89, 90, 96, 197, 199, 218, 222
Babylonian captivity, 92, 115, 217
Babylonians, 16, 65, 81, 100, 112, 113, 115, 116, 118, 144, 150, 171, 172, 202
Bacchus, 132
Bach, Johann Sebastian, 145, 250

Bacon, Roger, 246
Badawis, 107
Bahlul ben Dhu'aih, 107
Bakua, 110
Balfour, A. J., 246
Ballantine, William G., 300
Balmforth, Ramsden, 298
Baptism, 100, 125, 126, 127, 184, 185, 187, 225
Baptists, 10, 32, 41, 55, 58, 97, 104, 127, 196, 267, 279, 280, 284, 292, 301
Bar Abbas, 150, 151
Barbarossa, 16, 79
Barnabas, Book of, 190
Barnes, Harry Elmer, 299
Barrett, E. Boyd, 104
Bartimeus, 183
Baruch, Book of, 204
Basilides of Alexandria, 189
Beatitudes, 233, 234, 287
Bells, 120, 121, 124
Benedict, Rule of St., 84, 107
Bentham, Jeremy, 258
Bernard of Clairvaux, 7
Bethlehem, 116, 175
Bethlehem, Star of, 207
Bible Belt, 259
Bible, King James, 10, 32, 113, 116, 201, 205
Bible, translations of, 112
Bishop, 95, 101, 106, 174, 226, 260, 267, 270
Blasphemy, 101
Blessing of Mass, 118
Blood sacrifice, 136, 284
Bloody sweat, 185, 186
Book of Common Prayer, 204, 283
Book of the Dead, 192
Boshkoi, 107

Boswell, James, 192
Bovet, Pierre, 42, 296
Brahmanism, 7, 44, 122, 123, 288
Brahmans, 25, 92
Breasted, J. H., 114, 217, 218, 300
Briffault, R. S., 72, 126
Bronze Age, 115
Buddha, 149
Buddhism, 7, 68, 95, 122, 123, 125, 126, 141, 160 ff, 283, 284, 287, 288
Bull-roarer, 120
Bulls as gods, 78
Burgundians, 80
Burial clubs, 226
Burial customs, 40, 41
Burkitt, F. C., 298

Cabbala, 44
Cadoux, C. J., 279, 301
Caesar, Julius, 135
Caiaphas, 150
Calvinism, 8, 272, 283
Calvin, John, 26, 82, 244, 260, 280
Cana, miracle at, 102
Candler, Asa G., 131
Candles, 120, 124, 283
Cannibalism, 56, 284
Canossa, 239
Cardinal, 107
Carneades, 87
Carpenter, 62
Carter, J. B., 168
Caste, 93, 101
Castelius, 236
Castor and Pollux, 146
Catacombs, 226
Catharine of Siena, St., 7

Catholic Encyclopedia, 295
Catholic orders, 9
Catholics. See Roman Catholics
Cato, 84
Celibacy, 97, 101, 104, 136, 235 ff
Celts, 61, 62, 95, 155, 302
Centeotl, 136
Ceres, 83
Ceylon, 126
Charity, 117, 120
Chastity, 97, 104, 235 ff
Child, mind of the, 37 ff, 98
Children of the Sun, 76 ff
Chinese, 58, 67, 89, 115, 117, 123, 124, 142
Chippewa Indians, 137
Chosen People, 134, 147. See also Jews
Christian Science, 8, 88, 111, 280, 289
Christmas, 66
Chrysostom, St., 96, 272
Chu, 142
Ch'un Ch'iu, 142
Church and state, 26 ff, 89 ff, 94
Church-spire, 120
Cicero, 83
Cihuatcoatl, 125
Cinderella story, 288
Circumcision, 105, 133, 225
Civil War, American, 26
Clement of Alexandria, 186
Coca-cola, 41
Commandments, Ten, 267
Communion, 100, 117, 125, 127 ff
Communism, 26
Comstockery, 101
Con, 170

Confession, 124, 279
Confucianism, 68, 111, 285
Confucius, 142
Consciousness, 37
Constance, Council of, 242
Constantine, Emperor, 189, 238
Contraception, 97
Convert, 99
Copernicus, 259
Coppersmith, 62
Corinth, 177
Corn god, 130
Corn Mother, 60
Cosmogonies, 103, 169 ff, 252
Creation, 169 ff, 193
Credo. See Apostles' Creed
Cross, 115, 121. See also Crucifix
Cross, sign of the, 125
Crow Indians, 101, 110
Crucifix, 124
Crucifixion, 124, 150, 176, 177, 212, 220, 229
Crusades, 240
Cyprian, 230, 231
Cyrus, 217

Damasan canon of the Bible, 190, 191
Damasus, Pope, 190
Damiani, Cardinal, 107
Damien, Father, 279
Danaë, 146
Dante, 164, 167
Dark Ages, 240 ff
Darwin, Charles, 252
Dasgupta, S. N., 302
David, 25, 147, 195, 208, 221
Dawn-Man, 12, 15 ff
Death, primitive views of, 40 ff
Decii, 141, 142

deFlue, Nicholas, 107
Deformes, 156
Delos, 138
Demeter, 83, 85
Demiurge, 88
Democritus, 86
Demons, 91, 120, 244
Dendrites, 107
Dervishes, 107
Dervonnœ, 63
Deuteronomy, Book of, 194 ff, 269
Devil, 55, 121, 207, 230, 244, 266
Dhu'l-Hijjah, 133
Diaspora, 225
Didach, 190
Diderot, Denis, 247
Dinka, 142
Diodorus Siculus, 135
Dionysos, 85, 86, 88, 144
Disciples, 148, 151, 176, 209, 214, 223, 224, 226
Divorce, 97
Dominic, St., 124
Dominican rosary, 124
Dowie, Alexander, 231
Doxology, 185, 186
Druji-gereda, 163
Drujo-demana, 163
Dryads, 63
Duke, James G., 132
Dunkards, 196
Durant, Will, 302
Dushmata, 164
Dushukta, 164
Dushvarshta, 164
Dwarfs, 82

Eabani, 171
Earth Mother, 60 ff, 68, 69, 71,

Earth Mother (*continued*)
74, 76, 82, 83, 130, 132, 133, 136, 168, 202
Easter, 66
Easter duty, 97, 98, 175, 279
Eastern empires, 216
Ecclesiastes, Book of, 158
Ecclesiasticus, Book of, 204
Eckchuah, 80
Eckermann, J. P., 192
Eddington, A. S., 88, 261
Eddy, Mary Baker G., 16, 231
Eden, Garden of, 147, 172, 195
Education, 98 ff
Edwards, Jonathan, 160
Egalitarianism, 220
Egypt, 48, 59, 63, 89, 90, 91, 92, 96, 142, 175, 182, 227
Egyptians, 25, 57, 63, 70, 77, 81, 99, 105, 114, 115, 116, 124, 125, 131, 135, 137, 138, 142, 145, 169, 170
Einstein, Albert, 234, 258, 265
Ekkehard of St. Gall, 7
Eleazer, 135
Elias, 176
Elisha, 149
Elks, 251, 256
Elohim, 195 ff
Encyclopedia of Religion and Ethics, 294, 302
England, 101, 216
England, Church of, 204
England, King of, 25
Enoch, Book of, 159
Epicureanism, 88
Episcopalians, 55, 124, 283
Epistle of Mass, 118
Eridu, 171
Eucharist, 27, 28, 41, 127 ff, 284
Euchites, 107

Euphrates, 172
Euripides, 86
Eusebius of Cæsaræ, 181, 189, 231
Eve, 195
Evidences, Christian, 264
Evil, problem of, 173, 285
Evolution, 252, 259
Exodus, Book of, 194 ff, 269
Exorcism, 91, 121
Ezekiel, 137, 147, 210

Fairies, 63
Faith, 99, 228, 264, 276
Fall of Man, 173
Fasting, 125, 136
Fatalism, 111
Father, physiological rôle of, 44 ff, 75 ff
Fatherhood of God, 221
Fauns, 63
Fays, 63
Feralia, 156
Fez, 119
Fiji, 145
Finland, 126
Fire, the god, 53 ff, 62
Fire-Bringer, 11
Flight into Egypt, 175, 229
Flood myth, 16 ff, 172, 193
Flood, the god, 53
Flower, J. Cyril, 296
Fornication, 102, 184
Francis de Sales, St., 130
Frankincense, 116, 120
Franklin, Benjamin, 250, 251
Frazer, J. G., 128, 129, 296, 297
Frederick the Great, 250
Freemasons, 275, 279
Freudism, 262
Freya, 61

Fundamentalism, 264, 281, 282
Funeral, 91
Furiæ, 156

Gadarene swine, 183, 210
Gaia, 61
Galatians, Epistle to, 229
Galilee, Sea of, 211
Galileo, 246, 252
Galloway, George, 297
Ganges, 137
Gantry, Elmer, 279
Garo-demana, 163
Garonmana, 163
Garotman, 163
Gathas, 163
Gauls, 135, 181
Ge Ben-Himmom, 137
Geiermann, P., 300
Genesis, Book of, 103, 140, 171, 172, 173, 194 ff, 252, 260
Gentiles, 225
George III, King, 26
George, Henry, 289
Germans, 82
Germany, church and state in, 3, 26
Gethsemane, 213
Ghosts, 46 ff, 153, 162
Giants, 82
Gibbon, Edward, 247
Gibbons, James Cardinal, 300
Gilgamesh legend, 171
Gloria of the Mass, 118, 123
Gnomes, 63
Gnostics, 187, 227, 232
Gods: nature of, 5; origin of, 31 ff
Gofannon, 62
Golden Rule, 234
Goodspeed, Edgar J., 300

Good-will, 234
Gore, Charles, 298
Gospel of the Mass, 118
Goyim, 134
Great Mother, 62
Greece, 61, 86, 96, 215
Greek Church, 124
Greek language, 177, 179, 231
Greek Orthodox Church, 204
Greeks, 16, 63, 84 ff, 92, 116, 117, 125, 137, 142, 149, 151, 152, 155, 156, 197, 202, 218, 239, 260
Gregorian chant, 124
Gregory VII, Pope, 93, 107, 242
Guatemala, 80
Guignebert, Charles, 299

Hagar, 140
Hail Mary, 123
Haiti, 155
Halo, 125
Hamadryads, 63
Hambalites, 112
Hamistagan, 164
Hammurabi, 100
Hanifites, 112
Happy Hunting Grounds, 155
Harnack, Adolf, 129, 189, 232
Harvard University, 252
Harvey, William, 246, 252
Hastings, James, 294, 295
Hastings' Encyclopedia of Religion and Ethics, 171, 294, 302
Hathor, 57
Heaven, in general, 36, 49, 95, 117, 153 ff; of Oceania, 155; of American Indians, 155; of Haitians, 155; of Patagonians, 155; of Celts, 155; of

Heaven (*continued*)
Greeks, 155; of Teutons, 155; of Jews, 157 ff; of Buddhists, 160 ff; of Persians, 163; of Moslems, 165 ff, 246
Hebrew language, 112, 202
Hebrews, Epistle to the, 189
Hebrews, Gospel According to the, 186, 187, 190
Heinz, Henry J., 131
Hel, 155
Helen of Troy, 146
Hell, in general, 36, 49, 95, 153 ff; of Christians, 96, 98, 103, 175 ff, 242, 246, 252, 267, 268, 272; of Jews, 157 ff; of Buddhists, 160 ff; of Persians, 163, 284; of Moslems, 165 ff; of Parsees, 284
Henry IV, Emperor, 93, 239
Henry VII, King, 92
Herbermann, Charles G., 295
Heresy, 229, 234
Hermes, 149
Herod, 67, 147, 175, 214, 222
Herod Agrippa, 224
Herodotus, 116, 137
Herschel, William, 266
Herzog, J. J., 294
Heterousians, 152
Hexateuch, 194 ff
Hiddekel, 172
Hiel, 137
Higher criticism, 191 ff
Hilary, 231
Hilkiah, 198, 199
Hindus, 16, 106, 112, 302
Hiscox, E. T., 301
Hitler, Adolf, 194, 289
Hobbes, Thomas, 194

Holy Ghost, 102, 127, 151 ff, 165, 203, 227, 282
Holy Office, Congregation of the, 186, 259
Holy Rollers, 7, 122, 196, 280
Holy water, 124
Holy Week, 145
Homer, 86, 216
Homoiousians, 152
Homoousians, 152
Hoover, Herbert, 26
Hopi Indians, 117
Hopkins, E. Washburn, 297
Horus, 57, 63, 151
Hosea, 147
Hosea, Book of, 229
Hosius of Cordova, 238
Host, Elevation of the, 125
Huayna-Kapac, 64
Huitzilopochtli, 125, 128, 129, 136
Hukhta, 163
Humanism, 252
Humata, 163
Humility, 234
Hunabku, 80
Huns, 80
Huntington, Ellsworth, 273
Huxley, T. H., 234, 269, 300
Hvarshta, 163
Hymns, 113 ff

Iconium, 236
Ieoud, 150
Images, 124, 125, 128
Immaculate Conception, 188
Immortality, 40, 226, 262
Imperialism, 216
Incans, 64, 125, 146, 302
Incense, 115, 116, 117, 120, 121, 124

*Index Expurgatorius,* 258
India, 65, 88, 128, 133, 137, 149, 160, 169, 284
Indians, American, 48, 65, 105, 113, 155
Indians, Guatemalan, 79
Industrial Revolution, 36, 249 ff
Infallibility, papal, 30, 243
Inge, W. R., 301
Innocent III, Pope, 242
Inti, 64
Ioacim, 187
Iphigenia, 142
Irenæus, 179, 180, 189, 230
Iroquois Indians, 170
Isaac, 140
Isaiah, 137, 147, 158, 200
Isawis, 117
Ishtar, 171
Isis, 68, 151
Isles of the Blest, 155
Israelites, 67
Italians, 21, 53
Italy, church and state in, 26

Jacob, 196
James, Book of, 187, 190
James, Epistle of, 189
James, Montague Rhodes, 300
James the Apostle, 184, 210, 224
James, William, 291, 295
Jamnia, 204
Japan, 103, 123, 126, 284
Japanese, 67 ff, 170, 273
Jefferson, Thomas, 26, 250, 251, 269, 273, 289
Jeremiah, 137, 199
Jericho, 210
Jeroboam, 196
Jerome, St., 185, 186, 190, 204, 205, 229, 230, 231

Jerusalem, 175, 206, 225
Jesuits, 102, 104, 236
Jesus, 55, 60, 67, 95, 116, 134, 148 ff, 165, 174 ff, 192, 206 ff, 284
Jewish Encyclopedia, 295
Jews, 7, 16, 65, 92, 96, 115, 116, 119, 122, 124, 128, 132, 133, 137, 140, 147 ff, 171, 172, 184, 195 ff, 208, 213, 214, 216, 225, 273, 278, 286 ff. *See also* Judaism
Jih-pun-Kwoh, 67
Jinns, 63, 117
Job, Book of, 287
John, Epistles of, 189, 190
John, Gospel of, 148, 149, 176, 179 ff, 220, 228, 287
John-Joseph de la Croix, St., 107
John of the Cross, St., 107
John, St., 159, 160, 167, 180
John the Apostle, 184, 210
John the Baptist, 175, 187, 206, 207, 208, 214, 222
Jonah, 231
Joseph, 148, 175
Joseph of Arimathea, 223
Joseph of Copertius, St., 107
Josiah, 67, 198, 199
Judaism, 89, 226, 228, 229, 232, 284, 288. *See also* Jews
Judas, 176, 224, 229
Jude, Epistle of, 189, 190
Judgment, 165, 220
Judith, Book of, 204
Justin Martyr, 189, 230

Ka, 37
Kalasutta, 161
Kami, 68

Kami-musu-bi-no-kami, 170
Kanaloa, 170
Kant, Immanuel, 247
Kemal Pasha, 119
Kepler, Johann, 266
King of the World, 62
Kings, Book of, 137, 198, 200, 269
Kinichhau, 64
Kirkpatrick, Clifford, 299
Kneeling, 119
Kobolds, 63
Koran, 112, 165 ff, 273
Korea, 123
Krishma, 150
Kronos, 150
Kukkula, 162

Labriolle, Pierre de, 298
Lady Potter, 62
Lamas, 110, 122, 123, 126
Lamb of God, 134
Lammens, H., 113, 302
Land of the Rising Sun, 67
Lansbury, George, 274
Lapps, 126
Larvæ, 156
Last Supper, 212
Lateran Council, Fourth, 27
Latin language, 111, 177, 203
Latin War, 142
Laurent, Father, 107
Lavoisier, A. L., 258
Law, Jewish, 184, 199, 209, 232
Lazarus, 149
Leda, 146
Leeuwenhoek, Antony van, 246, 252
Leibniz, G. W., 246, 252
Lemuria, 156

Lent, 107, 117
Leo XIII, Pope, 124
Leuba, James H., 49, 274, 295
Levites, 25, 92
Leviticus, Book of, 137, 194 ff, 273
Lex talionis, 235
Li Chi, 111
Lightning, the god, 53, 62
Lights, 115
Limbo, 154, 165
Lincoln, Abraham, 26, 289
Little Bethel, 196, 286
Little Flower, 60
Locke, John, 258
Lodge, Oliver, 88
Logia, 178, 179
Logos, 88, 151, 197, 227
Lord's Prayer. See Paternoster
Lowie, Robert H., 109, 296
Loyola, Ignatius, 7
Lucian, 86
Luke, Gospel of, 148, 175, 176, 177 ff, 209, 210, 211, 213
Luke, St., 178, 224
Luther, Martin, 9, 114, 190, 191, 204, 237, 242, 244, 280
Lutherans, 9, 10, 191, 273
Lynd, Helen M., 288
Lynd, Robert S., 288

Maccabees, 92
Maccabees, Book of, 204
Magi, 66, 67, 116, 207
Magic, 13 ff, 27 ff, 297
Mahabharata, 145
Maia, 149
Malay language, 112
Malays, 48
Malikites, 112

# INDEX

Malinowski, Bronislaw, 44, 297
Manasseh, 137, 197, 198
Manes, 156
Manichæism, 227
Mansion of the Sun, 154
Manu, Laws of, 105, 106, 192
Mariolatry, 69
Maritala, 150
Mark, Gospel of, 148, 149, 177 ff, 207, 209, 210, 211, 212, 213, 219, 228, 264
Mars Hill, 232
Martin, Michael, 301
Martyrdom, 214, 215
Marx, Karl, 277, 289
Mary. *See* Virgin Mary
Mary Magdalene, 223
Mass, Catholic, 6, 7, 27, 28, 110, 113, 117, 118, 283, 287
Mather, Increase, 252
Mathew, Gospel of, 102, 116, 127, 148, 175, 176, 177 ff, 209, 210, 211, 212, 213, 219, 223, 228, 269
Mathew, St., 178, 187
Matriarchate, 72 ff
Matthias the Apostle, 224
Mauliwis, 107, 108, 117
Maya, 149
Mayas, 64, 79, 80, 170, 302
Mecca, 66, 119, 133, 167
Medals, 121
Medina, 107, 167
Melanesians, 44, 170
Mendel, Gregor, 258
Mennonites, 280
Merodach, 64, 65
Mesopotamia, 65, 77, 79, 119, 216, 227
Mesopotamians, 25
Messiah, 147 ff, 208 ff

Metaphysics, 87, 138, 151, 153, 169, 227, 228, 261, 298
Metempsychosis, 44 ff
Methodists, 55, 95, 101, 106, 113, 125, 127, 170, 196, 202, 234, 251, 257, 267, 273, 279, 281, 283, 301
Methodius, 231
Methusaleh, 172
Mew, James, 96
Mexicans, 16, 61, 65, 80, 115, 129, 135
Mexico, church and state in, 3
Micah, 137, 147
Mictlan, 154
Middle Ages, 36, 59, 237
Midsummer Eve, 67
Mikado of Japan, 67, 83
Milhakupa, 162
Mill, John Stuart, 258
Millennium, 208
Millikan, Robert A., 88, 261
Mind Force, 232
Minutius, 231
Miracles, 149, 183, 231, 259
Mishkat al-Masabih, 167
Missions, 57, 58, 181, 184, 229
Mithra, 65, 67, 144
Mithraism, 65, 66, 151, 226, 227
Moffatt, James, 300
Mogounus, 62
Mohammed, 167. *See also* Moslemism
Monasteries, 93
Monks, 93
Moore, George Foot, 297
Morality, its relation to religion, 4
Moral theology, 54, 96 ff
More, Paul Elmer, 87, 260, 269, 299

# INDEX

Moriah, 140
Mormons, 55, 264, 280
Morocco, 117
Moses, 16, 67, 134, 194, 196, 199
Moslemism, 7, 44, 66, 89, 107, 111, 112, 113, 117, 119, 122, 123, 128, 133, 165 ff, 284, 285, 288, 302
Mother of Gods, 62
Mother of Men, 62
Muazaga-gu-abzu, 122
Mundzuk, 81
Murray, Gilbert, 227, 298
Myrrh, 116, 120
Myrrha, 149
Mysticism, 7 ff, 272

Naiads, 63
Na-strand, 155
Nazareth, 175
Nazis, 80
Near East, 216 ff
Negritoes, 126
Negroes, American, 79
Neith, 57
Neolithic Man, 138
Neptune, 55
Nereids, 63
Nero, 224
Nestorians, 117
New Deal, 289
Newman, John H., 230
New Testament, 55, 60, 175 ff, 197, 200, 229, 236, 242, 243, 285, 286
Newton, Isaac, 246, 252
Nicæa, Council of, 152, 190, 238, 239, 283
Nicene Creed, 238
Nietzsche, F. W., 247, 291

Nifhel, 155
Nigeria, 136
Ninlil, 61
Nirvana, 163
Niskai, 63
Nixies, 63
Noah, 16, 196
Nogi, 214, 215
Numbers, Book of, 134, 135, 194 ff

Obedience, 136
Oceania, 155
Oceanids, 63
O'Connell, William H., 234, 265
Odin, 16, 144
Offertory, 117, 118
Oils, 115, 121, 124
Oktar, 80
Old Church Slavonic language, 112
Old Man, 23 ff, 33, 54, 76
Old Testament, 16, 55, 60, 67, 78, 116, 134, 147, 159, 184, 192 ff, 229, 231, 243, 263, 281, 285, 286
Olympus, 163
Om manipadme Hum, 122, 123
Oreads, 63
Origen, 186, 189, 204, 230, 231
Original Sin, 126, 174, 227
Orphism, 88
Osborn, Henry Fairfield, 88
Osiris, 114, 135, 151, 227

Pacha-Kamac, 64
Page, Kirby, 299
Palestine, 172, 203, 204
Pamphilus, 181
Pan, 85

Papias, 178
Papini, Giovanni, 298
Papuans, 126
Paradise, 167, 172
Parsees, 66, 164, 165, 284, 288
Paschal lamb, 134
Passover, 135, 150
Pasteur, Louis, 258
Patagonia, 155
Paternoster, 122, 123, 185, 186
Patrick, Mary Mills, 87
Paul, Acts of, 190
Paul, Epistles of, 148, 177, 182, 189, 200, 282
Paul III, Pope, 191
Paul, St., 89, 178, 180, 224, 228, 229, 232, 233, 234, 236, 244, 282
Peace of Augsburg, 70
Penance, 125
Pentateuch, 193 ff
Pentecost, 224
Pericles, 102, 138, 251
Pericope Adulteræ, 185, 186
Perry, W. J., 51, 62, 145, 297
Perseus, 146
Persia, 65, 92, 160, 163
Persian Gulf, 171
Persian language, 112
Persians, 16, 96, 116, 149, 163, 164
Personality, 37
Peruvians, 16, 70, 170
Peter, St., 176, 180, 211, 212, 224, 226
Peter, Apocalypse of, 190
Peter Celestine, St., 107
Peter, Epistles of, 179, 189, 190
Peter, Gospel of, 188
Pfleiderer, Otto, 299, 302

Pharisees, 150, 183, 209, 220, 222
Philippines, 126
Philo of Alexandria, 88
Philostratus, 150
Phlegethon, 96
Piaget, Jean, 37, 43
Pillar of Fire Brethren, 196
Pius II, Pope, 251
Pius IX, Pope, 30, 270, 279
Plato, 86, 87, 218, 260, 285
Poetry, 13, 286 ff
Polterberg, 244
Polynesia, 65, 73, 105, 170
Polynesians, 16, 21, 120, 124, 128
Pontius Pilate, 213, 222
Pope, his temporal power, 3. See also Infallibility, papal
Poverty, 136, 234
Pratapana, 161
Pratt, J. B., 295
Prayer, 25, 115, 121 ff, 168, 169
Prayer-wheel, 110, 115, 123
Predestination, 111
Preface of Mass, 118
Presbyterians, 8, 202, 281, 294
Presence, the, 88
President of the United States, 25, 256, 273, 279
Pretas, 162
Priests, the first, 11 ff; their rise, 89 ff; in Babylonia, 89, 90; in Egypt, 90, 91; Jewish, 91; in Persia, 92; in Asia Minor, 92; in Mexico, 92; in Greece, 92; in England, 92; in Spain, 92; in Germany, 92; in Tibet, 92; in India, 92; their duties, 104 ff
Prohibition, 3, 101, 256, 267

Prostration, 119
Protestants, 9 ff, 26, 60, 99, 103, 104, 117, 131, 191, 204, 205, 233, 237, 243, 259, 264, 280 ff, 301
Protoevangelium, 187
Proverbs, Book of, 287
Psalms, 229, 287, 293
Pueblo Indians, 51, 52
Punt, Land of, 116
Purgatory, 49
Puritanism, 245, 251, 283
Pyrrhonism, 87

Q, 177
Qadris, 107
Qat, 170
Quadrivœ, 63
Quakerism, 111

Radin, Paul, 296
Rain, the god, 53 ff, 62, 136
Rak'ahs, 119
Ramadan, 117
Rameses II, 64
Randall, John Herman, 299
Raymi, 125
Rê, 59, 63, 64, 114, 145, 170, 266
Real Presence, 243
Recessional, 125
Reformation, 70, 93, 98, 113, 190, 204, 239, 241 ff
Reform Bill of 1832, 26
Relics, 115
Reliquaries, 121
Renaissance, 242, 246 ff
Renan, Ernest, 286, 298
Requiem Mass, 118
Resurrection, 124, 176, 191, 222 ff, 264
Resurrection of the body, 227

Retreats, 283
Revelation, Book of, 7, 148, 159, 179, 189, 190, 228
Revised Versions of the Bible, 205
Rhodes, 150
Rifa'is, 107
Risorgimento, 26
Ritual, the first, 20
Rites, Book of, 111
Rivers, W. H. R., 297
Robertson, John M., 299
Robinson, James Harvey, 277
Rockefeller Institute, 267
Roman Catholic Church, 26, 27, 97, 98, 99, 110, 279 ff
Roman Catholics, 10, 103, 259, 273, 279, 283, 284, 300, 301
Roman Empire, 36
Roman religions, 82 ff
Romans, 65, 82, 116, 142, 148, 150, 151, 156, 168, 169, 207, 216, 219, 225, 226
Romans, Epistle to the, 234
Rome, 96, 216, 273
Rome, Council of, 190
Roosevelt, Eleanor, 290
Roosevelt, F. D., 25, 290
Roruva, 161
Rosary, 122 ff
Rotary, 284, 288, 289
Rousseau, J. J., 247
Russia, 216
Russia, church and state in, 3, 26, 93
Russia, Czar of, 25
Russians, 142
Ruth, Book of, 201, 205, 287

Sabbath, 134, 183
Sacco and Vanzetti, 289

Sacrifice, 91, 130 ff
Sadducees, 158
Sadhus, 106
Saints, 59, 62, 125, 143, 264
Salat, 113, 119, 122
Salvation Army, 125, 196, 280
Samghata, 161
Samoans, 139, 145
Samuel, Book of, 269
Sanchkara, Pharaoh, 116
San Cristoval, 145
Sanctus, 118
Sanjiva, 161
Sanskrit language, 112, 123, 126
Santa Claus, 288
Sarah, 140
Sargon I, 81
Satan. *See* Devil
Sayce, A. H., 171
Scandinavians, 82, 135
Scapular, 124
Schaff-Herzog Encyclopedia, 294
Schochet, 132
Schwann, Theodor, 258
Science and religion, 260 ff
Scientific spirit, 13, 253 ff
Second Coming, 228 ff
Segub, 137
Sentinum, 142
Septuagint, 203 ff
Sermon on the Mount, 176, 287
Servetus, 244
Seventh Day Adventists, 196, 280
Severus of Trèves, 80
Shadhilis, 107
Shakespeare, 289
Shamanism, 7, 100
Shamash, 65, 101, 113, 114
Shastri, P. D., 302
Shelley, P. B., 289

Sheol, 49, 157
Shepherd of Hermes, 190
Shiites, 44
Shilluks, 142
Shinto, 67 ff, 273, 283, 287
Shorey, Paul, 86
Shub-ad, Queen, 139
Sikhs, 284
Simon, Richard, 194
Sinclair, Upton, 289
Skepticism, 31, 86 ff, 98, 136, 156, 157, 159, 218, 248, 253, 270
Slavery, 26
Smith, G. Elliot, 297
Smith, Joseph, 16, 231
Snataka, 105
Socialism, 220
Social Justice, 283
Socrates, 86, 138, 218
Sodom, 196
Solomon, Song of, 201, 202, 205, 287
Solomon's temple, 67
Solomon, Wisdom of, 204
Son of Man, 210, 212
Sophocles, 87
Soul, 37 ff
Spain, church and state in, 26
Spaniards, 79, 115, 135, 143, 154
Species of Eucharist, 28
Spence, Lewis, 100, 105, 115, 125, 128, 154
Spinoza, Baruch, 194
Spirit, 37
Spiritualism, 88
Spring and Autumn Annals, 142
Srosh, 164
Stang, William, 121, 301

Starbuck, E. C., 295
Stoicism, 88
Stone Age, 40, 290
Stowe, Harriet Beecher, 192
Stratton, G. M., 296
Stylites, 107, 108
Styx, 156
Sulis, 62
Sumer, 81, 139, 145
Sumerian language, 112
Sumerians, 16, 61, 100, 113,
  114, 118, 125, 145
Sun, the god, 53, 87, 101, 115,
  130, 143, 144, 154, 160, 266
Sun worship, 63 ff
Sunday, 66
Sunday, Billy, 283
Sunday laws, 101
Sunday-school, 99, 202
Suras, 112, 167
Swan maidens, 82
Swedenborgians, 280
Syllabus of Errors, 270, 279
Sylphs, 63
Sylvester I, Pope, 238
Syncretism, 226
Synoptic Gospels, 175 ff, 211,
  213, 232, 288
Syrophenician woman, 219

Taaroa, 170
Tabernacles, Feast of, 135
Taboo, 173
Tahara, 119
Taka-mi-musu-bi-no-kami, 170
Talmud, 133
Tammuz, 144, 202
Tangaloa, 170
Taoism, 7, 122
Tapana, 161
Tchuktchi, 142

Teaching of the Twelve Apos-
  tles, 190
Temmangu, 68
Temptation in the Wilderness,
  148
Tennessee, 101, 273
Teocalli, 136
Teotl, 64
Teresa, St., 7
Terra Mater, 83
Tertullian, 230
Tetramorph, 189
Teutonic Pantheon, 82, 83
Teutons, 96, 115, 126, 144, 155,
  302
Teuzoi, 90
Tezcatlipoca, 59, 128, 143
Thamyris, 236
Thecla, 236, 237
Theology, 139, 145, 182, 226,
  230, 240, 251, 260, 282
Theophagy, 56, 127 ff
Theophilus, 178
Theosophy, 44, 45, 88
Thessalonians, Epistles to, 177
Thessaly, 85
Thomas Aquinas, 7, 241, 242,
  260
Thor, 115
Thrace, 85
Tiberius, Emperor, 191
Tibet, 92, 110, 122, 126, 168,
  284
Tigris, 172
Timeus, 183
Tlaloc, 136
Tlaxcaltecs, 142
Tobit, Book of, 204
Todas, 128
Tonatiah, 64
Totems, 128

Toy, C. H., 51, 271, 272, 297
Transubstantiation, 56, 127 ff
Trappists, 8, 104, 107
Trattner, E. R., 195, 196, 299
Trent, Council of, 191, 204, 283
Trinity, 102, 151 ff, 174, 185,
    190, 197, 226, 227, 247, 284
Trolls, 63
Ts'ai, 142
Tso, 142
Turkish language, 112
Turks, 112, 119, 273
Tylor, E. B., 96

Uniat Churches, 126
Unitarians, 95, 122, 152, 251,
    273
United States, 101, 216, 251, 252
Unknown God, 232
Ur, 139
Urdu language, 112
Uren, A. R., 296

Valerian, Emperor, 66
Valhalla, 70, 83, 154, 155
Valkyries, 82
Vatican Council, 202
Vedas, 65, 192
Verrill, A. Hyatt, 64, 80
Vestment, 283
Vetarani, 162
Victor, 238
Victoria, Queen, 25
Vincentius, 238
Vintius, 62
Virgin Birth, 148, 149, 150, 174,
    175, 183, 207, 226, 227, 247,
    264
Virgin Mary, 52, 61, 116, 149,
    165, 174, 175, 187
Vogels, Heinrich, 186

Voltaire, 247, 250
Vows, 168
Vulgate Bible, 112, 185, 191,
    205

Wagner, Richard, 82
Walsh, John, 117, 118, 120, 301
Washington, George, 26
Weems, Parson, 192
Weigall, Arthur, 150, 176, 299
Wells, H. G., 289
Wesley, John, 26
Weymouth, R. F., 300
Wheless, Joseph, 299
White, Andrew D., 258, 300
Whitehead, Alfred North, 269,
    270, 298
Whitney, Leon F., 273
Whole, the, 88
Wilberforce, Samuel, 233
Wilhelm II, 25, 194
Will, Free, 29
Willard, Frances E., 289
Wilmers, W., 301
Wind, the god, 58, 62
Wine of Eucharist, 41
Winnebago Indians, 4
Word, the, 151, 197
Word From the Abyss, 122
Wotan, 80

Xavier, Francis, 289
Xenophanes of Colophon, 86

Yahweh, 55, 60, 67, 82, 102,
    134, 137, 140, 141, 147, 149,
    150, 151, 157, 158, 159, 172,
    195 ff, 208, 213, 225, 232,
    243, 264, 268, 269, 274, 279,
    281

Yakuts, 110

Yerkes, R. M., 40

Y.M.C.A., 281, 284

Yucatan, 170

Zechariah, Book of, 184, 229

Zeus, 84, 88, 102, 138, 146

Zoroaster, 163

Zoroastrianism, 159

Maryland Paperback Bookshelf
*Other Titles in the Series:*

*The Tidewater Tales,* by John Barth
*The Friday Book: Essays and Other Nonfiction,* by John Barth
*The Amiable Baltimoreans,* by Francis F. Beirne
*The Oyster: A Popular Summary of a Scientific Study,* by
   William K. Brooks
*Run to the Lee,* by Kenneth F. Brooks, Jr.
*Maryland: A Middle Temperament,* by Robert J. Brugger
*The Lord's Oysters,* by Gilbert Byron
*The Mistress of Riversdale: The Plantation Letters of Rosalie
   Stier Calvert, 1795-1821,* edited by Margaret Law Callcott
*A. Aubrey Bodine: Baltimore Pictorialist, 1906-1970,* by
   Kathleen M. H. Ewing
*When the Colts Belonged to Baltimore: A Father and a Son, a
   Team and a Time,* by William Gildea
*The Potomac,* by Frederick Gutheim
*Spring in Washington,* by Louis J. Halle
*Bay Country,* by Tom Horton
*The Bay,* by Gilbert C. Klingel
*Home on the Canal,* by Elizabeth Kytle
*The Dawn's Early Light,* by Walter Lord
*The Tuesday Club: A Shorter Edition of "The History of the
   Ancient and Honorable Tuesday Club" by Alexander
   Hamilton,* edited by Robert Micklus
*Tobacco Coast,* by Arthur Pierce Middleton
*Watermen,* by Randall S. Peffer
*Young Frederick Douglass: The Maryland Years,* by
   Dickson J. Preston
*Crime and Punishment in Early Maryland,* by Raphael Semmes
*Maryland's Vanishing Lives,* by John Sherwood
*The Premier See: A History of the Archdiocese of Baltimore,
   1789-1994,* by Thomas W. Spalding
*Miss Susie Slagle's,* by Augusta Tucker
*Chesapeake Boyhood: Memoirs of a Farm Boy,* by William H.
   Turner
*Baltimore: When She Was What She Used to Be, 1850-1930,*
   by Marion E. Warren and Mame Warren